D0173887

TIPTIONARY 2

Also by Mary Hunt

Debt-Proof Living

Live Your Life For Half The Price

Debt-Proof Your Marriage

Debt-Proof Your Kids

Debt-Proof Your Holidays

The Financially Confident Woman

Tiptionary

Cheapskate Gourmet

Everyday Cheapskate's Greatest Tips

The Complete Cheapskate

Money Makeover

Best of Cheapskate Monthly

TIPTIONARY 2

MARY HUNT

Los Angeles

PRINTED IN THE UNITED STATES OF AMERICA

Cover Design: Jeremy Hunt, *www.SDMFX.com*

Cover Photo: Copyright Tim Agler, *tagler@cox.net*

For information regarding special discounts for bulk purchases, please contact:

DPL Press, Inc., P.O. Box 2135, Los Angeles, CA 90723; Special Sales: 800-550-3502. Visit us at *www.DPLPress.com*.

First edition published 2007

Library of Congress Cataloging-in-Publication Data
Information Available by Request from Publisher

ISBN 10 0-9760791-5-1
ISBN 13 978-0-9760791-5-6

1 2 3 4 5 6 7 8 9 10 11 12 13 14 15

This book is gratefully dedicated to the millions
of readers who have logged on to
DebtProofLiving.com
and joined us in our mission of providing hope
by contributing their clever, poignant, savvy,
and oftentimes humorous,
time- and money-saving tips.

CONTENTS

Acknowledgments xi

Introduction 1

Automobiles 3

Babies and Kids 13

Books and Computers 31

Cleaning 39

Clothing and Shoes 67

Food and Cooking 81

Gifts 135

Grocery Shopping 155

Health and Beauty 165

Home 191

Kitchen Tricks 227

Laundry 241

Money and Finance 253

Organization and Storage 279

Pets 295

Repairs and Maintenance 303

Special Occasions and Holidays 311

Travel and Entertainment 327

Yard and Garden 341

A Final Word 351

A Special Offer from Debt-Proof Living 355

Sign up for FREE Everyday Cheapskate 357

Index 361

ACKNOWLEDGMENTS

What you hold in your hands is the final product—the cream of the crop, the top of the heap of what started out as a gigantic pile of more than 10,000 possible candidates.

Winnowing down that pile to 2,300 ways to save time and money was no small feat. Without the tireless efforts of more a few people it could not have been accomplished.

Once we got it down to a manageable number the real work began—rewriting, testing, pondering, rewriting some more; typing, adjusting, editing and proofreading. It took a team of very smart people to make it look so easy.

To Wendy Hunt—who in the midst of our great tip adventure became my daughter-in-law—huge thanks for struggling through that first difficult cutting phase. We heard you laughing a lot and still wonder just which tips didn't make the first cut. That you kept your sanity through that mind-numbing process adds to the list of reasons why we think Josh chose the perfect wife. You've got tenacity, girl!

To Kristen Bergman—who joined us in progress—thanks for your tireless efforts, your keen eye and sweet spirit. Every author needs an editor who really knows her stuff. I hope this first project hasn't pushed you over the edge.

To Kim Penrose—who loves a technical challenge—thanks for your diligence in undertaking the task of indexing. We kept hearing you chuckle. We just hope that meant you were enjoying the book.

To Cathy Hollenbeck—my colleague, assistant, and friend who's worked so closely with me from the start, I have just one thing to say: We did it again. We finished another book! Okay, so I have one more thing to say, too: Thank you a million times over for being my editor, colleague, assistant and friend. I couldn't do any of this without you.

To the team at Screaming Death Monkey—great cover.

To Harold Hunt—Thanks for enjoying crackers and cheese for all these many months. I'm going to start making dinner again here really soon. Promise.

Introduction

It all started back in 1992 when I began publishing *Cheapskate Monthly* newsletter (now you know it as *Debt-Proof Living* newsletter) and invited readers to share with me their best money- and time-saving tips. They did and because the tips were so great—even entertaining—I shared them with my readers. The more tips I published the more I received.

I filed all the tips for a while, but that quickly became a logistical nightmare until I discovered a much easier method: Piling took hardly any time at all. And piles began to grow at an unprecedented rate into what I named Mt. Tip.

I knew I was headed for trouble the day I spent hours searching for one wonderful tip I knew was in there somewhere. And that's when I conceded that either I had to find a way to move mountains or call a rubbish-removal contractor. I couldn't go on living like this.

It was from that need to organize tips that the idea of *Tiptionary* was born. In your hands you hold *Tiptionary 2*, the second full-length, fabulously fun collection of tips—short, to-the-point suggestions for ways to do things cheaper, better and faster.

Readers of my daily syndicated newspaper column, *Everyday Cheapskate* (page 357) for how you can receive it every day by email), get their *Tiptionary* fix every time I share tips I receive that are particularly memorable. Subscribers to my monthly newsletter, *Debt-Proof Living* (page 355 for how you can get a free 3-month subscription), get a full page of tips in each issue as well. That's a lot of tips—and would you believe we still haven't scratched the surface? In fact, I now see an entire series of *Tiptionary* books on the horizon, which makes this the second in an ongoing series of an undetermined number.

Some of the best tips you will read have completely unknown origins because they've been passed from generation to generation, and someone along the line sent it my way. Some tips I receive are discarded because they turn out to be nothing more than myths—legends people believe with all their hearts, but when put to the test, they fail.

Some tips are discovered quite by accident. I think of the woman who wrote to me so excited that since her husband had started dumping his denture-soaking liquid into the commode each morning, she no longer needed to scrub the toilet on Saturday. Bingo! A great household tip.

Others will make you cringe if you're like me. It took me years to build up the courage to attempt sharpening my prized dressmaker scissors by cutting into metal. See? Sends chills down your spine, doesn't it? But I did and to my utter amazement, this tip works. You won't catch me paying to have scissors sharpened ever again.

You're about to learn that there are many different ways to accomplish goals. And that's good, because if you need to polish the copper in your kitchen and you don't have any lemons on hand, but you do have a bottle of ketchup, you'll be able to get the job done without running to the store to spend money needlessly. When there's more than one way to achieve the same result, *Tiptionary* will give you choices.

If you haven't thought to ask this question yet, you will, so here's the answer: No, I do not do everything featured in *Tiptionary 2*. There's not a person on the face of the earth who could do all of these things in a single lifetime, nor would I want to. Some of the tips are just not applicable to my life. And some won't apply to your life either. Some will grab your attention and cause you to respond, "Wow, what a great idea!" Others will make you laugh, while others might leave you wondering.

Think of *Tiptionary 2* as a grand smorgasbord loaded with every kind of delicacy you can possibly imagine—even some things you can't. As you pass by, look at everything, consider most things, and fill your plate with those that suit your taste. You might want to bring along a highlighter and Post-Its in case you get a hankering to take notes.

The best thing about *Tiptionary 2*, just like your favorite smorgasbord, is that you can come back again and again ... and again!

Mary Hunt
California
2007

AUTOMOBILES

Automobiles

Paint class

So your clunker doesn't look that great but it's paid for. And it runs like a top! You don't want to spend the big bucks to have it painted, but could you spring for just the paint? Call a local trade school or community college that offers courses in automobile painting. For the cost of materials you just might just be able to get Old Faithful painted by students—under the close supervision of very picky professors, of course.

New car notebook

New car shopping? First get a notebook. A BIG notebook. Fill it with cost comparisons and charts for the models of vehicles that hold your interest. Check related websites like in *www.edmunds.com*. Get price quotes at *www.kellybluebook.com* and a copy of the latest *Consumer Reports*, new car edition. Just having this with you shows the manager you've done your homework. Refer to it often—and without saying a word you'll get the respect you deserve. Prepare to be amazed.

Campus bargains

Looking for a used car? Check the posts on a college campus "For Sale" bulletin board. You know those students—often they take on cars they can't afford, and there are always graduates who are returning to their homes out of the area. When students need to get rid of their stuff fast, let their desperation sales of appliances, furniture, cars and computers be your excellent bargains.

Check for recalls

Whenever you purchase a used car be sure to call a local dealership with the vehicle identification number (VIN), which you will find on the inside door frame. Ask if this car needs to come in for any recalls. You wouldn't believe how many people just don't ever get their cars fixed. There's a good chance you will be eligible to get work done for free that should have been done before.

Free windshield repair

If your windshield has a crack or a "star," call your insurance agent. Some companies, like GEICO auto insurance, have a program where they will fix your windshield crack (smaller than a quarter) free—they even come out and do it at your work. They are interested in not having to replace that windshield later on.

Find a repo

Call your bank and ask to see the current list of cars the bank has repossesed that are now for sale. It's possible to pick up a car for little or no money down with bank financing ready to go. And you may even be able to bargain down on the quoted price.

Invoice secrets

Here's a little-known benefit of AAA membership: When shopping for a new car the folks at AAA will show you the dealer's invoice price on the car(s) you're considering. Now you can offer a dealer an amount close to this number, rather than starting from the sticker price and negotiating your way down.

Last customer of the month

Try to buy your new car at the end of the month. Most dealerships work on a calendar month, so the salespeople are anxious to meet or beat their quotas. You will be more likely to strike a great deal if your salesperson is just one sale from reaching that goal or is vying with others to qualify for a trip or other incentive. And if it just happens to be cold and rainy on that last day of the month, you'll be in an even better position. Not many people are out shopping during inclement weather, which gives you the decided advantage.

Battery shop

Before you buy a new battery or other parts from a car dealer, call around. The best price on a car battery is not likely to be at the dealership, but rather at a battery shop. Most are more than willing to quote a price over the phone. The same goes for just about every other automobile part and service, too. It pays to shop around.

Bumper un-stickers

To remove pesky bumper stickers from your car, first use a hair dryer on the sticker to soften the adhesive. Don't leave the dryer on for too long or you'll ruin the paint. Use a credit card to help lift the sticker off but don't use any sharp metal objects. Follow with a paint-safe solvent like Goo Gone, plus plenty of elbow grease, to remove the residue.

Car shades are more than cool

The cardboard car shades you can buy at the auto parts store for a couple of bucks will make your gasoline go farther. Not using as little as 1/20 of a gallon of gas to cool your vehicle with each start adds up over time. Car shades also protect the car's interior from sun damage.

Tire cleaner

A paste made of Bar Keepers Friend (a household cleanser available in most supermarkets) and water works well to clean tires. Spread it on and allow to sit for about 10 minutes. Rinse. This works as well as special whitewall cleaner, but for a fraction of the cost.

Fresh scent

Save your scented candle stubs to add fragrance to your car. Put the wax pieces in a small can or container and leave it in the car under the seat. On a warm day the wax will melt and fill the car with a nice fragrance.

Decals off!

Got a stubborn window decal that simply won't budge? Saturate it well with a baby wipe. It will scrape off easily, thanks to the oils in the wipe that soften the adhesive.

Find the missing cap

If you happen to leave your gas cap at the filling station, don't assume it's a lost cause. Go back and ask if it was turned in. If your station is like most, there's a big box full of gas caps under the counter. Try a few until you find one that fits. You'll do them a big favor by reducing the inventory.

Fragrant car

A new dryer fabric sheet will make your car smell great. Stuff it in the ashtray or under the seat. Or give a few used ones a second chance. They have enough fragrance remaining to keep your car smelling fresh and clean for several days.

Frozen doors, windows

If car doors are frozen shut, pour tepid (not hot) water around the locks and the doors will open with a firm tug.

Get tired

When buying replacement tires, inquire if they have any "take-offs" to fit your car. These are nearly new tires that are removed when someone replaces tires on a new car with special, fancy tires. Dealers want to get rid of "take-offs" and are likely to negotiate a great deal.

Good to the last mile

If your venerable car's headliner is

starting to fall, get some no-sew fabric glue from the fabric store and glue it back into place. It will still be in place long after you've driven the wheels right off that car!

Handy funnel

Need a funnel for adding oil or other fluids to your car? No problem. Grab a two-liter plastic bottle and remove the bottom with a razor knife. Now you have a terrific "funnel" for just about any messy job. Provided you did not remove the UPC code, you can still return it for your deposit. Keep a couple of these in the car for emergencies. Once cut, they nest together well for easy storage.

Just-in-time repairs

A few months before your warranty expires, take the car to a reputable mechanic for a thorough inspection and request a written report. If anything on that list is covered under your about-to-expire warranty, get those items fixed now. The small fee you may have to pay for that inspection is cheap insurance against discovering a problem after the warranty expires.

Wheel and tire cleaner

Lysol Basin Tub and Tile Cleaner is a great tire and wheel cleaner. It's much cheaper than buying a product marketed specifically for car tires and it cleans without much elbow grease.

Accident prep

Keep a 3x5 card with your information on it in your car's glove box. If you are in an accident you won't have to fumble and look for a pen while emotionally shaken. Include your name, address, phone, license plate number, make of car; plus your insurance company name, phone number and your policy number.

Repair it yourself

Before you have your car repaired by a professional, stop by the library. Find the Haynes Auto Repair Manual for your specific model. Written simply with step-by-step instructions, the manual can help you make the repairs yourself. Just think how much money you'll not spend.

Road tar remover

Use plain old baking soda on a damp rag to remove bugs, tar and anything else from your vehicle. Works great on chrome. Leaves no residue or odor and won't harm the paint. Rinse well. Works better than most pricey car wash products.

Run the A/C

If you live where you can go for months at a time without running the air conditioner, that's great for fuel economy but hard on the unit itself. Run the air conditioner for a short time at least once a month. This allows the refrigerant oil to lubricate the gaskets. If these gaskets dry out, they lose their seal. If that happens you can kiss your coolant good-bye.

Tidy backseat

A bed sheet (flat or fitted) makes a great cover for the backseat. Tuck it in well and the upholstery will be protected from pets and kids. When it gets dirty just pop it in the laundry.

Tire and rim cleaner

Fume-free, cold-oven cleaner works great to remove road dirt and grease from tires and chrome wheels. Just spray it on, wait a few minutes, sponge off and rinse with the hose.

Wiper blade cleaner

If you're a crafty person and have a bottle of rubber stamp cleaner around, use it to clean the rubber blades on your windshield wipers. It is designed to clean rubber without cracking. As a bonus it takes care of all that waxy build-up, too!

Alternative floor mats

Can't find reasonably priced floor mats for your car or van? Purchase clear plastic runner by the foot at the home improvement center. Use a box or utility knife to customize the fit around the seat hardware. You'll spend a fraction of the cost of auto floor mats and come out with attractive "mats" that fit perfectly.

Cruise control caution

If you are in the habit of using the cruise control, you're saving a lot in fuel costs. But don't use it on wet roads. If the tires hydroplane, the cruise keeps upping the speed of the tire. When the tire bites and gets traction again, the cruise control will make the car skid and swerve. No fun unless you're a stunt driver.

Frost-free windows

Wash your car's windshield and windows with a mixture of three parts white vinegar and one part water. Now they'll stay ice- and frost-free.

Half-price wiper fluid

Windshield wiper fluid can be diluted with water in warm weather and will still work just as well. While it should be used at full strength in freezing temperatures, in warmer seasons a one-half dilution works well.

Watch the heat control

Turning the heat on full blast in your car is hard on the blower. Keep it on the lower settings and you'll save on wear and tear for your vehicle's heating controls.

Kitty litter on oil

When you get a spot of oil, or even a major spill on your drive or garage floor, pour a generous amount of the cheapest kitty litter you can find over the spill. Now do the twist on the kitty litter until it is ground into a dust. The litter absorbs the oil so you can sweep it away. Keep the litter in your car because it also serves as a great traction aid when you are stuck on ice or snow. Just pour a generous amount in front of your drive wheels for needed traction.

Miles of money

Take an afternoon to plot three different routes you could take to get to work. Calculate the exact distance of each route. If you discover the shortest route also takes the longest amount of time, determine to allot the additional time to use less gas. Over a year's time this simple tactic will put dough back into your pocket.

Phone book save

Your old phone book can be a practical aid while driving in town. Keep a phone book tucked under the passenger seat—you just never know when you'll need to find a gas station or other address. This will save you the hassle of paying for the operator to look up a phone number for you or from having to scavenge the world of public phones for a phone book that isn't waterlogged or tattered.

Parking meter math

If you frequently use parking meters, do the math. If it costs 10 cents per 15 minutes or 25 cents per half-hour, it's cheaper to put four dimes (40 cents) in the meter than two quarters (50 cents). It all adds up.

Garage rental

If you live in an area where winters are severely cold and you have a garage you don't use, consider renting it out for the season. Most classic car enthusiasts need storage for their treasures and many end up paying a lot at self-storage facilities. If you can beat that price, you may be able to make a few bucks for space that would normally go unused. Just make sure you are covered by insurance and that you have a signed document that outlines the terms and conditions of this arrangement.

Kids' insurance

If your kids live away from home for college, either with or without a car, check with your insurance agent to see if you can get lower rates. If you live in a large city and your child goes to a college in a smaller city, your insurance should be lower.

Mystery leak

Does your car leak fluid from some mysterious place you cannot determine? Take a large sheet of butcher paper or a cardboard box that has been flattened. Place it under the car. Use a black marker to mark on the paper where each tire and where the front bumper is located. Leave it there until the leaks occur again. Now when you take your car to the mechanic you can place the paper back under the car positioning it as before using the notes as a guide. He will know where to look for the leak.

Handy trash bag

If your vehicle has bucket seats, a plastic grocery bag works perfectly for a car trash container. Hang a handle over the inner arm rests of both seats. It is cheap, convenient and works like a charm. When full, take it off, tie the handles, toss and replace. Keep extra bags stored up front.

Babies and Kids

Babies and Kids

Room re-do

If the cost of redecorating a child's room with matching sheets, comforter, pillows shams, dust ruffle and drapes sends you over the edge, here's a way to reduce that cost: Buy sheets in the pattern you want, then buy an extra sheet set that matches exactly or coordinates nicely. Cover the box springs with the extra fitted, which precludes the need for a bed skirt. Use the extra flat sheet to make curtains or a valance, and throw pillows. Two additional flat sheets would make a perfect duvet if you have even minimal sewing skills.

Eat peas

Doctors often recommend peas as the first vegetable to introduce to babies. And for some reason many babies hate peas. Here's a way to overcome this objection: Mix green peas with rice cereal. For some unknown reason it makes just enough change so baby has a change of heart. Works most every time.

Create a carnival

Summer boredom set in? Have your kids help you put on a carnival. Using resources such as *Family Fun* magazine, design a selection of simple games kids will like, such as shooting cotton swabs through straws to knock down paper cups, water balloon tosses, golf clubs with a sponge tied to a stick, and so on. Make up game tickets on your computer or draw by hand. Have your kids help with set-up and include some fun food, such as popcorn in paper bags or homemade popsicles. Set up prizes picked up from the local thrift shop and 'price' each with the number of tickets needed to win. Invite some friends, blow up some balloons and have a ball.

More than lunch

Free- and reduced-lunch programs in public schools offer more than food. Some districts offer reduced costs for sports, music lessons, field trips, tutoring and park and recreation activities, too. Programs like these are available for families who homeschool as well. If you think you might qualify (income limits are higher than you might imagine) even if you are only going through a season of low income, it can't hurt to apply. Pick up an application at your local public school.

Clean baby bottles

To clean the gook that sometimes accumulates in the bottom of plastic baby bottles, drop a teaspoon of regular rice and a few tablespoons of hot water into the bottle. Apply the lid and shake vigorously. Repeat as necessary. The kernels of rice act as tiny scrubbers to clean even the tightest spots inside the bottle.

Telephone toys

If your kids act up and misbehave when mom or dad are on the phone, here is a solution: Keep a large bag of small toys hidden until telephone time, at which time the toys are taken out of the closet and dumped on the floor. The children are so excited with their "new" toys, and mom or dad can have a pleasant conversation.

Prize box

In order to keep skills sharp during school vacations, give kids school work and chores each day. To improve their enthusiasm, decorate a big cardboard box and write Mom's and Dad's Really Fantastic Prize Box on the outside. Fill the box with assorted small toys, and small packages of mints and candy bars. This will stop the nagging and the groaning.

Off on the right foot

Mark your toddler's right shoe with a special mark like a heart or star. You'll be able to teach right from left while you teach how to put shoes on the correct feet.

Free paper dolls

When fabric stores receive the most current pattern books, they discard the older ones. By calling ahead of time, you can reserve one of these older pattern books. Then use the pattern illustrations as paper dolls for your children or grandchildren. The books are large, so there will be lots of "models" to cut out. You'll create hours of amusement and fun at absolutely no cost.

Gallery garage

If you can't bear to part with your children's artwork but don't have a refrigerator large enough to display each and every work, turn your garage into an art gallery. Tack or staple the masterpieces to the walls. This definitely beats plain garage walls, makes kids proud and gives the neighbors something to smile about, too.

Calendar recycle

Instead of tossing your calendar at the end of the year, cut off the pictures and hang them like mini-posters around baby's room and changing table. While changing, baby is occupied looking at all kinds of great pictures.

Babies and Kids

Diaper pin cushion

There you are, holding a squirming baby with one hand, trying to manage a cloth diaper with the other—all the while wondering how you will ever get that dull diaper pin in place to finish the job. Next time use a bar of soap for a diaper pin cushion. Those pins will glide through the diaper so easily and quickly, thanks to the soap that acts like wax.

Bubble party

Combine ten parts distilled water and one part Dawn original blue dishwashing liquid to make your own bubble solution. And add 1/4 part white corn syrup (like Karo) if you want to make more sturdy bubbles. Gather up things like clean soup cans that have both ends cut off or Hula-Hoops with makeshift handles attached. If you want to, you can pour the solution into a plastic kiddy pool and make huge bubbles. Turn it into a scientific experiment and go on a hunt for bubble-making items in your kitchen. This is a super cheap idea that's lots of fun.

Bubbles to go

Keep a bottle of bubble solution and a couple of wands in your purse. You won't believe all the times you'll be able to pull that out to keep the kids happily occupied while waiting.

Cheap baby food

Cook packages of frozen vegetables, blend in blender and then freeze in ice cube trays. Once frozen, pop cubes into a storage bag properly labeled. Now you have your own baby food without preservatives. You can do this with canned or fresh fruits, too. At dinner time put what the rest of the family is eating into the blender for baby. No more short order cooking at meal time.

Designer birthday party

Here's a great idea for a young girl's birthday. Buy inexpensive fabrics for the young guests to cut and create fancy dresses. You won't need to sew—just tie and pin with safety pins. Hold a fashion show so the small guests can model their creations.

Budding artists

An inexpensive acrylic box frame hung in a special place in your home make for an excellent display case for a child's artwork. Every week or so (depending on how many budding artists you are growing) change the art piece. Your kids will be proud to have their work so prominently displayed.

Tiny ponytails

Tiny rubber bands from the orthodontist office are perfect to hold ponytails in an infant's fine hair. Just one twist and that pony will stay all day.

Diaper rash cream

The price of creams and ointment formulated for diaper rash can be quite pricey. Instead, purchase zinc oxide in the first aid section of your store or pharmacy. For just a couple of bucks you can get a good supply of zinc oxide, which is the main ingredient in many of those expensive creams.

Toy boxes

Milk crates, washed and painted, make excellent stacking toy boxes that are just perfect for little organizers who love to keep their toys neatly separated.

Kid art

Go through the kids' toy boxes and find all the broken pieces, odd puzzle pieces and so on to make wall art. For example, put a child's photo or other important person in the center of a piece of cardboard and build a "frame." Take all misplaced or worn-out puzzle pieces and frame the outer edges of the cardboard. Kids love this kind of art better than expensive posters and frames.

Coupons are for kids

Watch how fast shopping with your kids turns to fun (and a great learning experience!) when you hand over the coupons to them to find the item on the shelf to match. At check-out give them the money saved from the coupons they searched. It teaches kids to appreciate saving at the grocery store while using their math and reading skills.

Formula samples

New parents get inundated with lots of baby formula samples and high-value coupons for future purchases. Don't throw these out, even if you will never use them. Instead collect the samples and purchase all the nearly-free items with the coupons at the cheapest discount or drugstore. Donate the entire lot to a local food bank or crisis pregnancy center where formula is always needed and much appreciated.

Storage tub

A ten-gallon storage tub makes a great baby bathtub for home or travel. Just load it up with bath toys, towels, washcloths and other items. Your baby can take a bath with familiar objects on vacation and not have to sit in a questionably "clean" motel bathtub.

Whiteboard

Instead of paying a fortune at the office supply store for a kid's whiteboard make your own. Buy six-foot sheet of shower board at the home improvement center for a fraction of the cost. It's the same material as commercially-made whiteboards. You can even make a simple frame for your board or mount it on the wall unframed.

Fire station birthday party

Some fire stations allow their facilities to be used for birthday parties—supervised by firemen, with access to the kitchen—in return for a small donation to a local charity. Check with yours. What kid wouldn't go nuts for a party at a real fire station?

Packing for kids

When traveling with small children put one day's outfit (shirt, pants, socks, underwear) into a gallon-size zip-type bag. Seal part way, push out air and seal the rest of the way to make it very compact. This saves space in the suitcase and allows you or your child to pick out their clothes without rummaging through everything. Keeps everything nice and clean, too.

Occupied baby

Keep a stack of family photos on your baby's changing table. Babies who can focus love to study the pictures, buying you enough time for a quick, non-combative diaper change. Just make sure these are photos you don't mind getting crumpled.

Kids on board

Road trips can be tricky with kids in the car, so start early in the morning. Each child gets a goodie bag of small toys, colored pencils, notebooks, cassettes, and so on—items that are usually leftover school supplies from the previous year. Travel for a few hours and stop for a breakfast picnic. At lunchtime, picnic again. Eat one meal a day in a restaurant (dinner) and you'll keep your costs down and everyone happy.

Chore cards

If your kids have daily chores but aren't readers yet, take photos of them doing their individual chores. Use these pictures as chore cards. They'll know exactly what their chore is for that day. No more fusses over who does what job.

Foaming soap refill

Here's a recipe that works well to refill a "non-refillable foaming hand soap container" (don't believe everything you read). Mix 3 tablespoons liquid hand soap, 1 drop food coloring and 7/8 cup water. This creates a mixture of 1 part soap to 5 parts water.

School supplies

Why pay the big bucks for tab dividers for your kids' school notebooks, when manila file folder 1/3-cut tabs do just as well—if not better? Just cut along the fold line and hole-punch. Can't get the kids to agree? Give them the money to buy the expensive tab dividers and tell them they can keep whatever they don't spend on dividers. You might be surprised just how quickly they see things your way. And as a bonus, no fussing with tiny inserts and working so hard to thread them into the plastic tabs.

Toy library exchange

If there isn't one in your area, start a toy library exchange. People can borrow toys like they do at a library or exchange gently used toys for different ones. It's an inexpensive way to keep renewing your toy and game supply without having to own everything.

Time to donate

Use a permanent marker to write the suggested age range on children's toys. This makes figuring out which toys are ready to be donated a snap and eliminates the confusion and clutter of keeping unwanted toys.

Year-round kids clothes

Estimate your kids' clothing sizes so you can buy a year in advance. Now you can buy fall clothes in February and March when they are on clearance, and summer clothes in September and October. Typically these are the months when kids' clothes are on sale at the greatest discounts.

Kids' art wrap

Don't know what to do with all the drawings and paintings your kids bring home? Give them a rotation on the refrigerator and then turn them into gift wrap. Relatives will get two presents in one.

Reusable worksheets

Buy plastic sleeves at the office supply store. Slip worksheets and fun papers into the sleeves, using dry erase markers to answer the questions. They are erasable and can be re-used over and over again.

Babies and Kids

Sleep under the stars

Instead of buying plastic stars or stickers for your child's ceiling, dab glow-in-the-dark paint on the tip of a dowel and randomly tap the ceiling in your child's room, reapplying paint as needed. The dots won't appear during the day, but at night these "stars" glow and even seem to twinkle. A cheap and easy way to surprise a child.

Car seat cover

To protect your child's car seat cut a plastic tablecloth to line the seat. You can find them at the dollar store and they are usually flannel backed, which make them nice to sit on. The vinyl on the other side keeps spills from going all the way through and staining or ruining the car seat fabric.

The other whiteboard

Instead of buying whiteboards for the kids' room, leave them notes on the bathroom mirror. A mirror can be written on just like a whiteboard, using dry erase markers.

Barstool covers

Large plastic quick covers designed to cover containers for the refrigerator make perfect seat covers for upholstered barstools. Stock up when they're on sale. Quick covers wash up easily.

Tidy tennies

Clean up the rubber soles and edges of kids' tennis shoes with Soft Scrub cleaner on a soft cloth. It wipes away scuff marks, chewing gum, play dough, dirt and so on from the rubber parts of the shoe.

Booster seat

A stack of old telephone books makes a great booster seat. Simply tape them with duct tape all around and cover with contact paper. Or use one as a desk footstool.

Lunch prep

If you have older kids in school and little ones at home, pack lunches for everyone. This way if you have to run out unexpectedly, the little ones have lunch all ready to go. No need to spend time or money on fast food.

Tiny toys

If you have young children in your home you've probably accumulated a plethora of small toys from meal deals. Get a supply of small eye screws at the hardware store and turn them into Christmas ornaments. It's a perfect solution for kids who like to decorate their own tree.

Fun bath

Are your kids sensitive to bubble bath but still want a fun and festive bath? Add a few drops of food coloring to the water and presto! Green, blue or whatever color you want. It doesn't stain, and they love it.

Rake 'em up

Keep a small plastic yard leaf rake for quickly picking up all those tiny toys kids love to scatter. Rake them into a pile. Now it's fast work to sort and put away.

Quick cut

Use a pizza cutter to quickly cut up pancakes, waffles and French toast for kids. Works great on peanut butter and jelly sandwiches and just about anything you need bite-sized in a flash.

Books on tape

Record your kids' favorites stories on tape using a bell or other noisemaker to signal a page turn. While not a perfect substitute for a warm lap, it's the next best thing when Mom or Dad is away or can't sit down to read a book.

Homemade play dough

Cheaper than store-bought, homemade play dough is also better because it lasts a long time—even when left uncovered. Mix 2 cups flour, 1 cup salt and 2 tablespoons cream of tartar. Add 2 tablespoons oil, 2 cups water and a few drops of food coloring. Stir together, then dump into a large fry pan and cook like scrambled eggs. Keep stirring a few minutes until it is no longer wet. When it looks like play dough, dump onto the counter and knead for a few minutes. That's it. Store in plastic bowls or storage bags.

Tidy drawers

Clear plastic shoe boxes from the dollar store make perfect organizers for a kid's drawers. Socks in one box, underwear in another and so on.

Lotion warmer

Lotion can be cold on a baby's skin after a nice warm bath. Warm it up by floating the closed bottle of lotion in the bath water with baby.

Costume box

Start saving clothes and accessories in a costume box for kids to play dress up. You'll be surprised how this becomes their favorite play thing.

Optional upgrade

Got kids with expensive tastes in

clothes? An effective way to nip designer labels in the bud without creating resentment is to agree that they can upgrade from the cost of the no-name item. But there's a catch. They pay the difference in cost, plus the cost of gas to get to the brand store. Once they have a say in the matter you might be surprised how quickly they see things your way.

Appliance safety

If you have small children in the house, attach large safety pins through the prongs of electrical plugs of all appliances not in use—both in the house and garage. In order for the appliance to be plugged in the pin has to be removed first. The safety pin blocks the prongs from going into the socket. Although it takes time for an adult to take the pin off for use, it also takes time for a frustrated little one who shouldn't be playing with the appliance in the first place.

Shoes fit

Every few months trace your kids' feet on paper, cut out the pattern and carry it with you. If you run into an outrageous shoe sale and the kids are not with you, you can fit shoes nearly perfectly using their drawn images.

Baby wipes

Surprisingly Kleenex Cold Care tissues make terrific baby wipes. These tissues are strong, extra soft and unscented. Simply dampen one with warm water for a terrific baby wipe substitute. Works perfectly.

Travel kids

Start each day's travel with a fresh roll of coins: one roll for each child for on-the-road expenses. Fine them one coin every time they ask, "Are we there yet?" By the time you stop to get your first tank of gas, they will have caught on.

Kids consignment

Children's clothing resale shops, like Once Upon A Child, are terrific bargain haunts. And when your kids outgrow clothes that are still in great shape, return them for cash or store credit.

Portrait package

Take the negative of your favorite snapshot of your child to your photofinisher. On the envelope under "special instructions" write "Portrait Package." You will receive a selection that includes an eight by ten, a five by seven and wallets, which you will treasure. Your custom pictures will bring years of delight because you took them yourself and took the time to get just the right shot. The price is comparable and the quality is far superior.

How to brush

Cut pictures from magazines of people brushing their teeth. Tape them to the bathroom wall or mirror where children can see them. Now teaching them what to do is reinforced by the pictures, and they catch on fast.

Bags to go

The cardboard center from a roll of toilet tissue makes the perfect sized container for storing empty plastic bags for the diaper bag. Two bags fit easily when stuffed into the tube. Have the roll on hand for soiled diapers or clothes as needed.

YOU the journal

Not into keeping detailed baby books? That's okay. Instead write your child a detailed letter for his or her birthday, citing the milestones of the past year. Keep each one and by the time the child is grown you will have an excellent Life Journal.

Forget the jammies

If a child goes through a season of making it impossible to get dressed in the morning, don't sweat it. Dress him or her for school the night before, after their bath, and let the child sleep in clothes for the next day. It won't hurt a thing and will ease the morning clashes. Sleeping in school clothes for a couple of weeks will help the phase to pass quickly.

Doctor visits

When you take your infant or child to the doctor, ask for samples of formula or pain reliever. Doctors receive many samples and stock bottles from the pharmaceutical salespeople and are happy to pass them along. This will also give you a chance to make sure your child is not allergic to medicine that might have cost a tidy sum.

Recycle envelopes

Save the envelopes from junk mail for teacher notes, school money and other information that needs to be sealed. It's economical and environmentally friendly, too.

Crayon cleanup

Even non-washable crayon will come right off painted surfaces and tile if you spray it with WD-40. Rinse it all away with warm water and a little liquid detergent.

Babies and Kids

Rainy day sandbox

A large plastic container (like those that slide under the bed) filled with uncooked rice makes a great rainy-day "sandbox." Add a funnel, measuring cups and other containers for hours of fun.

Tub of fun

This is an easy and fun way to get your child to take a bath: Fill each compartment of a muffin tin with shaving cream. Add food coloring to each compartment and stir. Makes great bathtub paints. Apply with sponge or fingers. Rinses away easily and cleans the tub in the process.

Waterproof mattress covers

Plastic mattress covers can be pricey, but shower curtain liners are cheap. One cut in half makes two twin-size waterproof mattress covers.

Too many toys

When you have too many toys and books at your house but aren't ready to part with them just yet, take the overage to the grandparents' house. The benefits are many: Grandparents don't have to fork out money for toys and books; kids have fewer choices at both places; and it's easier to keep things organized.

Senior pictures

Senior pictures can be expensive when taken in a studio. So visit the photo shop at Kmart (no one need know if your teen is sensitive about this), or take digital photos yourself and then have them printed professionally. You'll save a ton of dough and have great pictures, too.

Register kids

A spare check register makes a handy tool for a kid who wants to keep track of his or her money. Just don't let on that this is an excellent teaching tool for tracking expenses, and a practical math application, too.

Time management

A simple kitchen timer set for 10 minutes, for example, helps a child learn to manage time. When the timer sounds, it's time to feed the dog or pick up toys or get ready for bed.

Portion control

It's easy to go nuts with pretzels or other snacks that come packaged in large-size containers. But individual packaging can be expensive. So make your own by dividing these kinds of foods into small sandwich-size bags.

Push vegetables

The kids don't like vegetables? Don't despair. Smoothies may be the answer. Yes, smoothies! Start with fruit juice and frozen fruit in the blender, then sneak in small amounts of kale, broccoli, cabbage, carrots or sweet potatoes. Too weird? You'll never know till you try.

Tub toys

Store the kids' bath toys in a mesh laundry bag designed for washing delicates and underwear. The water drains out easily, and it keeps the toys organized and out of sight.

Save the knees

Kneeling on the hard bathroom floor while bathing a child is hard on your knees. To remedy this problem, pick up a kneeling pad used for gardening. Bath time will cease being a chore.

Bath seat

Find a five-gallon plastic bucket (like an empty laundry detergent pail) and bore drainage holes in the bottom. Now you have a perfect storage container for bathtub toys. Just load it up and keep it in the tub between baths. When bath time rolls around, empty the toys into the bath water and flip the bucket upside down to serve as a seat for the person supervising. and scrubbing.

Frisbee bowling

With what you have around the house you can make a Frisbee bowling set. Collect empty two-liter soda bottles, paint them white. Once dry, add numbers. To play, set them up like bowling pins, and attempt to knock them over with a Frisbee. Lots of fun for next to nothing.

Wash plush toys

Don't you wish there was a way to give stuffed animals a bath? Rejoice, there is. Place them in a pillowcase and tie or pin the case shut. Wash the whole thing in the washing machine on a gentle cycle, using warm water and detergent. Put the closed bag in the dryer for about 20 minutes, then remove the animals and allow them to finish air drying. They'll be like new.

Table talk

The Christmas cards you receive each holiday can have a new purpose throughout the year. Use them to stimulate family conversation at dinner. Take turns picking a card then spend time remembering good times and talking about that friend or relative.

Babies and Kids

Homework boxes

Make a homework box for each child in the family. Fill with sharpened pencils, erasers, rulers, compasses, colored pencils, crayons, markers, glue, scotch tape, note paper—everything a kid might need to complete homework. Buying the items when they are on sale and keeping them in one place will save you time and money when your child comes home and announces that a special project must be completed for the next day.

Shampoo pump

So how on earth are you supposed to hold the baby and manage the shampoo bottle at the same time? Don't even try. Instead pour the shampoo into an empty pump soap bottle. Now you can easily dispense the shampoo with one hand without letting go of baby.

Long live the crayons

Make crayons more resistant to breaking by wrapping each crayon with masking tape when you first take it from the box.

Dress up

What little girl doesn't love to play dress up? Adult camisoles, slips, shoes, scarves and sweaters are a great start. For dressier tastes, thrift shops are a cheap place to find bridesmaids' gowns, hats, night gowns, shoes, purses, scarves, gloves and dresses. For storage, use a big, old suitcase.

Five-minute birdfeeder

Coat a big pinecone with peanut butter, then roll it in sunflower seeds or other birdseeds. Use a wire, a piece of yarn, or a pipecleaner to top, and you have a homemade birdfeeder to hang. Great project for kids to make.

Changing table

Instead of expensive furniture, buy a workbench kit from a home improvement or hardware store. Cover a piece of foam you've cut to fit the bench top with flannel-backed vinyl from the fabric store. You'll have two shelves below for all of baby's stuff. And when baby's beyond needing to be changed, you'll have a great workbench.

Quick wean

To encourage your baby to give up the bottle in favor of a cup, fill the bottle with powdered milk, buttermilk or Kool-Aid—no sugar added. Put the good stuff in a sipper cup. Offer both to baby and just watch how fast he or she makes the switch without any fuss. Then use milk or juice in the sipper cup.

Energy smarts

Here's a great way to teach kids about the cost of utilities. Set a base month by showing the kids the bills for water, electricity, gas and so on. Tell them that if those bills go down in the future, you will pay them a portion of those savings. Then teach them ways to reduce energy usage such as hanging laundry on the line outside, turning off lights, taking shorter showers and so on.

Kids' checking accounts

Teach your older kids how to manage a checking account. Arrange this at your credit union or bank and then deposit their allowance to their bank account. Teach them to write a check, to balance the account and to track their spending carefully. They'll be miles ahead once they leave home.

Half-off

Cut ordinary store-bought baby wipes in half. Twice as much product without any noticeable change in performance.

Best bibs

Make the best baby bibs out of dish towels. Fold a new dish towel the long way. Starting about one-half of the way down, cut a half U-shape curve from the fold toward the outer edge, turning north about 2 inches from the outer edge. Continue to the top, removing the curved piece completely. This should leave two long strips approximately 2 inches wide at the end of a towel. Use these to tie around baby's neck. You have an instant bib that are three times larger than those dinky ones that cost a lot.

Lights out

Got kids who are constantly in and out of the refrigerator, eating the food faster than you can buy it? Remove the light bulb. If they are really hungry they will take the time to search, otherwise it won't be worth the effort.

Pacifier fade out

To help break a toddler's pacifier habit, substitute it with one that is infant size. Finding it is not as satisfying, the toddler will let the habit simply fade away.

Wish list

When your kids get a case of the "I Wants," affirm their desire by telling them to put that on their Wish List. Make sure they write it down with all the details including the price, the store, color and so on. Human nature what it is, several weeks hence it will likely be crossed off in favor of something else. If something stays on the list it could be a candidate for a birthday or Christmas—or worthy of saving one's allowance.

Baby bottle rack

Hang a 3-tiered wire vegetable basket high above the sink. This makes a perfect spot for baby bottles and all their parts to air-dry without making a mess on the counter.

Puzzle pouch

Nothing will make a kid's room and toy box a disaster zone like puzzle pieces—especially if several puzzles get mixed. To alleviate, take a puzzle when it is new and mark the back of the pieces alike (try a letter or shape corresponding to that particular puzzle). Now cut the picture of the puzzle from the flimsy box and pop it, together with all the pieces, into a strong gallon-size zip-type plastic bag. Toss the box because it's going to fall apart anyway. Now even if puzzles get mixed you can easily sort them, making cleanup a lot easier.

Quiet toy

Purchase several colorful elastic "coiled" key chain holders that fit on your wrist. Make sure you remove the rings that hold the keys. When you want your baby to play quietly, slip several of these elastic key chain bracelets on your wrists and let baby pull and snap away. They are soft and will not be harmful. Keeps baby quietly fascinated for long periods of time.

Artwork scrapbook

Instead of trying to figure out how and where to store the artwork your children bring home from school, take a picture of your child holding the picture or object. Then put it in a scrapbook for everyone to enjoy.

Artwork storage

Instead of trying to display every new piece of art your child creates, save wrapping paper and paper towel rolls and roll the items around the tube. Store these rolls in the closet.

Dressing baby

When trying to dress a newborn whose fingers seem to spread and get caught in the sleeves, try putting socks on the baby's hands.

Hidden patches

If your kids are really hard on the knees of their jeans, buy iron-on patches from a store like Wal-Mart and put them on the INSIDE of the jeans before they start wearing them. Now the knees will hold up great with no sign of patches.

Kids' lunch

If you pack the family's lunches for the next day in the evenings after dinner you may be tempted to pack everything in the lunch box and place that in the 'fridge. Don't. Lunch boxes get really dirty and can contaminate the contents of your refrigerator. Instead, just slip the lunch box inside a plastic grocery bag first.

Make your own paper

Here's a fun activity to do with your kids—make your own paper. Get instructions from a book at the library and use shredded junk mail for your paper-making material. You can even add in flower petals and grass to give it a decorative look. Homemade paper is great for stationary, gift wrap, cards and journals.

Recycled trophies

You can use old plaques and trophies over again. There is always a wide selection at the thrift store. Simply remove the names and have new plates made for a fraction of the cost of purchasing a whole trophy. Your kids will be just as pleased.

Matching game

This is a great way for toddlers to match their clothes and learn at the same time. On the inside of their clothes on the tag put a 2 and on the matching shirt or shorts put the same number. Letters can also be used. They know that 2 and 2 match or that A and A match.

Books and Computers

Books and Computers

Magazine co-op

Get your neighbors or a group of friends together and share magazine subscriptions. Just rotate each issue, and everyone gets to read their favorite.

Computer screen cleaner

Use old dryer sheets to clean the dust from your computer screen. The dust clings to the sheet and it won't scratch your monitor.

Printer cartridge refills

You can save big bucks at *www.oddparts.com/ink* for printer cartridge ink refills.

Change your IP

Before you change your Internet provider keep your old account active until the new installation is complete. Often times you'll need to download new software and will need Internet access to update your computer. Once everything is complete and all your incoming email has been transferred you can cancel the old account.

Library 411

The library is a good source for contact information on companies out of your area. Use the Internet or out-of-area phone books and there will be no need to spend money on dialing information anymore.

Cheaper books online

Before going to a bookstore, check out *www.google.com* and search online bookstores to get great deals. You can get up to 50 percent off the retail price at some websites.

Password amnesia

Keep a small Rolodex near your computer with all your passwords listed. For security reasons it's not recommended to use the same user name and password for all sites. This will also save time when you update your accounts, too.

Find promo codes

Before you visit online shopping websites, do a quick search for a "promo code" or "coupon code" in your favorite search engine.

Easy library access

Many county libraries have websites that include their catalog of books.

If you're looking for something specific you can order it to be delivered to your branch when it's available.

Recycle magazines

Recycle your magazines by cutting out your name and address information and donating them to nursing homes and hospital waiting rooms.

Find a book

Book Crossing (*www.bookcrossing.com*) is a website community where book lovers leave books in public places for others to find and read. Books are registered so they can be tracked. The site also features book trading.

Inkjet warning

Always leave a cartridge in your printer even if it's empty. While you're waiting for a replacement the connections need to be protected, and the empty cartridge will do this.

Cut-rate software

Try purchasing a trade-out package on computer software you're considering. Many larger computer stores—especially those that build custom computer systems or those that sell large volumes of software—will sell (at big savings) fully functional, complete software packages that have recently fallen prey to the newest upgrade.

Reuse? Maybe not

Be careful reusing paper that has already gone through the printer, as it can dirty your printer and get the rollers gummy.

Computer books

The best time to buy computer books at a steep discount is when the updated version of the computer software or hardware is released. Bookstores want to get these "obsolete" guides off the shelves and out of their stores.

Mailing books

Use fourth class or "media mail" when shipping books through the US postal service. The savings is amazing.

Communication savings

Ask yourself if you really need a telephone on a landline anymore. For those that have cable access and use cell phones to talk, a landline might be an expense that's no longer necessary.

Used paperbacks

Trade in your old paperbacks at used

bookstores for credit toward other books. Depending on the condition, some bookstores give up to one-half of the original purchase price.

Laptop case

Save money on a laptop computer case by purchasing a zip-type binder slightly larger than your computer. Remove the three-ring mechanism inside and voila! You have a padded zip-up case to house and protect your computer.

Best deals online

Use the Internet to check out deals before you go shopping in a store. Use a search engine like Google or visit stores' websites to get the best deals. You will quickly become a savvy shopper.

Unplug cable lines

When a lightning storm hits don't forget your cable line when unplugging your appliances and power cords. If lightning hits the cable box it can fry modems, ethernet cards, televisions and anything else that hooks up to the cable box.

Free greeting cards

Stop paying money for greeting cards. Go online and you'll find dozens of greeting card websites that offer free customized cards for all occasions.

Bargain children's books

Next time you are at your favorite children's resale shop, make sure you check the book section. You'll be surprised to find hardcover classics in excellent condition with very reasonable price tags.

Reuse mouse pads

Have more mouse pads than you know what to do with? They are great furniture protectors for indoor clay flower pots. Just cut to fit the size of the pot.

Fitness videos

The website *www.videofitness.com* is a fitness site where you can exchange fitness videos for the cost of postage only. This is a great way to test fitness routines without investing a lot of money for the unknown.

Schoolbook exchange

Set up a schoolbook exchange at your private school to off-set the enormous price of purchasing new books each year.

Books for sale

Your bookshelf clutter might be another person's treasure. Don't discard all those books, sell them. Online book selling websites like *www.half.com* offer wonderful tutorials and information on how to turn your classics into cash.

Website finder

Check out *www.quickfindit.com* to find products and services on the Internet. It's free and offers live guides that link to related information of interest.

Weekly printer use

Printer cartridges can dry up for lack of use, so it's wise to use your printer at least once a week.

Collection of cords

To corral a group of cords (telephone, lamp, computer) buy a plastic shower rod cover. Cut to your desired length, then spread it open and enclose the cords. You can even match it to your carpet color, and then those cords will be even less visible.

Library for bestsellers

The next time you are in a store that sells new books make a list of the ones you want to read. Then head for the library or its website and either check them out or put your name on the waiting list. No need to purchase when you can borrow.

Jumpy mouse

To fix a jumpy computer mouse, remove the cove from the bottom of the mouse, remove the ball and wash it with soap and water. Air dry or wipe with a lint-free cloth, and you're back in business. Check the rollers inside the mouse, since they can get dirty, too.

Free software

Open Source software at *www.openoffice.org* features office software that is very similar to Microsoft Office. You will find clones for Word, Excel and PowerPoint. This is stable, professional software that is free and legitimate. A great alternative to expensive software.

Empty printer cartridge?

To "buy" yourself a few more days before you replace it, give your printer cartridge a good shake. You'll be amazed how many pages you can print on an "empty" printer cartridge.

Magazine deals

Check the Internet for magazine deals. Many sites such as *www.magazines.com* offer low subscription rates. At *www.amazon.com* you can purchase single copies for less than the newsstand.

Books and Computers

Library summer savings

During the summer many libraries give children free certificates for restaurants and fun things around town, after they've read a certain number of books.

Kid's software exchange

Set up a neighborhood "Software Shelf" to offset the high cost of children's computer software and conquer the boredom factor. When a child is done with a game just exchange with a neighbor who has a different game, always being careful not to violate copyright laws. Set it up like a library and let neighborhood kids borrow in exchange for adding their own titles to the library.

Bookmarks in a snap

Those metal snap hair clips make great, inexpensive bookmarks. You can snap the point of the clip so it points directly to the place on the page where you stopped reading. The clips hold onto the pages without ripping them. You can buy a sheet of them at the dollar store.

Newspaper subscriptions

If you subscribe to a newspaper, make sure you check out current subscription offers before renewing at your regular annual rate. You can save a bundle by renewing at the lower advertised rate—and you might even get some sort of freebie thrown in with it.

Printer savings

Conserve the ink in your printer's cartridge by adjusting the print quality. Choose "Draft" or "Fast Draft" for documents where print quality is not an issue.

CLEANING

Cleaning

Clean club

What's as cheap as water but cleans windows, mirrors, counter tops, chrome fixtures and stainless steel sinks so they shine like the sun? Why it's club soda! Just fill a spray bottle and away you go.

Cleaning reminder

In order to remind everyone in your family what has to be done in order to call a room in the house "clean," take pictures of each room and put them in a flip photo album. On the reverse side of the photos, list the chores to be done in each room. If someone asks if a room is clean enough, you can just tell them to check the list.

Rez-free carpets

Forget all those commercial carpet cleaning solutions in the grocery store. They cause more problems than they solve because they leave behind sticky residue. Instead make a simple 50/50 solution of white vinegar or non-sudsing household ammonia (you get your choice—but don't use both) and cool water. Gently blot into the carpet with a clean white rag and allow to sit for 5 minutes. Blot again to transfer the stain to the clean cloth. Repeat with clear water and allow to dry. A tough stain may require some scrubbing.

Scum-free shower doors

Who knew that a dryer sheet—even one that has been used—will remove the soap scum from shower doors? Pair with white vinegar for stubborn build-up.

Remove blood

To remove blood stains from your favorite apron (a lovely memory of that juicy T-bone steak, right?) just soak the affected area in a small amount of cold water and pour table salt on it. Wait a minute or two and watch as the salt turns pink. Rinse. Repeat as necessary if the stain has been set for a while.

Silk flowers

Pop those dusty silk posies into a paper bag along with a cup of table salt. Close the bag and shake. All the dust will stay behind in the salt. While you can recycle that salt, best you reserve it for flower dusting.

Fan static!

There's nothing like static electricity to turn a fan blade into a dust magnet. But that's no match for a dryer sheet. Just take one of those gems and wipe down that blade to release dust, pet hair and cobwebs, too.

Diamond sparkle

Gather up your gems and drop them into a small container that has a secure lid. Add a small amount of liquid dish soap and fill about half way with boiling water. Careful! Apply the lid tightly and swirl the mixture. Allow to cool; remove items and brush gently with a very soft small brush (an old ratty toothbrush is ideal). Rinse in clear, cool water. Enjoy the sparkle and count the money you didn't spend on a commercial jewelry cleaner.

Permanent marker

It's a tough assignment but someone has to get that permanent marker off the wall. A little rubbing alcohol on a cotton ball is just the thing to do it.

Dry-erase boards

To add luster and restore the surface of a dry-erase memo board, polish it down with a dryer sheet. Never thought of that, did you? You're going to be so happy.

10-second cleanup

You're exhausted after a long day of painting. The last thing you want to face is cleaning that messy paintbrush. Got ten seconds? Pour 1/2 cup of liquid fabric softener into a gallon of water. Stick that brush in, swish it around while counting to ten (slowly, please). Pull it out and allow yourself to be filled with wonder. A clean brush, just like that! Hopefully you were painting with water-based paint. If not, you're on your own.

Bucket o' soda

If you long to use a lot of super washing soda for the laundry and other cleaning chores—and who doesn't?—zip on over to the local pool supply to pick up a big bucket of soda ash. It's exactly the same thing: 100% sodium carbonate. Please do not confuse with baking soda, which of course you remember from chemistry class is sodium bicarbonate.

Flute brush

Ever noticed while cleaning baby bottles that the brush is curiously shaped like a champagne flute? Talk about wild and crazy coincidences! Double duty for your bottle brush will keep your lovely stemware in tip-top shape, too.

All-purpose cleaner

Ever worry that you might become faint while cleaning the house? Well here's a concoction that ensures its user does not fall into a deep sleep. It's potent! Might want to open the window just a smidge. In a plastic spray bottle mix together 1/4 cup rubbing alcohol, 1/4 cup non-sudsing household ammonia and 2 drops liquid dishwashing detergent and fill with water. Clean mirrors, glass and bathroom fixtures to your heart's content.

Silver cleaner

To clean tarnished silver flatware, line the bottom of a dish with aluminum foil. Sprinkle a heaping teaspoon of baking soda on it. Pour about an inch of boiling water into the dish followed by the silver pieces. The tarnish will disappear, as if by magic, provided the silver is touching the foil.

Shampoo chase

A terrific way remove soap scum from shower walls is with cheap shampoo. Take a sponge, make a good lather and scrub away. Rinse clean.

Crayon-fix

Count on a crayon in the shade of wood to hide those unfortunate scratches on furniture and woodwork. If you're lucky enough to have kids with that big 96-pack you've got lots of colors choices. One's bound to match.

Scrubbing bubbles

Sure you can buy the expensive stuff, or you can sprinkle a bit of baking soda on that dirty sink, faucets or stove top and clean it with a sponge dipped in white vinegar. You just might be surprised to discover you really can make your own scrubbing bubbles.

Bye-bye hard water ring

Don those lovely rubber gloves then use a pumice stone to remove the hard water rings from the toilet bowl. Minimal effort, maximum results.

Oh, those sippy lids

Is there anything worse than a stained rubber insert in a sippy cup? Trust me when I say you'll be happy that you've stocked up on denture cleaning tablets. Soak those lids overnight. There. Clean as a whistle.

Candle mess

Don't struggle getting that melted wax out of the votive holder. Just stick it in the freezer for a few minutes. The mess will pop right out.

Spots be gone

Tired of all those scuff marks and

scratches on your painted walls? Pour a small amount of nail polish remover on a cotton ball, dab the spots, rub ever so gently and presto! Spots are gone. You won't have to pick up a paint brush for a long time.

Tough floor cleaner

You'll need to collect a few unusual ingredients, but when you do you'll never go back to commercial floor cleaner: Mix together 1 gallon hot water, 2 tablespoons Murphy's oil soap, 1/4 cup washing soda, 1 cup white vinegar and 20 drops eucalyptus, peppermint, or tea tree essential oil (not fragrance oil). Use this full strength for mopping floors. No rinsing necessary. Use essential oils, not fragrance oils. The oils listed are antibacterial, and eucalyptus oil is also antifungal.

Ugly skid marks

Black-soled shoes often leave marks on vinyl floors. But don't sweat it! Hit them with a bit of fingernail polish remover on a moist paper towel or rag. Scuff marks are almost instantly gone.

Soft scrub

Making your own "soft scrub," is much cheaper and better than a store-bought product. Mix 3/4 cup baking soda, 1/4 cup powdered milk, 1/8 cup Murphy's oil soap (or liquid castile soap) and 5 drops lavender essential oil (or your favorite), with enough water to make a smooth paste, in any squirt—not spray—bottle. Make sure you use essential oils, not fragrance oil.

Hand de-greaser

Forget those pricey automotive hand cleaners. Why? Because you have a better product right there in the kitchen under the sink! Full strength original blue Dawn liquid dishwashing liquid cuts through grease and gets hands and nails clean with no harsh chemicals.

Baked-on yuck!

Don't we all hate pots and pans with burnt-on food? What a mess! You'll never fret again with this slick solution: Dryer sheets! Even used ones will work. Just fill the pot or pan with hot water, pop in a sheet or two and let it sit for a while. Oh, 20 minutes might be good, but overnight is better. All that yuck will just slide out and down the drain. Just make sure the sheet doesn't go with it!

Half-price steel wool

Cut your steel wool scouring pads (like Brillo or SOS) in half. Now you can afford to use a new one every time. No more slimy, yucky mess.

Cleaning

Liquid hand soap

Grate a 3.5 oz bar of soap containing moisturizing cream (like Dove) into a large bowl. Add 3 cups of water. Microwave on High 5 to 6 minutes, or until the soap is dissolved, stirring every 2 minutes. It will thicken as it cools. Fill soap dispensers. Makes perfect liquid hand soap for the cost of a bar.

Cheap antibacterial

Mix 1/2 teaspoon liquid chlorine bleach with 1 quart of water in a spray bottle. Cost? Oh, about a penny for a highly effective, kitchen disinfecting antibacterial that's not going to bleach everything in site. Use it to clean the refrigerator interior, countertops, cutting boards, sink and stove.

Stovetop cleaner

Have you checked the price of cleaners made especially for smooth stovetops? Better brace yourself. Or make a paste of baking soda and water instead and just apply with a clean cloth. Picks up all the burned-on residue in a flash. Rinse, then buff with a clean cloth.

Drain cleaner

Mix together 1 cup baking soda and 1 cup table salt. Store in a closed container that you have labeled clearly. Put 1/4 cup of mixture into each drain once a week. Follow with a kettle full of boiling water (at least one quart per drain). For a clogged drain use 1 cup of the mixture plus 1/2 cup white vinegar. Stand back because it's going to gurgle and bubble away. Wait 15 minutes then follow with the boiling water.

Vacuum bag

In a pinch you can re-use a vacuum cleaner bag. Take the full bag outdoors, cut the bottom seam and empty contents in the trash. Carefully re-roll and staple closed, then cover the area with strong tape to restrict any dust from escaping and clogging your machine.

Save the CD

You could buy a spray-on product designed to restore damaged CDs. You could, but you'd be wasting your money because you already have such a product. It's that bottle of Windex. No kidding. Spray on, wipe off and presto—like new. No skipping, no sticking.

Fuzzy ceilings

Textured ceilings collect fuzz and tiny dust bunnies. Don't even try to wash that ceiling. Instead grab two lint roller refills and cram one onto each end of a paint roller. Now roll the ceiling clean as you would any other linty situation. All the fuzz will stick to the lint rollers and you'll be so happy.

Quick clean fiberglass

Clean your fiberglass or acrylic tub and shower with a wet dryer sheet. It won't scratch, but will leave your tub and shower as clean as it was when brand-new.

Clean granite top

Stained granite? Sprinkle table salt on a cut lemon and scrub that stain. Allow the juice to remain for an hour, then rinse away. Don't worry. The salt is non-abrasive to granite.

Porcelain

Clean porcelain sinks or tubs by sprinkling cream of tartar on a damp cloth soaked in white vinegar. Works like a charm.

Clean grimy windows

To clean grimy windows use approximately one tablespoon of Cascade automatic dishwasher rinse agent in two gallons of water. Apply with a new sponge that has no soap residue. Windows will shine with no spots. If windows are extremely dirty, this may require a repeat performance.

Anti-rust magic

To keep steel wool scouring pads from rusting between uses, store the pad in a soap dish you've lined with aluminum foil. Don't ask why. It just works.

Septic tank activator

Calling all septic tank owners: Here is a cheap alternative to expensive activators you've been buying with your hard-earned cash: Dissolve one pound brown sugar in one quart of hot water. Allow to cool to lukewarm then stir in 2 teaspoons active dry yeast. Immediately flush the mixture down the toilet. That ought to do it.

Candle wax on carpet

Okay, so you didn't realize the candle was actually leaking all over the carpet. First let the wax harden. Next place an old dish towel on top of the wax and run a hot iron over the towel. Pick up the towel and place a clean area of the towel over the rest of the wax and continue to "iron" it up. Repeat this until all the wax has been absorbed into the towel. Depending on how much wax you're dealing with, you may need to use more than one towel.

Clean and minty-fresh

Want to remove a stain without

damaging the smooth surface of furniture and countertops? Give toothpaste a test on an inconspicuous place. The extra mild abrasives in toothpaste remove stains without scratching. Even works on rust. Simply rub a dab into the stain for about 30 seconds then wipe it away.

Salted fleas

Got fleas? Sprinkle the carpet with ordinary table salt. Allow to sit for several hours to dehydrate fleas and eggs. Vacuum well to pick up all salt.

Scuff marks

To get scuff marks off white patent leather shoes, dab a little fingernail polish remover on a paper towel and gently rub off the scuff mark.

Clean, by George!

You love your George Foreman grill—if only it was self-cleaning. Well, here's the next-best thing: Throw a soaking wet folded paper towel on the grill after you unplug it but while it is still hot. Close the lid. It will steam clean itself. When cooled just wipe off the residue. Easy.

Candle black

Don't you hate that black, smoky build-up that accumulates around your candle jars? Remove it with a dryer sheet—a new one or even one you've already used. Get it wet first and then just run the sheet around the rim. You'll see.

Burned coffee carafe

It happens to the best of us, so don't fret if you've burned the bottom of the coffee carafe. Drop a couple of ice cubes into that blackened pot followed by a tablespoon or so of table salt. Now start swirling those cubes in a frantic manner. Round and round the salt will scrub that mess clean off! Rinse clean, and you're back in business.

De-foggy mirror

Clean your bathroom mirrors with shaving cream and they will resist fogging up even when Junior takes his 45-minute shower.

Nail polish vs. carpet

Carpet will never win against spilled nail polish. But you'll give it a fighting chance if you move in with Windex as quickly as possible. Apply generously, then scrub vigorously with a clean white rag. May take some elbow grease, but it works on most types of carpet, particularly nylon.

Not just the toilet

Stubborn, ugly hard water deposits on porcelain sinks and tubs can be resistant to almost everything. But not toilet bowl cleaner. Wear gloves, apply sparingly, scrub appropriately, then rinse. Admire.

Germ-free sponge

Every time you run the dishwasher, stick in your kitchen sponge, too. Just hook it onto the rack with a clothespin so it can't go flying and land on the heating element. What a quick and efficient way to sanitize that little helper.

Ink stains

Why do pens wait to leak until dropped head first into a shirt pocket? There are several remedies: Cheap hairspray, the cheaper the better because it's mostly acetone. Soak that stain and blot out the ink with a clean white cloth. Or soak it in milk. Yep, good old milk that contains lactic acid. If the stain is fresh that will leach it right out of the fabric and into the milk, depending on the type of fabric you're dealing with. Formula 409, the commercial all-purpose cleaner, also does a good job on ink. Next time put the cap on first, okay?

Hold the elbow grease

For quick, easy clean-up of cookware, especially after cooking anything fried, generously sprinkle the hot pot with baking soda, add water, and let set till clean-up time. Any cooked-on food particles will wipe right out—no need for elbow grease.

Soap scum

To avoid having to clean soap scum from your soap dish, cut a sponge to the size of your dish, set it in the dish and put the soap on top. The soap drippings will be collected on the sponge, and all you have to do is rinse the sponge instead of scraping the dish.

Narrow containers

It's easy to clean baby bottles and small-mouthed containers with a little dish soap and uncooked rice kernels. Apply the top and shake. Rinse well. That bottle will come out spotless. The food or juice waste will disappear. Rinse afterwards.

Rust rings

Before putting your new can of shaving cream on a wet bathroom surface, cover the base rim with a thin coat of clear nail polish. No more irritating rust rings on the tub.

Cleaning

Wet vac

Spots on your light colored carpet? Flood the spot with warm, clean water, then vacuum dry with your shop vacuum set on "wet" to remove all of the water. Provided you get to each stain quickly, your carpet will stay clean and bright without the need for professional cleaning.

Flawless needlework

You've worked on it for months. The cross-stitch piece is done, but sadly your dingy fingerprints are not adding to its beauty. To give it a good cleaning, place the finished piece in a bowl, cover with table salt and leave it there for 2 to 3 hours. Remove the piece, shake off the salt and place in clothes dryer on warm for 15 minutes. Remove from dryer. The salt absorbs the oils and dirt from your hands without using water—leaving the piece as fresh as if never touched by human hands.

Scent of clean

When you change vacuum cleaner bags, add a drop of essential oil to the new bag. Now as you vacuum, your home will be filled with the subtle fragrance of your scent of choice. Lavender oil is the least expensive and a good choice for room fragrance. A 1-ounce bottle can last for 5 years.

Laminate countertops

To deep clean your laminate countertops—and remove sticky residue and most stains—use lacquer thinner. Uh-huh. Lacquer thinner. Use cautiously and with ventilation.

Fiberglass cleaner

Imagine such a simple solution for cleaning fiberglass: shampoo. Inexpensive shampoo on a damp cloth cleans fiberglass tubs and showers really well—also the surrounding walls. Rub the cloth on the tub to remove scum and dirt, then rinse.

Squeaky clean dishwasher

Sometimes even your dishwasher needs a good cleaning. Find two packages of unsweetened lemon Kool-Aid drink powder—that's right, the small packet with the familiar smiling pitcher on the front—and pour one into each of the dishwasher's detergent cups. Lemon Kool-Aid is loaded with citric acid—just the thing to clean out all the soap residue and hard water minerals that tend to collect inside a dishwasher. Run the dishwasher empty on the longest and hottest cycle available.

Egg cleanup

If you drop an egg on your linoleum

floor or your countertop, don't use a dish cloth or paper towel to wipe it up—simply sprinkle an ample amount of salt on the entire spill. Pick up with a cloth or a paper towel. Comes right up.

Steam cleaner solution

Instead of the pricey cleaning solution made especially for your home carpet steam cleaner, substitute with non-sudsing household ammonia. It does an amazing job. Be sure to test a small area first to check for carpet colorfastness.

Recycled air freshener

You can use dryer sheets to make your home smell good by attaching them to your furnace filter. Every time your furnace runs, you'll get a burst of fragrance throughout the entire house. You can also lay one in a vent to quickly freshen up a room.

Instant hand sanitizer

Mix together 2 parts rubbing alcohol, one part water, and enough petroleum jelly (Vaseline) to make it gel-like. Pour into a pump bottle for a homemade version of instant hand sanitizer.

Air freshener

Use a spray bottle filled with a 50/50 solution of water and white vinegar to freshen the air and to get rid of odors. The vinegar smell dissipates quickly, leaving the air smelling clean. For stubborn smells, spray the source.

Crayon marks

Need to remove "artwork" from walls, windows, floors, plastic toys or goodness knows what else? Grab a can of WD-40. This very versatile product lubricates and softens the wax, making it simple to wipe away the "art" with a paper towel.

Clean hands

Instead of paying $3 to $4 for a bottle of hand washing soap, pick up a bottle of bubble bath from the dollar store and use it to refill your empty bottles.

Easy candle removal

Pour a few drops of water into the bottom of a candle holder before inserting the new candle. Once that candle has burned down, the remaining wax will just pop out without much coaxing at all.

Odor remover

To remove musty odors from wet carpet place about six charcoal briquettes and a cup of Epsom salts in a shallow container. Place container in the offending area. Because these products are absorbent, odors will be gone in no time.

Slick sinks

Clean the sink as you normally would, then apply a small amount of paste car wax, following the same procedure as you would to wax a car: Apply, then allow to dry, then remove the haze with a soft cloth and a buffing motion. Keep the sink stopper closed so none of the residue goes down the drain. The sinks remain shiny and cleaner longer. Water will bead off and resist water marks. This works on the chrome faucets, too.

Easy oven clean

To clean your oven fill an old aluminum pie pan half full of household ammonia. Place the pie pan on the bottom shelf of your cold oven overnight, uncovered. Wipe down the oven with a sponge that has been dampened with warm water the following morning. Do this once a week for a month, and your oven will sparkle. Follow once monthly for maintenance. No messy foams, no harsh chemicals and no added expense beyond a cheap bottle of household ammonia and an old pie plate.

Shower curtain rescue

Every few weeks wash your shower curtains—along with a couple of white bath towels—in the washing machine with detergent and bleach. You'll kill and prevent mildew. Spin dry, re-hang. Now you will never have to face that gross black slimy action at the bottom of the shower curtain again.

Double duty

Rather than grabbing a bucket when preparing to mop the floor, reach for your trash can instead. It's the perfect "bucket" for hot soapy cleaning solution and a quick and handy way to clean and disinfect your trash can at the same time.

Dishwasher rinse aid

Most dishwashers have a special reservoir for liquid rinse aid. You can stop buying that expensive product and instead fill the compartment with white vinegar. A small amount will dispense with every wash, keeping dishes sparkling along with the inside of the dishwasher.

More than lemonade

Lemon cleans chrome and stainless steel so don't throw out those lemon rinds before first putting them to work. Run the cut edge of the lemon over the sink surface and faucets for a quick cleanup. Rinse well.

Glue gun cleanup

A used dryer sheet—like we're at all surprised there is yet another use—works well to remove "glue strings" from the nozzle of your gunky glue gun. Let the gun cool slightly so you won't burn yourself, then wipe the nozzle until the stuff comes off. May take a few repeats if your glue gun has suffered from your repeated neglect.

Vinyl floors

To clean black marks off vinyl floors, grab that can of WD-40 lubricant from the garage. Spray directly on the marks and use an absorbent paper towel to wipe those marks clean away. Now follow with a good rinse of soap and water because that WD-40 is slicker than grease.

Daily shower cleaner

To make a homemade version of daily shower cleaner spray, pour 1 part rubbing alcohol and 3 parts water into a spray bottle. Spray down the shower each day to keep on top of things.

Dust blaster

Got an air compressor in the garage? Great. Take your lampshades out there and blast them with that compressed air. Not only is this highly effective, it's likely the most fun you'll have all day.

Shower floor cleaner

Wonder how to get the ugly, dingy gray off the shower floor and return it to sparkling white? Toilet bowl cleaner that contains bleach. Squirt a generous amount around the floor of the shower. Allow it to sit for a few minutes. Scrub with hand brush and a little water. Now you can wash all that grayness down the drain.

Clean sink secret

Hotel housekeeping staffs have a secret: Shampoo—the cheap stuff, sample stuff—is a very effective sink cleaner. Who knew that just a bit on a wet cloth would clean and shine that sink like it's never shone before!

Pine sap

A cheap and safe way to remove pine tree sap from your car without damaging the finish is to rub it with a soft cloth soaked with plain 70 percent isopropyl rubbing alcohol, available at the pharmacy or drug store for less than a buck.

Cleaning

Sparkling dishes

If you love sparkling clean dishes and crystal clear glassware enough to go the second mile, here is a little trick you are going to love. First, mix up a batch of 1 part baking soda and 1 part borax (Twenty Mule Team Borax is in the laundry aisle). Keep this in a covered container. During the dishwasher's rinse cycle open the machine and throw in just 1 tablespoon of this mixture plus 1/2 cup of vinegar. This will remove all traces of soap and residue and leave your dishes squeaky, sparkly clean and spot-free. Warning: Do not use this method if you have installed a water softener. Chemical reactions could permanently etch your glassware.

Quick-clean baking dishes

Baking dishes and pans can become terribly greasy and downright gross with a build-up of baked-on miscellany. Here's a quick fix: Spray a light coating of oven cleaner on all surfaces. Allow to sit for at least 15 minutes. Now all that stuff should come off with a light scrubbing. Wash as usual.

Iron glide

Use a dryer sheet to clean the bottom of your iron. Let your iron cool down, then rub it across the plate when it's still somewhat warm and the gunk will slide right off onto the sheet. Now it will glide with amazing ease.

Dust Buster filters

Can you believe how much those replacement filters cost? Yikes. And did you know that you can re-use a filter several times before sending it to its final reward? You can. Simply remove that filter, empty the particulates and then rinse it carefully under warm water. Shake dry and pop it back into the Dust Buster. Carry on.

Clean grimy caulk

Okay, so we aren't so anxious to admit it, but doesn't everyone battle with dingy caulk? You know, that white "filler" between tub and wall, tub and floor, and shower floor and wall? Here's a reasonable way to clean it. Load an old toothbrush with toothpaste. Just as you would brush your child's teeth, brush that caulk. Gently, please—you do not want it to tear. In just a few minutes, it'll be as good as new. And minty-fresh, too!

Clean is blind

Never again go through the horror of taking your blinds down, soaking them in the tub, scrubbing them and laying them in the sun to dry. Simply use a dryer fabric softener sheet (such as Bounce or Snuggles, or something comparable in texture) to clean your blinds while they are hanging. Close the blinds and use the dryer sheet to wipe each blind. The rough texture of the dryer sheet removes all dust build-up easily and quickly and leaves your blinds shining.

Foil a toddler

What is it about toddlers and permanent markers? If that phenomenon for you means throwing out that dry erase board, stop. A can of Lysol spray could be your counteraction. Spray the board generously. Allow to sit for a few minutes, then wipe over all the leftover marks with a paper towel.

The last drop

It can be frustrating to be down to the last few drops of a product dispensed in a spray bottle and be unable to spray it out. To get the last bit of cleaner out, drop a few marbles or small stones right into the bottle. This will raise the level of the cleaner.

Soap? On carpet?

A bar of Fels Naptha laundry soap just might be the carpet spot cleaner that wins you over. Just get the area damp, rub with a small amount of Fels Naptha and work in with your fingers. Blot it up with a clean white cloth, and the stain will be gone. Best that you rinse well so as not to leave behind even a hint of soap. Try this on old, stubborn stains. Prepare to be pleasantly surprised.

'Fridge shelf "paper"

Cover the glass shelves in your refrigerator with clear plastic wrap. No more washing shelves. When they get sticky and icky, just remove and replace the shelf "paper."

Hairspray over spray

If your bathroom floor, counter and mirror have a build-up of hairspray over spray, here's the solution: Rubbing alcohol. Just wipe those offending areas with a generous amount. It cuts right through the hairspray and disinfects at the same time.

Spin-fresh deodorizer

Add a couple of drops of your favorite essential oil to the inside of the cardboard toilet tissue roll. With each turn, a subtle hint of fragrance is released into the room.

Dishwasher soap savings

It's not good to overdo on the

amount of automatic dishwasher detergent you use. Depending on the hardness of your water, it could permanently etch or cloud your glassware. Better that you measure carefully according to the dishwasher manufacturer's instructions. So instead of pouring or dumping, empty the entire contents of that box of detergent into an airtight container. Now use a measuring spoon to measure the exact amount of detergent.

Berry stains

When you get a stain from any kind of berry on a tablecloth, placemat or napkin, pour boiling water through the stain over the sink. This method will remove most stains immediately, but sometimes it takes more than one session of pouring through.

Dust mitts

A pair of old mittens makes for handy dusting cloths, and old worn tube socks come in as a close second. Just put them on your hands and away you go. Occasionally step outdoors and clap your hands together to remove the dust.

Extended labeling

When you make up household solutions, write the recipe right on the plastic bottle with a permanent marker. Now you won't have to look it up to make a refill.

Carpet spotter

To remove spots from carpet in between cleanings: Mix 3 tablespoons dish soap, 1 teaspoon white vinegar, 1/2 teaspoons household ammonia and 3/4 cup water. Use a spray bottle that makes this mixture into a foam (or you can stir with a whisk to make foam). Place only the foam on the spot. Rub in; let set briefly. Then rub back and forth with a clean rag. Spot's gone!

Lipstick stainage

If you've ever suffered the heartbreak of a lipstick going through the laundry, you know the feeling of despair. But cheer up! That can of WD-40 will take care of the problem. Saturate the stains, allow to sit for 30 minutes, then re-launder as usual.

Miracle bathroom cleaner

It's simple but it works. Original blue Dawn dishwashing liquid has some kind of miraculous quality about it that makes it "melt" through stubborn soap scum and hideous build-up on showers and tubs, no matter whether porcelain, acrylic or fiberglass. Use it straight up and you'll bless the day you read this tip.

Java hands

The best way to really get the dirt and stains out of the lines in your hands, especially after painting, gardening or polishing silver, is to rub your hands with coffee grounds for several minutes. Then rinse and wash with soap, and you'll have the smoothest hands ever. And make sure those are used coffee grounds, ok?

Cleanest windows ever

A uniquely effective way to clean windows and mirrors to a sparkling streak-free shine is to spray on a 50/50 mix of vinegar and water then buff dry with newspaper. No streaks even when the sun shines.

Polishing antique furniture

Never polish antiques with a penetrating formula such as oil because it will change the color of the wood over time and reduce the future value. Only use a wax polish that can later be removed without damaging the highly-prized, original finish.

Furniture polish

Homemade furniture polish is better than anything you buy because it polishes, cleans and protects furniture. Use 1/3 cup each of boiled linseed oil, turpentine and white vinegar. Mix together and shake well. Apply with a soft cloth and wipe completely dry with another clean, soft cloth. Buy the boiled (it must be boiled, but do not attempt this yourself) linseed oil at the hardware store.

Shower door spots

Hard water stains or film on your glass shower doors can be easily removed with a soft cloth and any cheap baby oil. Be very careful not to get it on the floor of the shower/tub because it will be slippery. Repeat when necessary. It will also prevent future build-up.

Silver cleaner

To clean silver make a thick paste of baking soda and water and massage gently into the silver with an old, very soft toothbrush. Rinse under warm water, or if the piece is too big, wipe off with a wet washcloth and buff to a shine with a clean all-cotton towel.

Slippery slide

Take a piece of wax paper large enough to wrap around your hand and "dust" or "clean" the shower curtain rod as well as your clothes closet rod. The little bit of wax on the wax paper stays behind, keeping hangers and shower rings moving well.

Swiffer Wet Jet refills

There are multiple ways to refill a Swiffer Wet Jet liquid container with your own solution of white vinegar and water, but none so quick and easy as boring a hole at the top of the container. Refill 1/3 full and away you go. Filling the container full might result in the liquid sloshing out unless you figured that you could simply stop it with a cork. Use a turkey baster to get the liquid in there quickly without spills.

Kid-safe cleaner

This all-purpose cleaner is safe for kids and pets as it contains no ammonia or other harsh ingredients: One cup distilled white vinegar, 1 gallon water, a few drops of essential oil and just *a drop* of dishwashing liquid. Keep in a tightly closed container and label the container. This works wonders on hardwood floors.

Tight squeeze

Turn your big vacuum cleaner into one that can get into microscopic spaces with the help of a drinking straw. Attach it as an extension to the smallest attachment, using duct tape to seal the openings. Now you can vacuum tight places like keyboards and drawers with ease.

Shower door cleaner

Are you sick and tired of buying expensive cleaners for your shower doors, only to be disappointed again? The answer is cheap shampoo. The cheapest shampoo applied to a wet wash cloth and used to clean the shower doors works better than any expensive cleanser. Your shower doors will once again be crystal clear and beautiful.

Cleaning blitz

Don't have all day to clean? No problem. Set the timer for 10 (20, 30) minutes. Do all you can in one room until it sounds. That's it. Move on to another room and repeat. Or if you're really strapped for time, challenge yourself to clean like crazy for 5 minutes. You'll be surprised how much you can get done if you are that focused.

Spot be gone

Got a stubborn, burned-on spot? Saturate it with rubbing alcohol (carefully if that spot is on your gas stovetop) then scrub it with a sponge. Works when other products do not.

Newsprint

Forget the expensive paper towels.

Today's newspaper is still the best paper to clean windows and mirrors. Okay, yesterday's paper works just as well.

Scouring pads

Perhaps someday someone will tell us why this works, but until then just believe. A scouring pad like Brillo or SOS is rarely spent with just one use. But leave it out and it will turn into a mess. So do this: Return the partially used pad to the box and close it. Next time you need it, it will be as good as new.

Blind success

Here's a miraculous way to clean blinds—even horrible, dirty blinds that do not respond to normal kinds of cleaning. Run hot water in the bathtub. Drop in 3 or 4 Cascade Action Pacs (they contain Dawn liquid as well as Cascade powder). Once dissolved, place a blind in the water. Allow to sit for 20 to 30 minutes. Then lift the blind up and down a few times to allow all that dirt to fall off. Rinse in clear water. Hang to dry.

Wooden spoons

You may not be stuck with stains on your wooden spoons if you follow this procedure: Soak the spoon in plain tap water for 15 minutes. Now place it in the microwave on a paper towel and heat on High for 30 seconds. Carefully remove the spoon (it will be hot) and toss the towel. Your spoon should look great.

Last ditch effort

Lysol Mildew Remover with bleach is manufactured to combat mildew in tubs and showers. But this product has another use. Some have success removing spots that even the dry cleaners could not get out of a garment. Be sure to check for colorfastness. Surprisingly, while the spot goes away, even colored items are not harmed. Think of this as a last-ditch effort—just in case your results are not so stellar.

De-sticker

Whenever you have a sticky situation, think baby oil. Just apply a little oil to the sticker, let it soften and off it comes. Simple.

General cleaner

You can't get much simpler or cheaper than this: Mix rubbing alcohol 50/50 with water in a spray bottle. That's it. Cleans everything, is safe for the environment and easy on the wallet.

Cleaning

Sash brush

Invest a few bucks in a painter's sash brush. The bristles are very soft and cut to a sharp angle. This is the best handy tool for dusting the most intricate cracks and crevices of everything from window sills to fine collectibles.

Baking soda

Fill a Parmesan cheese shaker with baking soda. It's attractive enough to leave out on the counter and handy enough to use for scrubbing anything. Baking soda is a non-abrasive cleanser.

Diapers double duty

A large cloth diaper fits a Swiffer Wet Jet floor cleaner perfectly. It's absorbent, soft, and best of all, reusable.

Washer scum

Use any bathroom soap scum remover to clean the inside of your washing machine. Spray it all around the rim where scum collects and then just wipe it all away.

Another oven cleaner

A great non-smelly way to clean your oven is with baking soda. Just mix it with water to make a paste. Wearing rubber gloves, smear it all over the inside of the oven and leave overnight. In the morning it will be dry. Now use a wet sponge to remove the dried mixture. All that icky oven stuff will come right off with it.

Too many bubbles

If you ever have the unfortunate experience of mixing up liquid dishwashing soap with automatic dishwasher detergent, you will be overcome with soap bubbles. In fact, they could spill out of the machine all over the kitchen. Here's the handy solution: White vinegar. Open the door and pour in a cup full, then allow the cycle to finish. It will dissipate all those bubbles.

Cleaning whiteboards

Can't get all traces of the dry marker from the whiteboard? There are three solutions that we know of, depending on which item you have handy. Toothpaste does a great job. Liquid car wax (like Turtle Wax) also takes away all the shadows and leaves the board white and shiny as new. Or, believe it or not, black coffee on a cloth works, too.

Microwave cleaner

Fill a 2-quart bowl half way with water and add 2 tablespoons of baking soda. Microwave on High for 5 minutes so the liquid has a chance to create a lot of steam. Carefully remove the bowl and wipe down the inside of the oven. No scrubbing.

Where the janitor shops

Want to pay wholesale prices for high quality, specialty cleaning products—like those that contain enzymes? Check a janitorial supply store.

Lipstick stains

If you ever decide to leave a tube of lipstick on your cloth car seat on a very hot day for a very long time, using isopropyl (rubbing) alcohol removes all traces. Saturate, blot, saturate, blot. Blot some more until it's all gone.

Carpet stains

If you have off-white or beige carpet, Lysol Basin Tub and Tile Cleaner removes just about everything. Spray the area and blot with a clean cloth. It may take a couple sprays, but the stain will be gone. This even works on those unknown stains.

Odor control

Bowls of white vinegar will absorb the odor of cigarette smoke after a party or gathering. After the party, just put out two or three bowls of white vinegar overnight. In the morning there will be no smoke odor left. It's cheap and it works like a charm.

The best tub scrubber

Don't throw away your used mesh loofah sponges. They are the absolute best thing for cleaning a bathtub that has a soap or scum ring. Use the cleaner of your choice then scrub the scum away effortlessly with your mesh sponge. It works wonders and also recycles the sponge.

Lampshade cleaning

Got fabric lampshades with very fine pleats that are hard to clean and harbor dust? Use a baby hair brush. The bristles get between the pleats to remove the dust and dirt, and a baby brush is so soft it will not crush or damage the pleats. Your shades will look like new.

More rust stains

Use regular white toothpaste to remove stains from vinyl floors, countertops and dishes that may have come in contact with a cast iron pan.

Cleaning

Vaulted ceilings

If you have very high ceilings, here's a way to get rid of all those cobwebs. Get a length of PVC pipe from the home improvement store that is close in diameter to the hose attachment of your vacuum cleaner. Stick the hose end into the pipe and wrap a bit of duct tape around it to seal the connection. Now you can reach those cobwebs no problem. PVC is really cheap, by the way.

Window cleaning

Sure, newsprint is the best material for cleaning windows. But the ink makes a real mess on your hands. So use unprinted newsprint. Call your local newspaper company and ask if they have any end rolls. Some give them away for free; others charge a couple of bucks. Either way it's worth it to find out. This paper is also great for kids' drawings, crafts and picnic table covers.

Spectacles cleaner

A drop of shampoo cleans eyeglasses as well if not better than optical cleaner. Shampoo is formulated to remove grease and natural body oils.

Dust cloths

You are going to love making your own pre-treated dusting cloths because they are so much cheaper than the ones you buy. Mix together 2 parts hot water and 1 part lemon oil. Dip lint-free cloths (like old kitchen towels) into the mixture. Squeeze thoroughly, then hang to air dry. Store in a clean coffee can or other air-tight metal container.

All-purpose cleaner

Here's a recipe for a natural, all-purpose cleaner that costs pennies to make. To one quart water, add one teaspoon each of liquid dish soap, borax, lemon juice and vinegar. Mix well and pour into a spray bottle. Hard water option: If you have very hard water or need to clean stubborn soap scum, add two teaspoons each of lemon juice and white vinegar.

Fake snow

Spray-on snow looks so pretty when sprayed on windows at Christmas time, but have you tried to get the stuff off? It's not easy. Unless you know to grab that cheap bottle of shampoo you keep on hand just for tough cleaning jobs. Works on mirrors, too.

Burned-on food

We all know how difficult it is to remove burned-on food from kitchen pots. Try sprinkling some dishwasher detergent in the pot and soaking overnight. It's like magic!

Erase restore

Sometimes pencil erasers get dirty and smudge, leaving a black smear on the page. Clean pencil erasers by lightly sanding on an emery board until the eraser is clean. No more smudges!

Thermos cleaner

Does your coffee thermos look like a science experiment inside? The easiest way to clean it is with 2 or 3 effervescent denture cleanser tablets. Go for the store brand. Let them fizz and do the cleaning for you.

Sliding doors

After cleaning the track of your sliding glass patio door, run a piece of paraffin wax or a candle back and forth along the track. That door will slide like a brand-new door.

Shiny commode

Toilet bowl cleaners all claim to be the very best and make your bowl shine. Here is a tip that does not even involve any cleaner. Put 3 tablets of Vitamin C in the toilet—do not flush, but allow to sit overnight. Then scrub the bowl in the morning. Amazing results.

Votive candle removal

To get your votive candles out of the votive cups, just spray the votive cup with a little non-stick cooking spray before putting in the candle. When the candle burns down and it is time to remove the remainder, you will find that it removes VERY easily.

Crushed glass

When a glass breaks pick up the large pieces as you normally would. But to ensure you get all of it—even the tiny pieces you cannot see—take a slice of bread and lay it directly on top of the glass and press gently, then throw away bread slice. This picks up all broken glass. You won't have to worry that you missed any.

Unlikely duster

Pantyhose material makes for soft and easy-to-use dust cloths which very quickly can be run along baseboards, behind doors and on hardwood floors. Dust and loose hair cling to the fibers and make a real neat cleanup job. Since you'll use ruined hose anyway, just toss the them—dirt and all—into the trash.

Crevice cleaner

Use a toothbrush to give your

kitchen sink fixtures a good cleaning. Toothbrushes also work well to clean meat tenderizing mallets and the grinding plates of juicers. When you're done, sterilize the brush with isopropyl alcohol or hydrogen peroxide.

Drip-proof cleaning

To clean your chandelier hang an umbrella upside down from the light fixture. Fill a small spray bottle with warm water and two tablespoons rubbing alcohol and give the chandelier a good spray. Any drips will be caught by the umbrella.

Easy vacuuming

Keep an extension cord on your vacuum cleaner so you can continue to vacuum larger areas without having to stop and plug in the vacuum somewhere else. And whenever you need an extension cord, you'll know right where to find it.

Foil dustpan

If you have a small pile of dirt and debris that needs to be swept up but you can't find your dustpan, try this tip: Wet a small piece of aluminum foil on both sides and flatten it against the floor. Sweep your mess onto the foil and throw the whole thing out.

Grinder cleaner

To keep your coffee grinder clean run cornmeal through it from time to time. Then just pour it out and brush any remaining debris with a small paintbrush set aside for this purpose.

Hairspray removal

To remove hairspray that has baked onto your curling iron, use a few drops of rubbing alcohol on a cotton ball or cloth and wipe down the cool iron. Then wipe the iron with a wet cloth.

Ink solution

To remove ink of felt pens, markers and ink jet cartridges from your hands use antibacterial hand sanitizer. Keep it by your desk and use as needed. Hand sanitizer can remove ink stains from other objects, too.

Mop your walls

For anyone who has difficulty getting on their hands and knees or stretching to scrub the bathtub and walls around it, use your kitchen mop. You get great leverage to apply pressure without killing your knees or straining your back. A long handled scrub brush works well to clean grout.

Moth ball odor

To rid a cedar chest of a mothball smell, put some crumpled up newspaper in the chest for several days. You may need to replace it several times, but eventually it will get rid of the odor.

Pouring cleaning products

If you like your "soft scrub" cleaning products but have trouble getting them out of the bottle, fill the container with water. This makes the products much easier to pour without a loss of cleaning power. Of course, they will last longer, too.

Recycle paint thinner

After using a paint thinner, pour the used thinner into a wide mouth plastic container, put the lid on and leave it until the next time you need to clean something. The sludge will have settled and you can pour off the clear liquid for cleaning. When there is too much sludge, you can label the container and send it off to the hazardous waste depot.

Rolling clean

Instead of using a vacuum attachment to dust cloth lamp shades, try using a lint roller to pick up the dust.

Rust remover

Shaving cream cans often leave ugly rings on your tile and bathroom counters. To clean these rings put a little toothpaste on a wet washcloth and very gently rub the stains in a circular motion. The very fine grit of the toothpaste removes the stains almost immediately without doing any damage to the counter. Toothpaste will even take rust stains off marble surfaces.

Scuffs be gone

To remove scuff marks from the floor without getting down on all fours cut a small "X" in a tennis ball and attach it to the end of a broomstick to hold the ball in place. Then rub the tennis ball over the marks to remove them easily and quickly.

Life of a sponge

If you use sponges to wash dishes, don't throw them away when they get too dirty. Keep them in a bucket and use for jobs like cleaning the litter box or washing tires. When the job is done, you can just throw that old sponge away.

Sparkle plenty

When you clean around your bathroom or kitchen sink instead of a toothbrush to get around the base of the faucet, use hydrogen peroxide. Pour some into the cap and with a cotton swab apply it all around the edges. It bubbles up and pulls the dirt right off just like it does on a cut. Then take another swab and wipe up the dirt and peroxide. Your faucet will sparkle.

Stain sanitizer

If you get ink on something at work, hand sanitizer can dissolve the ink. Use it on clothes (just dab on fingertips, rub it in and blot with a tissue), desk top, phone, and key board when it gets accidentally marked by a pen. It sanitizes the desk top and phone, too!

Sticker remover

Rub a dryer sheet on stubborn stickers or sticky residue to remove it.

Swiffer dusting sheet

Think those dusting sheets are only good for one use? Think again. Run a few through the washer and dryer and they'll come out good as new.

Vacuum care

When your vacuum cleaner's rotating brush gets tangled in the strings and hairs that it has picked up from the carpet, use a seam ripper to easily cut through the mess so you can untangle the brush.

Coffee stain magic

To clean a coffee pot, put a few drops of automatic dishwasher liquid inside and fill up the pot with hot water. After soaking for a few minutes give the inside a quick swish with a cloth or sponge and all the stains will be gone. No scrubbing necessary.

Clothing and Shoes

Clothing and Shoes

Bottled knee highs

Keep your knee highs in a large prescription bottle. You can write the color of the knee highs on the plastic top. The bottles will protect the hose from runs and don't take up much space in a drawer or cabinet.

Button at the ready

When you buy a garment that comes with extra buttons, sew them to an inside seam allowance of the garment. Then they are always with the garment and you won't have to hunt for a replacement when you need one.

Button bond

If you dab a bit of clear nail polish on the thread going through a button, it will hold much longer. The polish locks the threads in place.

Button fix

When sewing a large button onto a coat, use dental floss instead of regular thread. You can also use heavy thread and put a small button on the other side to strengthen the stitches. Your buttons won't pop off so easily.

Final use

When sorting through worn socks, shirts or other small clothing items, set some aside for one more use. Use them on the next camping trip, road trip or when you have a dirty job to do—then throw them out. This makes for less dirty laundry to carry if you are backpacking or camping.

Kool colors

If you want to dye a garment but don't have any clothing dye on hand, use a packet or two of Kool-Aid. Pour the drink mix along with some hot water into a tub and let your garment soak in it. Your clothes will be dyed in a few hours.

Mending jeans

If the metal button on your jeans comes apart and falls off, it is impossible to sew back on. Instead use some super glue to affix the knob and back stud through the fabric. Let it set for a few days, then wash and dry it. Your jeans should be perfectly wearable again.

Pin holder

A magnetic business card (like the ones you receive from local Realtor's and pizza deliveries) laid magnetic side up is perfect for keeping straight pins from rolling off the table and onto the floor.

Purse saver

To pack away your winter scarves and hats, store them inside a handbag or purse that you don't plan on using during the spring and summer. The winter accessories will help the purse keep its shape. Just make sure not to over stuff.

Quick button fix

If you are at work or out in public and your button pops off, see if you can find a twist tie (the kind that closes a bread wrapper). Tear the paper off and use the wire in place of thread to secure the button until you get home.

Shoe protector

It is easy for heels or other nice shoes to get scratched when packed in a suitcase. Before you put the shoes in the bag, slip each one in an old sock and they will be protected. Your clothes will stay cleaner, too.

Shoes for less

If you are a female, you can purchase top quality sneakers in boy's and men's sizes at huge savings. Women's sizes are about a shoe size smaller in the men's department.

Freshen shoes

Stick a used dryer sheet in your smelly shoes. Leave the sheet there overnight, and the shoes will smell fresh again the next day.

Waterproofing stick

Don't spend a lot of money on products to waterproof shoes. Clean your shoes or boots really well and buy a stick of lip moisturizer like Chapstick. Rub the moisturizer all over your shoes. This is a great way to waterproof during the winter months.

Remnant clothing

Keep a list of yardage and notions needed for your favorite clothing patterns in your purse. When you're out shopping stop by the yardage store or sewing department and check out the remnant table. If you find fabric you like check your list to see if it works for any patterns you have. This is an easy way to add a cute skirt or blouse to your wardrobe for hardly any cost, and keeps you from buying fabric or notions that won't work with the patterns you like.

Cleaning sneakers

To get white leather sneakers clean and white again, use a baby wipe to get the dirt off and avoid drying the leather like a wet cloth can.

Sparkling clean

Hand sanitizers work great cleaning leather tennis shoes. Get the dirt and scuff marks off in a jiffy.

Stop the runs

Should your nylons begin to run while you're at work put a little drop of liquid paper (white out) on the run and it will stop. Try to put it in a spot that's not visible. Hair spray and nail polish also stop nylon runs, but since these are not usually available in an office setting liquid paper will work just as well.

Pants to shorts

Kids generally start school in the fall with new jeans, but generally by Christmas they're ready for a new pair, and by summer the knees are shot and the pants too short. The solution? Make shorts. Don't sew? Take them to a dry cleaner or tailor in your area that does small alterations. It's usually not more than $2 a pair, which is a lot less expensive than buying new shorts. Plus, you're recycling.

Get rid of hanger marks

If you have pointed hanger marks in the shoulders of your knit tops put on the top and relax the hanger bump with your hand-held blowdryer. It's amazing how quickly the hanger bumps disappear.

Moth-proofing

Rather than buying expensive cedar hangers, tiles or drawer liners, it is much cheaper to buy a package of cedar chips packaged for hamster bedding. Simply tie the chips into cheesecloth bundles or old pantyhose material. These can then be placed in drawers or hung in closets.

Cover that V

If the V-neck in a dress or blouse is too low make a matching insert. Cut a piece of the material from the inside back of the neck (sometimes the tag is very easy to remove or none is there at all), finish one of the edges, and sew the insert into the V-neck. The material is free, easy to add and it looks like it's part of the design.

Hanger organizing

Not sure what you've worn from one season to the next? When you change your closets over for a new season, put the hangers (with the clothes attached) on the rod backwards. When you wear an item, turn the hangers around facing the conventional way. At the end of the season you can easily see what you've worn, what needs to be cleaned, and what you need to think about giving away.

Designer deals online

Don't pay retail for designer clothes. There are many websites that have great deals on clothing from all kinds of designers including clothing for women, kids and men. A very popular website to visit is *www.bluefly.com*, which has a lot of clothes at 50% off retail.

Shorten your slip

If you're rushing to get ready and find that your slip is too long for your outfit shorten it temporarily. Cut the waist from an old pair of pantyhose, placing the elastic around your waist over the slip. The elastic holds the slip to just the right length.

Clothes for twins

If you have kids the same gender who are also about the same size, buy their clothes in different colors-everything from sock to underwear, shirts, pants, etc. You'll have a much easier time sorting the clean clothes. Sears KidVantage Wearout Warranty will replace Sears clothes for free if a kid wears them out before he outgrows the item. This is a great program especially for little boys who go through the knees of their jeans long before they're outgrown.

Keep white shoes white

Nurses know a thing or two about white shoes and white shoe polish: The best and cheapest way to keep white shoes white is with a can of flat white spray paint. A large can is often on sale and works better than any shoe polish. And it takes only a few minutes to "polish" the shoes.

Shipping charges

When ordering online find out if the item can be shipped to the company's retail store near you. You may be able to eliminate all shipping charges if you agree to pick up the merchandise at the store.

Color coordinates

Pick a color palette that you like and looks good on you and stick with it. Buying clothes in every color of the rainbow is a surefire way to make sure you have a closet filled with clothes you'll never wear.

Hanging scarves

Take shower curtain rings and snap them together to make a long chain. Take a hanger and pit the hook through the top ring. Now you have a hanging scarf holder that will keep dozens of scarves neat, visible and completely organized.

Belt ends

To keep longer ends of belts in place use double-stick tape. Having the belt end attached to the belt makes for a cleaner look.

Pantyhose life

When you get a small run in your pantyhose above the ankle, mark an x on the inside tag with a marker. That lets you know to wear that pair with slacks or a long skirt. Saves time and frustration in the morning.

Boot stuffing

Instead of using expensive boot stuffers to keep your boot tops from falling over and creating a crease while they are stored in the closet, get one of those long, dense foam pool toys called "noodles" that kids play with in the swimming pool. Cut it in two and you have a pair of perfect boot stuffers. Foam noodles are a lot cleaner and easier to handle and sturdier than rolled up newspaper.

Pattern weights

If you are a seamstress, you know the joy of using pattern weights instead of pins to hold a pattern in place while cutting. Here's a way to make your own very effective weight: Reuse your old, empty spice containers, filling them with clean, fine sand. Once filled, glue the tops on well so the sand will not leak out. Lastly, glue a piece of scrap felt to the bottom so they will not slip on the pattern.

Fuzzballs

You can easily remove pilling from shirts, sweaters, even upholstery—with a new disposable razor. Simply shave all those tiny fabric balls away. Do make sure you do this carefully so you do not slash the fabric. Test your skills in an inconspicuous place first.

Recycle plastic

Instead of buying a tie or scarf holder, use the plastic holder from a six-pack of beverages. Hook it over a hanger in your closet. Tie scarves and hang ties from the rims.

Tighten a snap

To tighten up a snap that isn't holding it together anymore (especially irritating on the legs of otherwise perfect baby and toddler clothes) take a very small flathead screwdriver into the groove of the female side of the snap. Push back the little metal rim all along the circle until the little gaps are gone and the connection is tight again.

Never-retrieved clothes

For great clothing bargains, check your dry cleaner for clothes they have For Sale that were never picked up. Often these are high-end items that are in good shape and nicely cleaned.

Cheap shoe cleaner

Scrubbing Bubbles bathroom cleaner works great to clean expensive leather tennis shoes. It also works wonders on sandals made of any kind of foamy or spongy material. It takes away that dirty footprint, and the sandals smell better, too. Be sure to test this carefully in an inconspicuous place.

Stubborn lint

You can win the battle with stubborn lint stuck to wool pants or other items if you come armed with a new Scotch Teflon scrubbing pad. Not only will it loosen the stuck-on lint when rubbed across it, it will also pick it up and remove it. Happy days are here again.

Watch savings

Can't find the right watch for your small wrist? Check the kid's department. You'll be thrilled with the selection and the prices, too.

Like-new sneakers

A Clorox Gel pen will clean up old discolored white tennis shoes and makes them look new again.

Static cure

If you find when you are dressing that your slacks, dress or skirt is clinging (static electricity), don't fret, just spray the inside lightly with hair spray. You don't need to let it dry, just turn back to the right side and slip it on.

A measure of success

When going to yard sales and thrift stores carry a fabric tape measure and a little notebook of your family's clothing measurements. Often times on used clothing the size labels are missing so measuring is essential.

New again

If the uppers on your good leather shoes are still in great shape, have them re-soled and re-heeled. For a fraction of the cost of a new pair, yours will look like brand-new again.

Zap static cling

Use a dab of hand lotion right over your pantyhose to eliminate static cling. Always carry a travel-size bottle of lotion for this purpose.

Spare pair

When buying colored or patterned socks buy an extra pair. Now if one is lost in the washer or dryer you'll have a spare.

Little girls clothing

Buy jumpers and overalls a size larger than required then move the buttons up a few inches on the straps. As your little one grows, move the buttons. You'll get a couple of seasons from the same garment and save money in the process.

Save wear and tear

Instead of wearing your dress shoes to work, wear tennis shoes and bring your dress shoes separately. This will save wear and tear on your shoes from walking and also from driving. Here's your bonus: You'll have your sneakers with you so you can take a walk at lunchtime.

Shirt recycle

Often it's the cuffs that are the first to go on a man's long sleeved shirt. No problem. Cut back the sleeves and hem them up for an instant summer shirt. Not a seamstress? You do the cutting, ask the dry cleaner to finish the edge.

Women's shoe trick

If you wear size seven or smaller, look for casual shoes in the boy's department. You'll find great tennis shoes, deck shoes, hiking boots, cowboy boots and sandals for half the price of the same thing in the women's shoe department. This also works for ski boots and skates, even cleats and golf shoes, too.

Tough hose

Before wearing hose for the first time wash by hand using a gentle detergent. After washing and squeezing out the water, roll hose into a ball and wrap with plastic wrap. Place in freezer until frozen. Take out of freezer, allow to thaw, and then hang to dry as usual. This toughens the fibers making them more durable.

Scuffs off patent leather

Use fingernail polish remover to remove scuff marks from patent leather shoes. Works great but you should test in an inconspicuous place first just to be on the safe side.

Renewed leather

Restore color to leather shoes, belts, bags, etc. by re-dyeing them.

Leather dyes are found in many places but the most reliable is a shoe repair shop. Take in anything of leather and a good shoe repairman can re-dye with either the same or a darker color.

Hanging blazers

When hanging suit jackets or blazers on a curved, shaped, wooden or plastic clothes hanger, turn the hanger around and hang the jacket or blazer facing you. Placing the hanger backwards keeps the shape of the shoulders in a sturdier, tighter position.

Great belt deal

The discount clothing stores seem to frequently have excellent buys and a large selection of high quality, designer brand, men's leather belts. The only problem is they're all in very large sizes. Not a problem. Buy according to the style you prefer then stop at the shoe repair shop on the way home. Ask them to remove the buckle, cut off the extra inches and reattach the buckles. The charge to shorten, even added to the cost of the belt is still less than half of the retail price of a designer belt.

Altering to fit

Finding a good tailor is the key to dressing well for less. Now you can shop for color, style and design at consignment, vintage, thrift or discount stores. A good tailor can take a garment down by two sizes, so this gives you a lot of leeway when it comes to sizing and fit.

Mitten extenders

Cut the tops from socks that have become worn and sew them to the top of your kids' mittens. No more mittens filling up with snow or slipping off.

Fix slippery socks

If you have hardwood, or slippery floors, use fabric paint on the bottoms of your kids socks to give them extra "traction." This is especially helpful when babies grow into toddlers and their balance isn't the best. Ironically, it's just when they start walking that they stop making toddler socks with rubberized decorations on the bottoms. Wavy lines make for the best traction.

Free hangers

Some department stores have a policy of giving the customer the high-quality hanger on which the garment is hung, but only if the customer requests this. If you could use another hanger, be sure to ask.

Clothing and Shoes

Donate clothes

When cleaning your closet, give everything you're not keeping to charity—even the old, worn, stained and otherwise un-salable clothing. Most charities band together to send clothing overseas to needy areas. Things that are not sent overseas are recycled by lint or rag recyclers. Charity thrift stores keep a dumpster that gets emptied weekly. When they recycle, they make 4 cents a pound or so, but it adds up. Don't put your cast-off clothes in landfills. Donate them.

Uniforms for less

If you are a healthcare worker who must wear scrubs to work, here's how to save a bundle: Call the local medical center and ask for the operating room. Speak to a supervisor and ask for a referral to the company who provides their uniforms. They'll know and be happy to tell you the cheapest place to buy gently worn but still serviceable scrubs.

Seam ripper

If you need to rip out a black seam or another dark fabric and have trouble seeing the stitches, lightly rub a piece of chalk over the stitching line. The individual stitches then become very visible. Saves time and eye strain.

Jeans to dye for

If you have a pair of jeans that were inky-black when you first purchased them, but they are gradually turning streaky gray from too much wash and wear, don't despair. Instead of springing for a new pair, pick up a package of Rit dye and turn them back to black. Just follow all the instructions on the package. Add 2 cups of salt to the dying process to get the blackest black possible. To keep them that way in the future, wash them inside out in cold water with a small amount of detergent only.

Wrinkled clothes

If your clothes stay in the dryer for too long they become wrinkled and need ironing. When this happens, dampen a clean cloth, put it in the dryer with the clothes and run on touch-up cycle for about 10-15 minutes. The items will come out wrinkle-free.

Shorts and ponytail holders

When kids wear out the knees in their sweatpants, cut them off for shorts. The fullness in the legs allows air to circulate, and the heavy material really holds up to outside playing. As an added bonus, the covered elastic at the bottom of the pants makes two ponytail holders. Since the material rarely ravels, this is a true no-sew proposition.

Wrinkles away

For washable wrinkle-resistant slacks, wash them and put them into the clothes dryer for just a few minutes. Remove them while still wet and hang upside down lining up the creases and clipping the hem edges to the clips on pants hangers. The weight of the still-wet pants will be just enough to pull out all wrinkles, leaving them perfectly creased and the right length, too.

Saving white canvas shoes

To make white canvas shoes look like new, wash them first and then clean the rubber parts with baking soda and a wash cloth. For the canvas, you will need a wet toothbrush and white shoe polish—foam polish works best. Apply a small amount of polish and work into the canvas. If it's not soaking in, it is too dry so add more water to the brush. The white will splatter so do this in an area that is well protected. Allow to dry overnight and in the morning you'll have shoes that look nearly new.

Stretch tight shoes

Do you have a good pair of leather shoes that are just too tight? Follow this procedure practiced by shoe professionals: Spray the inside with a 50/50 mixture of rubbing alcohol and water. Put on a pair of extra-thick socks and wear the shoes for a few hours. They will stretch sufficiently to make them comfortable to wear.

Temporary relocation

If you have trouble thinking of getting rid of any of your clothes, do this: Take the ones you haven't worn recently and move them to another closet, basement or attic. Now you can see what you do wear without feeling you've lost your close friend. After a year or so you'll be less emotional about getting rid of them. But for now, just consider them relocated—and enjoy the extra closet space.

Purse renew

If you have a high-quality handbag that is looking tired and slightly shabby, stop by the shoe repair shop. Pick up a bottle of leather sole and heel dressing, and polish in the color of your bag. Now clean it up. Your bag should look like new.

Shop with the men

Ladies, check the men's or boy's departments when buying clothes that are not gender specific. In some stores and states where this policy is not restricted, the same Levi's 501 will be $3 or $4 more in the women's department than the men's or boy's. It's sure worth checking.

Upscale thrift shopping

Shopping at thrift stores in upscale communities is like finding buried treasure. Those in the know find designer label apparel with high end department store tags still attached. This approach takes time and discipline to not buy more than you need, but it can be a lot of fun, too.

Uniform socks

If you have a large family and wonder why you always end up with mismatched and missing socks at the end of laundry day, here's a solution. Buy only white (or black) tube socks that are one-size-fits all. Now laundry will be a snap because all the socks match.

Scuff cover

Use black magic markers to color in scuffs on your black boots and pumps. It works better than the special "scuff repair" shoe polishes and does not wear off so quickly.

Squeaky orthotics

If your shoe inserts or custom-made orthotics cause a squeak when you walk, simply sprinkle a little talcum powder under the inserts. Squeaks will vanish.

Teen technique

If you have a teen who's talked you into a winter coat or other pricey item that ends up in the closet with little or no wear—or gets lost or permanently loaned—here's a great idea: Approve the next purchase, but require the teen to pay for this out of his or her allowance or savings. At the end of the school year if he or she has worn the coat or item to your satisfaction, has taken care of it satisfactorily and you didn't have to argue about wearing it, then and only then agree to reimburse the full price of the item, plus the interest he or she would have earned had the money not been touched. You're going to like the results of this money-teaching event.

Static cling

That spray stuff to remove static cling is not always the most long-lasting solution for pants, hose, slips and skirts that cling due to dry, electricity-charged air. Here's a better solution. Apply a healthy amount of lotion to your legs and rub it in well. Now stuff a dryer sheet into each of your pants pockets. Enjoy your cling-free day.

A month of outfits

Before the start of a new month, print out a blank month-at-a-glance calendar from your computer. Proceed to your closet. Write down the different outfits you will wear next month. Start with the week-days, particularly important if you work outside the home. Switch things up, come up with different combinations. Now fill in the week-ends if that is appealing to you. Once your calendar is full, place the clothes in your closet in the order you plan to wear them. Treat it as a game and it will keep you from last-minute purchases on your lunch break because you fear that you have nothing to wear. As a bonus you will save time because you know what you'll be wearing in advance.

Denim softening

Make sure you put 1/2 cup of white vinegar in the rinse of your favorite jeans and they'll come out soft with that "well-worn" feel.

FOOD AND COOKING

Food and Cooking

Where's the beef?

Instead of buying regular prepackaged hamburger meat, buy a side of round roast or brisket instead. Then have the butcher grind it for you. Stock up when brisket is on sale and get more burger for your buck.

Cooking in bulk

Cooking three times as much as you need of staples like spaghetti sauce or pinto beans and freezing some for later doesn't take three times longer to prepare. Ease into cooking mass quantities by first cooking twice as much. After that it's easy.

Hard-to-peel eggs

For hard-boiled eggs that just won't peel, try the plastic peeler used for slicing and removing the peel from oranges. Just slide it under the membrane attached to the shell.

One good egg

To determine whether an egg is still fresh enough to eat, immerse it in a pan of cool, salted water. If it sinks, it's fresh—if it rises to the surface, toss it.

Out of sight

Having a storage area and freezer away from the kitchen can save a lot of money when buying in bulk. Most people when looking for something to eat will only check out items in a kitchen and won't bother with the extra trip to the basement or garage. Distance not only makes the heart grow fonder, but the treats last longer!

Weepy icing

When using real whipping cream for icing a cake, mix one teaspoon of dry instant vanilla pudding mix per one cup of cream before whipping. Add sugar to taste while beating. Adding the pudding prevents the whipped cream from separating and "weeping."

Crunchy celery

Wrap celery in aluminum foil when storing in the refrigerator and it will last for weeks.

Lunch treats

Prepackaged snacks can really break the food budget. Instead package your own. Gather the kids and institute a time for "bagging" the lunchbox snacks like chips, pretzels, cookies, brownies, carrots and celery or string cheese. Bag enough for the week. All that needs to be added in the morning is a sandwich. Saves time and money.

Ham for less

A cheaper alternative to expensive deli ham is to buy a whole, fully-cooked, boneless, smoked ham and take it to the meat counter at your grocery store for slicing. Most butchers are more than happy to do this. You'll spend several dollars less for each pound.

Slippery chicken

Pulling the skin off chicken can be tough when it's slippery because it's difficult to get a good grip. Dip your hands in flour first and the skin will pull right off.

Leftover meat

Don't throw away leftover meat that might be dried out. Put it in the blender or food processor and shred it. Mix with mayonnaise and your favorite seasonings for a great sandwich filling.

Coffee creamer

Mix together evaporated milk, vanilla extract and sugar for a very yummy French vanilla coffee creamer.

Grapefruit slush

Purchase the largest size bottle of ruby red grapefruit juice and divide it into 10 or 12 freezer-safe cups. Cover with plastic wrap and secure with a rubber band. Freeze solid. To serve, remove from freezer and microwave on high for 40 seconds. Using a long spoon, stir until slushy. Refreshing on a hot day!

Freezer labels

Use inexpensive labels that are used for file folders as freezer labels. They work great in the freezer and easily peel off plastic containers.

Freezing eggs

When eggs are on sale, stock up. Break the eggs into a freezer-safe container and whisk well to blend. When you need an egg in a recipe use an ice cream scoop to portion out what you need. One scoop = one egg.

Keep bananas longer

Bananas kept in a zip-type plastic bag last longer. As soon as you get home from the market put them in the bag and they'll last a week before getting those brown spots.

Grease the grater

To get more cheese in the recipe and less stuck on the grater, spray both sides of the grater lightly with cooking spray before grating the cheese.

Freeze the 'nog

Freeze eggnog in ice cube trays to use in coffee and other recipes. Place the frozen cubes in zip-type bags in the freezer and they'll last until the holidays come around again.

Canned vegetable juice

When baking casseroles or other dishes that call for canned vegetables, save the juice and use it to replace part of the liquid (milk, water) in the recipe. No one will be able to tell and it's a great way to use the vitamin-rich juice that is in every can.

Don't boil fresh

Fresh eggs that are boiled are usually harder to peel. Boil up your older eggs first.

Can opener

When opening a can of vegetables, first use a bottle opener to puncture holes in the can and drain the liquid. Then use a can opener to open the lid.

Flavored ice tea

Flavored tea bags (like raspberry or peach) are a lot more expensive than plain tea. Here's how to cut the cost and still have fruit-flavored tea: Use three regular-size tea bags and one fruit-flavored tea bag. Boil water, pour over tea bags, and then steep for five minutes. That's it! One box of flavored tea will last three times as long.

Meatloaf in a bag

If you've stored and then thawed hamburger meat in a freezer bag, don't throw it out—mix your meatloaf in the bag! Add all the ingredients and knead until thoroughly mixed. Remove the meatloaf to the proper baking pan. Now toss the bag. No mess, no fuss.

Flavored cream cheese

No need to pay extra for flavored cream cheese. Purchase any type of cream cheese and beat until smooth, adding jam or preserves to taste.

Soft brown sugar

Put those bread heels in the same container with your brown sugar. The sugar will absorb the moisture from the bread, and will stay softer, for longer. Plus, it's a great use for those often-disregarded bread ends!

Pan prep

Mix equal amounts of shortening,

vegetable oil and flour together to form a paste. Now "grease" your pans with this concoction. No more cakes stuck to the pan.

Lettuce wrap-up

Wrap lettuce in white paper towels and keep in a gallon zip-type bag. Lettuce stays fresher longer.

Crispy lettuce

Want grab-and-go lettuce? Prepare it like this: Separate the leaves and place in barely lukewarm water. Pour about 1/4 cup of regular salt in the water and let the lettuce leaves soak for a few minutes. Drain and rinse. Dry the leaves. Place two paper towels in a gallon zip-type bag and lay all the clean, dry lettuce leaves on top of the paper towels. Press out some of the air in the bag. Your cold crispy lettuce will last for longer than a week in the refrigerator.

Guacamole

Do you hate it when your homemade guacamole dip turns brown? Add the avocado pit back into the bowl of guacamole. It retards the browning process.

No-tear onions

When cutting onions, light one or two candles and place them as close as you can to the knife while you are slicing the onions. The flame from the candle burns away the "fumes" from the onion.

Meat wrappers

Before you hit the meat counter, go to the produce area of the supermarket and pick up a few extra plastic bags to store your meat that is destined for the freezer. Double bag if you're going to freeze the meat, and use twist ties to secure the bags.

Frosting-free cake

Skip the frosting by coating the pan with sugar instead of flour before baking. When cool, just dump the cake out upside down. The sugar will have formed a slightly crispy crust on what is now the top of the cake.

Gourmet coffee

Mix equal parts of your favorite gourmet coffee with the cheaper store brand. Tastes as good and you'll get twice as much.

Gourmet instant coffee

It's easy to make your own gourmet instant coffee, and it's so much less expensive. Combine 4 tablespoons sugar, 1 small package chocolate instant pudding, 2 tablespoons cocoa, 1 1/2 cups non-dairy creamer, 3/4 cup instant coffee. Mix in blender. To use: Add 2 teaspoons to 7 ounces of hot water. Change up the pudding flavors and omit the cocoa for different flavors.

Fresher food

Don't transfer snack foods like cereal, chips, crackers or cookies to zip-type bags—they won't stay any fresher. Fold over the original packaging and secure with a clothespin.

Taco supreme

Take advantage of those ground beef sales and cook taco filling to freeze. Portion-pack the meat into containers, and keep a stash of tortillas and grated cheese in the freezer. It's nice to know you have dinner in the freezer.

Freezing soups and sauces

Make batches of soups or sauces and freeze in a baking pan. When frozen, cut into one-serving squares and place in a zip-type bag. Easy to reheat one serving or the whole batch—whatever you need.

Freshest bread

Bread companies deliver fresh bread to the market five days a week: Monday, Tuesday, Thursday, Friday and Saturday. The bread from each day has a different plastic closure tab. Monday is blue, Tuesday is green, Thursday is red, Friday is white, and Saturday is yellow. The colors are in alphabetical order so it's easy to remember. Now you can make sure you pick up the freshest bread.

Fresh frozen bread

To keep frozen bread fresh, place a paper towel on top of the loaf inside the bread bag immediately after purchase. Secure bag and freeze. Works well for hot dog and hamburger buns, too.

Flip those heels

Stop throwing out the bread heels because you think no one wants them. Just turn them inside out and picky eaters will not be the wiser.

Bread pudding

Make your own savory bread pudding by saving the bread heels, stale hamburger and hot dog buns, bagels and any bread products. Just keep the bag in the refrigerator and when it gets full, shred the bread. Mix with milk and eggs and add shredded cheddar cheese, Worcestershire sauce and Dijon mustard. You can also flavor your bread with apples, cinnamon and raisins.

Stale bread

Bread that's too stale for sandwiches makes great Melba toast. Toast it and cut it diagonally to make four triangles. Put all the pieces on a baking tray and put it in the oven to dry out completely. Toast keeps for weeks in an airtight container.

Spring herbs

When storing herbs in the refrigerator, wrap them in a damp paper towel and store in a plastic bag in the vegetable crisper. This keeps them fresh for days.

Ice cream add-ons

Buy store-brand vanilla ice cream, which is cheaper than name-brands, and add your own flavors. Pancake syrup and cinnamon are great additions to vanilla. This works with frozen yogurt, too.

Powdered milk

Using powdered milk in recipes that call for milk can save you a lot of money, but not affect the taste at all.

Iced coffee

Begin by making either coffee or espresso. Fill a coffee cup with ice, pour the coffee over the ice, and follow with milk to taste. Add your favorite flavored creamer.

Season the bird

Wait until you've placed your chicken or turkey into the roasting pan before you start seasoning it. Shaking salt and pepper onto a bird while trying to hold on to it will only make you spill most of the seasoning.

Soda fizz stopper

Increase the refrigerator shelf life for 2-liter bottles of soda by slowly tipping the bottle back and forth after you've put the cap back onto the opened bottle. The trick is to agitate the liquid just enough to get good pressure. Too much pressure and it'll be hard to open next time. This restores the pressure it had when the bottle was unopened. The more liquid that is missing the more tipping it takes (press your thumb against the shoulder of the bottle and you'll feel the pressure building). Always open your bottles carefully to avoid a soda shower.

Flavored oils

Check your natural foods store for inexpensive bottles of flavored oils for cooking.

Fake sour cream

Whip low-fat cottage cheese in your blender, add a little lemon juice and chives (if desired) and you have a very tasty topping for your baked potato. You'll be amazed how much it tastes like sour cream.

Protein singles

Place one fresh, boneless, skinless chicken breast in a zip-type bag with marinade, and freeze. When you are ready for a quick meal, just take it out of the bag and stick it in your oven or in a pan on top of the burner. It's seasoned, low-fat, and delicious.

Drip-less cones

When serving ice cream cones to children, put one or two small marshmallows inside the cone before adding the ice cream. This keeps the ice cream from melting through the hole at the bottom of the cone. It also adds a little sweet surprise at the bottom!

Bowl covers

Purchase cheap shower caps at beauty supply stores and use them for bowl covers when putting leftovers in the refrigerator. They fit most any size bowl.

Recycle charcoal

After barbecuing, close the air vents to your grill. The charcoal will go out and can be relit for the next cookout. Add fresh charcoal as required. Half of your charcoal can be saved by doing this.

Oil savings

When you purchase a new bottle of cooking oil, don't rip off the round seal at the top. Just stab a few holes in it with a sharp knife and squeeze the bottle to dispense the oil. You'll have better control over how much oil you use.

Pork patties

If your family likes pork chops then chances are they'll like pork patties. Just mold ground pork into patties, season with salt and pepper and fry in a pan. You'll save a lot buying ground pork over pork chops.

Quick soups

Ready-to-serve soups can be very expensive, but they sure are convenient. Make your own by placing any flavor of condensed soup in a container, add a can of milk and shake. Pour one serving into a microwavable bowl to heat. Save the rest in the refrigerator.

Banana buns

What to do with those extra hot dog buns we end up with for some unknown reason? Make banana sandwiches. Spread with peanut butter and top with a peeled banana. It's quick, easy and no banana pieces fall out like they do on "normal" sandwich bread.

Ditch the oil

Substitute applesauce for the oil called for in cakes, breads and muffins. It's just as moist and healthier, too.

Easy husking

For a quick and easy way to husk corn-on-the-cob, wrap the corn in plastic wrap and microwave for two to three minutes. Be careful not to burn yourself when removing plastic wrap. The husks and silks fall right off.

Gelatin to-go

Wash those empty yogurt cups and save the extra plastic spoons from restaurant to-go orders, and make your own gelatin cups. These are easy to grab and go, and everything is disposable.

Leftover popcorn

Store leftover microwave popcorn in the refrigerator. Just microwave for a few seconds when you're ready to eat again.

No drippy popsicles

Save the lids from yogurt containers and Pringles. Cut a small slit in the middle of the lid. Place lid upside down on the popsicle stick so any juice can collect and stay within the rim of the lid. No more cold, sticky hands.

Spice life

Spices stay fresher longer when stored in the refrigerator. Once opened they generally lose their strength within a few months. In the refrigerator spices maintain their color, aroma and taste much longer.

Shortening mess

Before adding shortening to a measuring cup first add an egg from the recipe to coat the cup. Remove the egg. The shortening measured will now slide right out of the cup. No waste, no mess.

Meals to-go

When cleaning up from a meal put leftovers right into containers for lunch or another meal on the go. If you have room, designate a shelf in the freezer for your "to-go" meals.

Food and Cooking

Get sauced

Always buy the large size of broth or tomato sauce because it's cheapest that way. Use for your immediate needs, then freeze the rest in ice cube trays. When frozen store in zip-type baggies. Drop them into soup or defrost for pizza. They instantly add flavoring and liquid to almost anything.

Mixing instructions

For bulk items that you repackage at home into smaller bags or containers, make sure you remember the contents and the instructions for preparation. Cut out the information from the original package and stick it inside the bag. Now you know what you've got.

Freezer fast food

When preparing multiple batches of casseroles and entrées to freeze, line loaf pans with plastic wrap and spoon in desired number of servings for each meal. Pull the ends and sides of the wrap over the food and place in your freezer. When frozen, remove the block, wrap and all, from the pan and place in a freezer bag. Label and return to freezer. These blocks stack well and take up less room in the freezer than round containers.

Frozen yogurt treats

Make your own homemade version of the commercial yogurt treats. Place a pinch of nonpareils, rainbow mix, or other cupcake sprinkles into popsicle molds. Fill halfway with vanilla yogurt. Add more sprinkles, fill with yogurt, and top with sprinkles before adding sticks. These are a big hit with children and healthier than the commercially-processed brands.

Healthy "sherbet"

Turn calcium-fortified frozen orange juice from concentrate into orange sherbet. Divide one large can of frozen concentrate into four serving bowls, cover each bowl and freeze. The cost per serving can't be beat, and there's no sugar or artificial coloring. Each serving is loaded with vitamin C, potassium, folic acid and calcium.

Mini brownies

Use mini muffin pans to make your own mini brownies. Prepare batter as usual, and spray the tins to make sure that the brownies come out perfectly. Fill the pans 2/3 full and bake approximately 12 minutes at 350 F. Cool and enjoy.

Cheap cereal

When grocery shopping, keep your eyes open for the small trial-size (typically 9 ounces) boxes of cereal, generally sold for under $1. This can be a huge savings over the larger boxes and if purchased with a coupon, your savings are more dramatic. But don't wait, they don't last long on the store shelves.

Big omelets

The best omelets are made with beaten eggs that have been frozen. This is a great opportunity to use up eggs if they are getting near the "use by" date. Use two eggs per person and beat them with a little milk. Place in zip-type plastic bags in the freezer. When ready to use, defrost for a couple of hours. Beat eggs again and cook in a hot pan. Using this frozen method gives you the size and density of a three-egg omelet, but with only two eggs.

Slow cooker turkey stuffing

Grease the inside of a slow cooker with butter. Make your favorite stuffing and add 1 can of cream of celery or cream of mushroom soup. Place stuffing mix in prepared slow cooker. Cook on low heat 1 to 1 1/2 hours before your turkey is due to be finished. It will be perfect, and you don't have to dig it out of the bird or take up room in the oven.

Simple ham glaze

Bake your ham in a cooking bag, according to directions. After the ham is done, remove and place it in a large roaster. Using a full jar of sweet and sour sauce, brush the sauce onto the ham. Put back in heated oven for 10 minutes. After the ham is heated through remove from oven and let set for 10 minutes. You'll get rave reviews for your "homemade" glaze.

Fruit tea-licious

Instead of buying expensive flavored iced tea, buy a large canister of unsweetened instant tea. Add your desired sweetener, water and a small can of fruit juice—raspberry goes especially well with tea.

Easy meal planning

Tweak your meal planning to match the number of days between paychecks. Instead of planning meals around a seven day week, plan out and prepare the number of meals between pay periods. This way you'll never come up short when it's dinner time, or have surprises when you hit the check out line since you've planned every meal.

Food and Cooking

Slow down the spices

Almost all spice bottles now have big holes on top and if you're not careful, it's easy to use too much and then use it up too quickly. Take a little piece of tape and cover up all but a couple of holes. Presto! No more waste.

Lunch bag popcorn

Make inexpensive bagged popcorn that is easy and portable. Place 1/2 cup un-popped corn kernels in a paper lunch bag, spray lightly with cooking oil, fold open end closed and place horizontally in your microwave. Cook for about 4 minutes on high. Cooking time varies with microwaves.

Pizza kits

Make basic pizza dough almost effortlessly in a bread machine. Make enough to freeze in slightly flattened disks, and put together pizza kits with your favorite meat, cheese and sauce. All the ingredients are quick to thaw and you'll say goodbye to expensive take-out pizza.

Spice grinder

To chop fresh or revive old store-bought spices, simply toss into your cleaned coffee bean grinder and give it a whirl.

No burned ice cream

Avoid freezer burn and funny tasting ice cream. Take big piece of plastic wrap and cover your ice cream. Press the plastic wrap down on the surface, carefully making sure there are no pockets of air between the wrap and the ice cream. Replace the lid. You'll have fresh-tasting ice cream down to the very last bite.

Fresh leftover salad

If you have leftover salad that you want to save, but you've already tossed it with dressing, put a couple of crackers (Ritz or any brand) on top of the salad, then wrap it with plastic wrap and put in the refrigerator. The crackers absorb the moisture, preventing the lettuce leaves from wilting. It will be ready to eat again the next day.

Drinkable yogurt

Kids go crazy for drinkable yogurt in those cute little containers. Avoid the cost and make your own. Mix together in a blender about 1/2 cup of plain, low-fat yogurt with about 1/4 cup of milk and 1 tablespoon of strawberry jam (more or less to suit your taste). Blend at the 'liquefy' setting until smooth. Enjoy!

Eggs for picky eaters

Put food coloring in your kids'

scrambled eggs, a la Dr. Seuss. They'll love it and will ask for eggs more often.

Hard-boiled eggs

While you're cooking hard-boiled eggs, add food coloring to the water. When the eggs are finished cooking they will be tinted the color of the die. At a glance, you'll be able to know which eggs are raw and which are cooked.

Onion flavor

Onion adds great flavor to stews and sauces, but many don't like to eat them. Add the chopped onion to a tea ball and drop it into the stew.

Easy refills

Here's a quick and easy way to refill the handy-size ketchup, mayonnaise and mustard containers. Pour the contents into a gallon-sized, zip-type bag. Snip the corner with scissors and squeeze the contents into the container. Works just like a pastry bag. Toss the bag when when you're done.

Lemon freeze

When you find yourself with an abundant supply of lemons just freeze them whole in freezer bags. The texture changes a little after the lemon has thawed, but for juicing purposes there's no change. Now you can enjoy lemons year-round.

Recycling egg cartons

Many area farmers' markets offer food and vegetables to purchase in bulk. This includes chicken farmers who will trade your empty egg cartons for farm, fresh eggs.

Frozen potato chips

Sealing bags of potato chips and storing in the freezer prolongs the freshness of the chips. They also don't taste too bad when they're cold, otherwise just set out for a while to "defrost."

Pie cleanup

Before rolling out pie dough, spray your counter and rolling pin with cooking spray. This will keep the dough from sticking and make cleanup a breeze.

Flavorful soup

Add a packet of instant gravy mix to your homemade soup to add flavor and richness. Use 1 to 2 packs for a medium to large pot. This also gives it a nice, rich color.

Save that tomato paste

A lot of recipes call for just a small

Food and Cooking

amount of tomato paste, or only a little dab is needed for flavor. So what to do with the rest? Lay a piece of waxed paper or plastic wrap on the counter and place about a tablespoon of paste every so many inches. Then just fold the wrap over the individual mounds of paste. You can also wrap them individually. Then just pop them into a zip-type bag and freeze. You'll have those little amounts of paste whenever you need them.

Hot oil

To determine when your grease is hot enough for deep frying, drop one un-popped popcorn kernel into the grease. When the kernel pops, you're ready to roll.

Beet tricks

After boiling beets for canning, dip them in ice-cold water and the skins will come off easily. To slice them, use an egg slicer or a French fry cutter, depending on what you're going to do with the beets after they're sliced.

Crispy cones

Keep your unused ice cream cones in the refrigerator or freezer to keep them fresh. They stay fresh up to three months in the refrigerator and up to six months in the freezer. Just seal tightly in a zip-type bag and you're in business.

Keep your cool

Keep an insulated bag in your trunk to hold your cold items while you're driving home after grocery shopping. If you need to make some stops you won't have to worry about anything melting or spoiling before you get home. When not in use those bags fold flat.

Forget sprays

Keep your cooking oil in a jar with a lid, with a pastry brush close by. Use this to coat your pans when cooking and baking. Just add flour if it's suggested when baking.

Egg substitute

If you come up one egg short when baking, try substituting one heaping tablespoon of mayonnaise for an egg. This works really well in pie crust recipes that call for an egg. The crusts roll out easier and thinner, too.

Meat for less

If you live near a university that has an agricultural or food science program, check to see if you can buy meat, dairy or produce from their farm. Chances are you can get meat and eggs for very low prices.

Salt shaker

If your ceramic salt shaker is constantly moist on the inside, but you cannot add rice to absorb the moisture because the shaker has large holes, use macaroni noodles. They absorb the moisture in the same way, but are larger than the holes and will not fall through.

Poor man's steak

If you love the taste of steak but not the price, buy rolled rump roast and cut into 1/2 to 1 inch thick slices. These cuts are fairly tender, however you can further tenderize by using a meat mallet.

Ripe melons

Follow these guidelines to pick out a good cantaloupe or musk melon. Do not purchase if the skin is too green—that means it was picked too early. The melon should be a good tan color, firm not soft. The end of the melon that was picked from the vine should be soft when you press your thumb on it. If it is hard the melon was picked prematurely. Another test is to smell the end of the melon that was picked from the vine. It should smell sweet like a ripe melon.

Easy-open clams

You'll never struggle with opening clams if you wash them in cold water, then pop them into a plastic bag. Stick the bag in the freezer for one hour. They'll pop right open with ease. Works for oysters, too.

Yesterday's grind

Check out the meat department at your local store. Each morning they grind up the beef from the night before and sell it as "yesterday's grind hamburger." Some stores make it available around 9:00 in the morning. You can get great deals on this cut of meat. It's worth checking out.

Vanilla coffee

Want to have gourmet-tasting vanilla coffee without the gourmet price? Measure your coffee as usual and add the water. Pour two teaspoons of vanilla extract into the bottom of the carafe and then run your coffee maker as usual. Great Flavor without spending a fortune.

Cool cukes

Wrap your cucumbers individually, cut or uncut in a paper towel, and they will last up to two weeks. No more mushy surprises when you reach inside the veggie bin.

Rinse the ground beef

Instead of purchasing ground

turkey (low-fat, but not as flavorful), or lean ground beef (low-fat, but can be expensive) purchase regular ground beef on sale. After browning it for casseroles, chili, and so on, drain the grease then rinse and drain the beef with hot water in the same pot. Saves money and the fat content is actually less than that of ground turkey.

Save on restaurant pizza

Many pizza restaurants have lunch buffet pizza left over that they have to toss. Offer to buy the leftovers for a reduced price. Any money the pizza place gets from you will be more than they will get if they throw the pizza out. You can take home a large amount of pizza and simply freeze it, defrosting one or two pieces whenever you want.

Kids and veggies mix

When you have leftover veggies in the refrigerator, place homemade pie crusts in the bottom of small casserole dishes and tell your kids it is time for them to make their own "veggie pie." Have them pick the veggies they want to put in their pie and mix them with a small amount of cream of chicken, mushroom or potato soup and milk. Cover with a top crust and bake at 400 F. for 20 minutes or until browned.

Homemade chocolate "squares"

Instead of buying expensive baker's chocolate chocolate squares mix three tablespoons of baking cocoa with one tablespoon of oil. Now you have homemade chocolate "squares." Since most recipes call for the squares to be melted, not only have you saved money, you've saved time, too.

Tenderize cheap steak

You can tenderize cheaper cuts of meat by marinating them in Coke. Several hours before you grill, place the steaks in a bowl and cover them with a cola drink. You can even use flat Coke. Add approximately 2 tablespoons of soy sauce and 1 teaspoon of garlic powder.

Freezer energy saver

An empty freezer uses more power than a full one. If yours is not filled with food, fill it up with milk jugs or with water. Besides saving on your power bill, you will also have plenty of ice for coolers and cold water if the power goes out during an emergency.

Power saving coffee pot

If you like to have hot coffee available throughout the day, save energy and wear and tear on the coffee maker by putting your freshly brewed coffee in a thermal insulated pot. It will remain hot and fresh all day.

Moist carrot cake

To make an especially moist and delicious carrot cake, substitute Junior's baby food carrots for the specified amount of grated carrots. No one will suspect they are eating baby food.

Homemade popsicles

Keep some plastic molds for homemade popsicles on hand. When you open a can of fruit—whether it's packed in syrup, light syrup or juice—pour it into the popsicle molds right away and freeze. This makes a healthy, low cost, tasty popsicle.

Easy tomato soup

For quick, easy and good tomato soup, mix canned spaghetti sauce (any kind) with water or milk to thin, a little sugar and salt, and then heat. Add croutons and a sprinkle of shredded cheese.

Make ahead pastry

When making pastry during the holiday season, prepare extra dough and store it in a zip-type bag in the refrigerator. Shortly after the next holiday feast, when you have leftovers from a ham or turkey dinner, use the extra dough to make a pot pie.

Coffee filter substitute

Out of coffee filters? Try a single-ply, high-quality paper towel—like Bounty—in place of the filter. Just cut it to size. You may find it works as well as a coffee filter for a lot less money.

Frozen meat in the slow cooker

You can take a roast out of the freezer and put it straight into your slow cooker, set on High. Add seasoning, onion and several unpeeled cloves of garlic. Let it cook all day, and by dinner time it should be exceptionally tender and flavorful.

Quick microwave rice

In a glass microwave-safe bowl add one cup of rice and two cups of water. With microwave on High and bowl uncovered, cook for 11 minutes. If rice is not completely cooked, stir and cook for an additional two minutes. Ordinary white ice is about half the cost of instant rice, so you'll be saving money while not sacrificing convenience.

Food and Cooking

Low-fat with high-fat flavor

If you don't like the taste of skim milk but wouldn't mind cutting back on your fat intake, mix a couple of teaspoons of whole milk with a cup of skim. It will taste and look more like whole milk but without all the fat.

Cooking pasta

To save money on gas or electricity, heat the water for pasta to a rolling boil, add the pasta as you normally would. Cover the pot and turn the burner off. Within 5-10 minutes the pasta will be cooked perfectly.

Eat cheap at work

If you are often tempted to buy food from local restaurants to satisfy your hunger while at work, you know the cost eventually adds up. Get in the habit of grabbing a yogurt or piece of fruit on your way out the door for when those sudden snack cravings hit. A dollar on healthy snacks is much more attractive than five dollars on junk.

Almost free pizza

If you have a weakness for expensive gourmet pizza, you can still have it once a week almost for free. At many pizza shops, orders that are called in and not picked up are sold for a couple bucks each. Call ahead and find out what they have available for pick up.

Food by any other name

Kids can't stand a certain food item? Give it a new name. Call bread pudding "cinnamon roll delight" and you'll soon have requests for seconds.

Taco mix measure

When making tacos with the seasoning packets that call for added water, the empty packet usually has the capacity of the amount of water called for in the recipe. Measure water in the packet and you'll save the bother of getting out a measuring cup. You'll also be sure to get every bit of flavoring out of that packet.

Oil carafe

Clean out a five fluid ounce soy sauce bottle and put vegetable oil in it. Since the bottle is lighter and the spout is smaller, it's easier to pour into a measuring spoon without spilling.

Flavored iced tea

Flavored tea mixes are delicious, but they also are expensive and contain high amounts of sugar and caffeine. So make your own fresh tea by the pitcher. In a two-quart container, put in six decaffeinated tea bags, one package of unsweetened soft drink mix (such as Kool-Aid) and 1/2 or 3/4 cup sugar. Pour four cups boiling water over it, then cover and stick in the refrigerator. When cool, remove tea bags and fill to the brim with water. Enjoy!

Chicken meals

Get two or three meals out of one whole chicken. Meal one: Serve a whole chicken done on rotisserie. Meal two: Use the leftover chicken carcass to make homemade chicken soup with chicken broth, vegetables and noodles. Meal three: Make chicken salad from the leftover chicken.

Gummy mess

During the hot, humid summer months, the moisture in the air makes sugarless gum really messy. Store it in the refrigerator to prevent this problem.

Long-lasting onions

Buy a large bag of onions and once home, spend half an hour chopping up all the onions at once. Put the onions in snack size zip-type bags and put them into the freezer. Anytime you need onions for a recipe, grab a bag.

Plastic wrap vs. baggies

Save money using plastic wrap instead of baggies, especially when packing lunches. Baggies might be easier, but plastic wrap works just as well keeping lunches fresh.

Grapes last longer

Take the grapes off of the stem when you get home from the grocery store, then store in the refrigerator. Grapes stay fresher longer when separated from the vine.

Yummy veggie burgers

Cut down on the cost of veggie burgers and make your own. With a fork, mash one can of beans with liquid (kidney, black, adzuki) in a large bowl. Add about 1 cup of texturized vegetable protein (TVP) and 1/4 cup corn flour. For seasonings, add onion and garlic powder, chili spices, A1 sauce, or other spices. Let sit in refrigerator for an hour to firm up. Make into patties and freeze.

Protect your ingredients

To keep the family from eating ingredients that have been earmarked for a recipe, place a fluorescent dot on the item. These colorful dots will very clearly get the message across—hands off!

Food and Cooking

Multi-talented applesauce

Use applesauce as more than just a fruit serving. Add to hot cereal and substitute in baked goods when the recipe calls for oil. Gives cakes and muffins extra moisture and taste, too.

Chocolate bunnies anytime

Instead of buying expensive chocolate bars to grate for recipes, stock up at the holidays. Chocolate bunnies, hearts and Santas can be frozen and used as needed.

Pizza disks

Use the little three-prong plastic disk in your pizza box to keep other foods from sticking to the plastic wrap, foil or wax paper.

Fast mashed

Cook potatoes in your pressure cooker in half the time of boiling or steaming. Just follow the manufacturer instructions for pressure cooking.

More lemon juice

Don't just stop at rolling that lemon on the counter. After rolling, put it in the microwave for up to 30 seconds. The quantity and ease of juicing by hand will be noticeable.

Spices for less

Save your empty spice jars and refill with spices purchased in bags. Savings on spices in bags can be up to 75% over prices on jar spices. Look in the International foods aisle for bagged spices.

Casserole crunchies

Save the tiny broken pieces of potato or tortilla chips in the bottom of the bag and keep in a zip-type bag in the freezer. Crushed up, this makes the perfect crunchy topping for any casserole and a little bit goes a long way.

Easy potato salad

When making potato salad cut up the potatoes before they are boiled. This speeds the process since it only takes about seven minutes to cook diced potatoes.

Thermos jug odors

When storing a thermos, cooler or drinking jugs, wash and air dry. Before storing add crumpled-up newspaper inside and close or replace the lid. Moisture and odors will not make the cooler smell funny because the paper absorbs the odors.

Easy cheese grating

To make blocks of cheese easier for

grating, just stick the block in the freezer for about 30-minutes before grating. This works especially well in the food processor for softer cheeses like mozzarella that tend to gum-up.

DIY Rice-A-Roni

Make your own "Rice-A-Roni" for pennies with plain white rice and spaghettini. Melt butter in a pan and add the rice (any amount), then add the spaghettini that you've broken into small pieces; brown. Add chicken stock or bouillon, and water; cover pan. Cook until liquid is fully absorbed.

Cheap herbs

Buy spices and herbs at a health food store. You'll be amazed at how much you'll save over grocery store prices.

Homemade fudgcicles

Make your own fudgcicles with instant chocolate pudding. Simply follow the directions on the package, but after mixing pour into popsicle molds instead of bowls.

Yogurt mix-in

Make up your own combinations of yogurt and fruit flavors. Purchase plain or vanilla yogurt and bags of frozen fruit. Select the fruit you want and microwave for 10-15 seconds. Mix the yogurt with the fruit and enjoy this delicious, healthy snack. It's so easy even the kids can do it.

Ice cream cone cupcakes

When you make cupcakes for special occasions, bake them in ice cream cones—the kind that will stand on their own. They bake perfectly, you can add a little frosting and best of all—there's no paper liners to peel off.

Cherry pitter

If you can cherries and cherry pie filling you've got a lot of cherries to pit. Instead of buying an expensive pitter, just use a corn on cob holder. The type that has two metal prongs works perfectly. Simply put both prongs into the cherry and lift the seed out. If you choose to leave the seed in the cherry, the prongs work well to prick each cherry to prevent bursting during the canning process.

Beat the messies

When using a measuring cup to pour pancake batter, tie a garbage twistie tie thru the hole in the handle of the measuring cup. You can now rest your cup on the side of the bowl and it won't slip in. Plus you won't have to clean up wasted batter from resting the cup on a counter or a plate. More batter, less mess!

Meatloaf muffins

Instead of a loaf pan, use a muffin pan to make mini-meatloaves. They bake in less than half the time (about 20 minutes at 450 F.) and are perfect to freeze for individual portions. They can also double as meatballs for spaghetti or subs. If you make a basic recipe and leave out the extras, when serving you can offer "toppings" such as ketchup, gravy, barbecue sauce, soup and so on.

Over-ripe bananas

When bananas become more ripe than edible it's time for banana "ice cream." Peel bananas, break into chunks and keep in an airtight container in the freezer until ready to use. Put a few chunks at a time into either a food processor with the S-blade (preferred), or a blender (works, but capacity is smaller). Pulse either machine until the bananas look like course grits, similar to pie dough. Although it looks lumpy, it feels smooth when eaten. Serve and enjoy.

Banana wipes

It's not a mystery of the universe, but it's close: use the peel of any banana as a quick shoe polish wipe on your leather shoes!

Ice cube trays

Rather than buying ice for parties, save your Styrofoam egg cartons and fill them with water. They stack nicely and when the party's over, you can toss them. They also make great popsicle trays, too. Just fill with juice, close the top and insert a toothpick or popsicle stick through the lid. The lid holds the stick in place.

No more top bananas

Bananas can bruise so easily just by sitting in a bowl or basket, simply from the weight of the other bananas. Instead, break up the bunch and lay the individual bananas along the edge of the basket. They will last much longer by themselves.

Hull strawberries

Take a drinking straw and push it up from the center bottom of the strawberry. The stem and the hard center will pop right out.

Deviled eggs

An easy way to fill deviled eggs is to prepare the filling in a quart-size freezer bag. Put the egg yolks and all your favorite ingredients right into the bag, zip it shut and mash together until well mixed. Snip off a corner of the bag and squeeze your filling back into the whites just as you would with a pastry bag. It's quick, easy and cleanup is a snap.

Baked bacon

Cook your bacon in the oven and it'll turn out perfect every time. Lay the bacon out on a cookie sheet (with sides) and cover the bacon with foil. Lay another cookie sheet on top of the bacon to weigh it down a bit. Bake for approximately 30 minutes at 350 F. Your bacon will be flat, just like it looks in the package, and the paper towels absorb the grease better because the bacon isn't curly.

Directory of leftovers

Get a small magnetic dry erase whiteboard and place it on your refrigerator. Every time you put leftovers in the refrigerator, write the name of the item and the date on the whiteboard. Next time you're packing a lunch, or looking for a snack, or planning the next meal, scan the Directory of Leftovers for ideas. If you use up a leftover food item, erase it or cross it off the whiteboard. You'll be amazed at the amount of food that WON'T go bad in your refrigerator. You'll even save money on your electric bill because you'll stop opening the refrigerator door and staring inside, trying to figure out what's in there and how old it is.

Low-cost gelatin cups

Purchase a bunch of those disposable 4-ounce plastic portion cups (with lids) from a restaurant supply store. They're cheap and come in quantities of 100 cups. Prepare your favorite gelatin and pour into the cups. Keep in the refrigerator and pop into lunch boxes and on-the-go snack packs.

Refrigerator food chart

While you're out for the day or at work, post a chart for everyone at home featuring ideas on what they can eat for breakfast and lunch. This helps them by giving them ideas and suggestions of what is already prepared or on-hand for them. Don't forget ideas for snacks, too. Older kids love this because it gives them choices and saves them from feeling it's easier to head to the fast food joint.

No-waste honey

When making a recipe that calls for honey, it usually calls for oil, too. If you measure and add the oil first, when you measure the honey it will slide right out of the measuring cup.

Mini chips

To make chocolate chip cookies cheaper, buy the mini-chocolate chips and use only half a bag for your recipe. No one will notice. Store the rest of the chips in the freezer until the next batch.

Bell pepper freeze

Bell peppers can be expensive, but they are very popular. When they are on sale stock up. Just wash, cut up, remove seeds and freeze. Use zip-type freezer bags or other special containers to avoid getting freezer burn. Freezing fresh peppers are much better quality than the ones that come in the frozen section of the store.

Corn on the frozen cob

Corn on the cob freezes really well. Buy fresh, remove the husk, wrap in foil and place in plastic bags. To serve, remove from the freezer and put them on the barbecue.

No more tears

Wearing glasses while chopping onions deflects the tear-causing fumes. Sunglasses work just great, too.

Sweet pickles to tenderize

Use a less expensive cut of beef when making stew. Just brown the beef and add sweet pickle juice to the water you add to the stew. This tenderizes and adds a flavor to the stew that brings out all the goodness of the beef. And remember, never add salt, as it toughens the meat.

Free coffee grinder

To make your own coffee grinder unscrew the blade from the bottom of your blender pitcher and screw it onto a small jar with matching threads (small canning jars work great). The confined space keeps the contents close to the blades and makes it grind evenly. Now you can buy whole bean coffee in bulk when it goes on sale and store it in an airtight container until needed. Grinding the beans when you make your coffee gives it super fresh taste and you can grind it as fine as you like—which allows you to get away with using less.

Warm tortilla chips

Take a stack of corn tortillas, cut them into quarters and arrange on a greased baking sheet. Bake at 400 F for 10 minutes per side.

Fresh green onions

Grow your own green onions right

in your kitchen After you've used the tops, save the bottoms (the white root end) of the green onions you bought at the grocery store. Just let the roots sit in water for a week and you get fresh green onions in your kitchen for free.

Designer muesli

Make your muesli cereal go farther by mixing the pricey fruit and nut cereal with less expensive filler cereals like rolled oats, grape nuts, and generic bran flakes. Adding the cereals increases the fiber content, while reducing the sugar and the price per serving—but you still get all the wonderful different textures and tastes.

Turkey tip

Buy a frozen Tom (20 pounds or more) and have the butcher saw it in half, north to south through the breastbone. This makes cleaning and stuffing the cavity easy. Prepare for roasting as usual, timing for half the total weight. Freeze the other half for later. This is more economical than buying two 10 to 12 pound birds, as large birds have a higher meat-to-bone ratio.

Donation time

Twice a year when it's time to change the clocks for Daylight Savings Time, clean out your food cupboards and donate anything you cannot use right away to the Salvation Army, food pantry or perhaps a women's shelter. This way you always know your food supply is fresh and you don't have to worry about finding cans of food that you have no idea how long they've been hiding.

French toast sticks

Homemade French toast sticks are a snap to make, just cut the bread into strips and prepare as you would regular French toast. Make a large batch at a time and freeze. It's easy to reheat as many as needed on any given morning. This is cheaper than buying them, and they taste better, too. Dipping sticks use less syrup than pouring it over a stack. For picky eaters that don't like the crust, keep the crusts for bread crumbs or other recipes.

Flavored water

Instead of paying 50 cents or more for a bottle of name brand, fruit-flavored, sweetened water, make your own for pennies. Buy a five ounce bottle of Luzianne Raspberry Flavoring (unsweetened) and your favorite sweetener. To two quarts of water, add one tablespoon of the raspberry flavoring and about 3/4 cup (more or less, to taste) of Splenda. Stir. Enjoy.

Food and Cooking

Bacon prep

Next time you buy a package of bacon, come home and cook the entire package. Freeze the individual pieces of bacon in a zip-type freezer bag. Grab your desired quantity and microwave. Hot bacon just the way you like it in seconds.

Freeze buttermilk

Recipes containing buttermilk usually call for small amounts, but you can't find buttermilk in small amounts. The solution? Buttermilk can be frozen. Measure 1/4 cup servings in baggies and store a bunch of servings in a larger zip-type freezer bag.

DIY veggie cocktail

V8 Vegetable Cocktail is loaded with great nutritious stuff. But you can make your own by putting a 48-ounce can of plain tomato juice into a pitcher with 1 teaspoon celery salt, 1/2 teaspoon onion salt, 1/2 teaspoon garlic powder and any other seasonings you prefer. Stir thoroughly and enjoy the savings.

Sandwich cookies

Combine leftover canned frosting and a half-eaten package of graham crackers and you've got a favorite dessert for kids.

Flavored syrup

Pancake syrup is so easy to make and you can add your favorite flavors. Pour two cups of granulated sugar into a saucepan. Meanwhile measure two cups of very hot water and have ready beside the stove. Turn the burner on high to melt the sugar. At the first sign of bubbles in the caramelizing (browning) process, quickly pour in the hot water. Boil on high for about five minutes. Don't stir. Turn off heat and add one teaspoon flavoring of your liking—almond, vanilla, maple—whatever you prefer. Cool and store in a sealed container.

Recipe organizer

What to do with all those recipes you've cut out of magazines and newspapers, off food labels, or the backs of food products? They are often misplaced in kitchen drawers and cabinets. A great way to keep them all in one place is to take a small photo album with clear drop-in sleeves. The recipes are sometimes so small you can fit two, sometimes three, per page. If you have a lot of recipes, start organizing the albums by categories. What a great recipe library you will have, with everything at your fingertips.

Homemade frozen dinners

Purchase clear plastic containers

and after each evening meal distribute the leftovers in containers so you have complete meals to freeze. This makes a great quick meal, you don't waste food, and no one gets tired of the same leftovers night after night.

A can of marinade

Instead of buying expensive bottles of barbecue sauce to marinate meat, pour ketchup in a bowl and add a can of cola. Mix to desired consistency and add your meat to marinate. De-licious!

Tea organizer

Tea lovers seem to accumulate tea bags. And with all those boxes and bags it's hard to know what exactly you have in your tasty stash. Cut the label off the box (generally the flap) and put it in a quart-size baggy, then put the tea bags in behind it and store file folder-like in a little plastic rectangular container. You'll free up a ton of space and now all you have to do is flip through the baggies instead of scrounging through all the boxes. You'll also know very quickly when your inventory gets low.

Frozen milk

Stock up on milk and freeze. The plastic containers are designed for freezing. They even have room at the top to expand when liquids expand when frozen. Skim or 2% milk freeze with the best results. Whole milk seems to separate once thawed, so you need to shake the container before pouring. Thaw frozen milk in the refrigerator.

Bacon, by George

Use your indoor grilling machine (like a George Foreman grill) to cook bacon. The grease drains off so the bacon is not soaked in fat. It's flat and very crispy. Perfect!

Food saver

Instead of spending money on a food saver machine, buy some drinking straws. Insert a straw into an almost-closed zip-type baggie and suck out as much air as you can. The result is close to what a food saver machine does and you don't have to buy special plastic.

Pasta sauce with baby food

Do you have kids that don't always eat right? If they enjoy foods like lasagna, pizza and spaghetti you can sneak in some nutrition and they won't even suspect. It's easy to sneak in a jar of baby food carrots when making pasta sauce. One little jar has tons of vitamin A and the taste is not even noticeable in the pasta sauce.

Food and Cooking

Reusable scoopers

The scoops in your laundry soap containers make great scoops in your flour and sugar canisters. Just wash and dry them and you're ready to scoop.

Coffee filters

Use coffee filters to make different sized tea bags, coffee bags, and aroma bathing bags for the tub. Staple the filter in the shape you need, usually one staple will do it, then add string. Filters are also good for straining liquids from cottage cheese and yogurt when you use them in recipes for spreads and dips.

Foreman gets foiled

Use aluminum foil next time you use your George Foreman grill. Add a layer of foil on the bottom of the grill and then cover whatever you're cooking. You'll avoid having to clean up a big mess.

No-egg substitute

If you're trying to cut down on your egg consumption, or are avoiding eggs all together, here's a great substitute. In recipes, instead of substituting one whole egg or two egg whites, use one tablespoon soy flour mixed with one tablespoon water. The mixture works just as well as an egg—a vegan substitute.

Slicing strawberries

The easiest way to slice strawberries is with an egg slicer. You'll get almost-perfect slices and very little mess.

Gourmet croutons

Instead of throwing away the first and last slice of bread, make croutons with the heels. Slice the bread into large cubes, and lay them in a single layer on an ungreased cookie sheet. Drizzle the bread cubes with extra virgin olive oil and generous doses of kosher salt (feel free to sprinkle any other favorite seasonings at this time). Bake in 400 F. oven for 10 minutes, with one rotation of the cookie sheet halfway through. These gourmet croutons are far better than the too-potent croutons at the grocery store, and you no longer waste perfectly good bread.

Healthier sauces

Always keep a bag of frozen chopped spinach in the freezer. Add a handful of spinach to spaghetti sauce, pizza sauce, stews and sauces. Just tell the kids it's "spices," if anyone asks.

Spices and more

Buy spices for a fraction of the regular price at ethnic supermarkets. Whatever spice you need you'll find it at the appropriate market, plus a lot more seasonings and foods at great prices. The savings are remarkable.

Once-a-month lunch

Save time and money by packing your lunch once a month. Purchase a large plastic storage container that will fit into the refrigerator at work. Load it up with a month's worth of healthy lunch fixings such as crackers, small tuna cans, fat-free pudding packs, fresh whole fruits, cut up veggies, lunch meat, small containers of condiments, cheeses, and whatever you like for lunch. At lunchtime you can "make" your lunch from the stuff in your stash. Use perishable items first and replenish your lunch kit with fresh items periodically. If refrigerator space is limited at work check with co-workers first about taking up so much space. You might need to alter the size of the container you use for your perishables. Write your name on your lunchbox. Once your co-workers see your great lunches other lunch boxes will most likely appear.

Make it sweet

An expensive ingredient, sweetened condensed milk, can be made right at home. Mix 1 stick butter, 1 cup boiling water, 2 cups sugar, and 2 cups powdered milk. Pour all ingredients in a blender and blend thoroughly. Mixture will be thin, but will thicken as it cools. This makes more than the equivalent of one can, but the rest can be refrigerated for 5-6 days, or frozen.

Floss and cut

The easiest way to cut your homemade cinnamon rolls is to use a piece of dental floss. Slide the floss under the rolled-up dough and pick up the ends of the floss and cross them until the roll is cut through.

Chicken again?

When you're stumped for what to fix for dinner check out the free cooking websites that have a ton of information and inspiration. Websites like *www.epicurious.com*, *www.foodtv.com* and *www.cookingbynumbers.com* are just a few of the Internet sources that offer recipes and ideas on what to do with leftovers or what to do with specific ingredients that you have in your cupboards.

Don't chop that lettuce

When making tacos with ground beef instead of chopping or shredding lettuce just line the warmed taco shell with a leaf of lettuce or two, before adding beef and other ingredients. It keeps the shell from getting soggy and breaking and you save yourself time by not having to chop or shred.

Making the last drop count

When you think the container of liquid coffee creamer is empty, give it one last chance: Pour a cup of hot coffee into the container, swish it around and pour it back into your cup. There, now it's empty.

Meatloaf on the Bar-b

Don't want to heat up your oven, but you still want to fix your favorite meatloaf in the summer? Why not cook it on the barbecue? Prepare your recipe as usual and put the mixture into an aluminum pan. Cover with aluminum foil, place it in the barbecue on the rack and place foil-wrapped potatoes around the pan. Put the barbecue cover on and cook for one hour.

Cornbread Panini-style

No need to make corn bread in the oven. A waffle iron or sandwich machine works great cooking corn bread. Mix up your cornbread mix, let sit 2 or 3 minutes, then bake in the appliance. Simple.

Fresh bread

Stock up when bread and bread products are on sale and keep it fresh-tasting in the freezer. Without opening them wrap each loaf or bag completely in aluminum foil before putting them in the freezer.

Small plate—big savings

Save on your grocery bill while you're saving on calories. Eat off smaller plates. Anyone who has dieted knows that filling up a smaller plate tricks your brain into thinking you're getting a nice big meal. This will stretch your food into leftovers and you will find you are satisfied after eating, without being overly stuffed. Your money will go farther, too.

Healthy "soda pop"

To save money and cut down on drinking all that sugar, make your own refreshing, carbonated drinks. Mix frozen concentrated juice with club soda instead of plain water. It will satisfy your craving for something sweet and refreshing, but without the calories.

Stockpiling

Create your own grocery store right in your own home. You'll save loads of money and will cut down on the need to run to the store all the time. Come up with what you will need to completely stock your pantry for two or three weeks. Depending on your budget either shop for those items all at once, or gradually create your stockpile. As you use the items write it down on a list. This includes food and personal care items. You'll find you'll only need to shop every other week and the only thing you'll have to buy on the alternate week is milk. Stock your freezer with meat when it's on sale and you've got your meals covered.

Chopping eggs

No need to buy an egg slicer if you have a good pastry cutter. Works just as well.

French toast supreme

Whenever you see day-old egg bread or cheese bread snap it up. It will give you the richest-tasting French toast.

Skip the eggs and oil

Instead of adding oil or eggs to cake mixes add 4-5 creamed bananas, one 15-ounce can of pumpkin, applesauce, blueberries, crushed pineapple or other fruit. Use with any of your favorite flavored cake mixes like yellow, white, spice, carrot, and chocolate. You can also add additional flavors like cinnamon, raisins or chopped almonds, too.

Tomato bounty

During the summer when tomatoes are in abundance wash a bunch, place on a cookie sheet (skins on) and stick in the freezer. Once frozen, remove from the pan and store in a zip-type freezer bag. When making chili, stew, spaghetti, or something that needs tomatoes, run the frozen tomatoes under warm water for a few seconds and the skins pop right off. Just throw the frozen, whole tomato into whatever you're cooking. Fresh tomatoes in your soups and casseroles—all winter long.

Frosted S'mores

When camping or having backyard fun, use a can of chocolate frosting for your S'mores instead of candy bars. It travels better and it doesn't get soggy when it's left in the cooler. Try adding peanut butter to your S'mores, too. Very yummy.

Cooking by numbers

Check out *www.cookingbynumbers.com* to help with get recipes using what you have in your pantry, refrigerator or freezer.

Slicing cheese

If you wait for a good sale on cheddar cheese in the two pound block you can save a lot of money. But before you head to the check out, stop by the meat department or the service deli and ask them to slice it for you. They'll do this for you for free, too. Just make sure they leave the UPC code attached so it will scan properly.

Camping chow

Before you go camping prepare large batches of three or four casseroles your family likes. Freeze in large zip-type bags. When packing put them in your cooler, which helps leave more room since they keep things cool until they're thawed. Eat the first one that thaws by heating in a cast iron pan on your camping stove. Saves time and there's no meal prep. Also works when staying in hotel rooms with a kitchenette.

Scraper cover

Do you hesitate to use your rubber food scraper for tomato and other red sauces because they have a tendency to get stained? Cover that scraper with plastic wrap. No stains and no wasted food either.

Carrot pancakes

To get kids to eat more carrots, add them to pancake batter. But you have to be sneaky. Cut up 2-3 carrots and cook with a little water and 1/2 teaspoon cinnamon. Allow to cool. Mash up carrots and liquid together, along with the amount of liquid called for in the batter recipe (less about 1/2 cup). Blend until it's the consistency of applesauce, and add it to your pancake or waffle batter. They'll never know they're eating carrot pancakes.

Mystery breading

Empty out your cupboards and pantry and haul all the cookies, crackers, cereals over to your food processor. Put everything in the food processor and grind them up. Yes, even the cookies—just skip the ones with cream centers. You can determine how fine or coarse you want the mixture to be. By mixing all of them together, you get a very unique flavor. Store the mix in a large zip-type freezer bag, add a few of your favorite seasonings, and put them in my freezer. When you need coatings for chicken, fish or pork, just pull it out of the freezer, pour what you need in a bowl and return the unused portion to the freezer. Quick, tasteful and economic.

Easy-off liners

To keep from losing half your muffin to the liner just spray the liners lightly with the vegetable cooking spray of your choice. Your liners will peel right off with almost no muffin residue and cleaning those muffin pans will be much easier!

Mail order co-op

Ordering extracts and flavorings from mail order companies enables you to find unique products. Unfortunately it can be rather expensive. To cut costs, ask your friends if they would like to split the cost and the products with you. It's a fun and economical way to sample different flavorings, but not get stuck with large bottles or hefty costs. This might turn out to be so much fun that you'll make it an annual event.

Freezing buns

Most buns are created equal. It's the quality of the plastic wrap that the buns are stored in that affects the freshness and quality of the bun, especially when freezing. So instead of opting for more expensive buns, buy whatever you like and then store in zip-type freezer bags.

Freezer bags

Freezer bags are expensive, but if you go to your local bulk food department in the grocery store and talk to the manager you may be able to buy a roll (1,000 bags) of the same bags they use there. If the manager agrees you'll score bags for about 2 cents a piece. It's a great deal and you get exactly what you want.

Spaghetti sauce

Tomatoes can be a bit on the acidic side when making homemade sauce. Just add a few pinches of baking soda. It will fizz up at first, but just continue to stir it in and the result is a much sweeter sauce with a lot less acid. This will definitely be appreciated by those that are affected by heartburn from tomato sauce.

Stretch-a-meal

If you use the pre-packaged meal kits you've probably found that the portions are a bit on the small side. You can stretch the meal by adding 2-3 packages of ramen that you've prepared. Just stir the hot noodles into the meal before serving. This addition costs pennies and will fill everyone up at your table.

Potato hose

Instead of throwing away torn or snagged pantyhose and stockings, wash them out and then hang them up in the food pantry to hold potatoes. Believe it or not those potatoes will last for months without sprouting and they will also remain nice and firm. They also make a heck of a conversation piece when company opens the pantry door.

Frozen pops

Freezing popcorn kernels is a good option for extending their shelf life. Also, it seems like more of the kernels pop after being frozen.

Last chance veggies

Before your veggies go bad and have to be tossed, save them and turn them into vegetable stock. Use whatever's in your crisper including the limp celery, dried out carrots, sprouting onion, dried out garlic, and soft bell peppers—anything that hasn't gone bad yet. Simmer for several hours with your spices and herbs. Strain the stock and toss the veggies. Freeze the stock so you have it for soup, rice, casseroles, roasts, stir-fry, and so on.

Oatmeal tricks

Kids love flavored oatmeal, but it's expensive and loaded with sugar. Go ahead and buy a few boxes when it's on sale along with a large canister of plain, store-brand oatmeal. Add 2-3 packets of the flavored kind to the plain canister. It will stretch a long way. Use a 1/3 cup measure for one serving.

Non-chip cookies

To bake a quick, vanilla drop cookie, make up a batch of your regular chocolate chip cookies-just omit the chips. Sprinkle with regular or colored sugar before putting in the oven, if you want them decorated. This is much easier that rolling out dough that has to be refrigerated before baking.

Canned juice cocktail

If a recipe calls for canned pineapple, drain the juice and add it to your orange juice you've got in your refrigerator. Pineapple orange juice is expensive when purchased premixed. Never discard the fruit juice from recipes calling for fruit. You can always combine fruit juice with seasoning for a great chicken or pork marinade.

Coffee leftovers

Don't throw out leftover coffee. Store it in the refrigerator and reheat by the cup in the microwave.

Boiling buddies

When you boil pasta for a veggie dish, throw in fresh cut up broccoli or other veggies during the last 5 minutes to save time and the need to use another pot. Drain both and toss with butter, parmesan and sauce—whatever your recipe requires. Only takes 15 minutes to fix. Another combination to try is boiling potatoes and eggs together for salad. It's amazing how many combinations you'll start to come up with. Saves on cleanup time, too.

Coffee creamers

Try powdered milk instead of dry creamers in your coffee. It's cheaper and has less fat and calories. At holiday time get fancy and add vanilla to taste and top it off with Cool Whip or real whipped cream.

Milk mixture

Here's a great way to stretch your milk money, but you'll need three empty gallon milk jugs to start. Buy a gallon of whole milk and divide equally between the three plastic jugs. Mix up 2 quarts of powdered milk and add to each jug. The jugs will be approximately 3/4 full, but that is okay. Freeze two of the jugs. When it looks like you're running low on milk, take a jug out of the freezer and put in the refrigerator for a day. Voila! No more running to the convenience store because you ran out of milk. And the best part? It tastes great!

Party leftovers

Here's how to keep all those party leftovers from going to waste. In a large slow cooker, add the leftover meat (ham, turkey, roast beef), the cheese, and veggies from the party trays. Then add the ranch dip from the veggie tray, three cups of cooked rice (you might have to actually prepare this), and a can of cream of celery or mushroom soup mixed with one can water. Add pepper, 1 tablespoon dried minced onion, and 1 teaspoon garlic powder. Mix all ingredients thoroughly. Cook on low for about three to four hours to heat through until the veggies are crisp tender. Serve with leftover bread from the deli tray. Delicious and you haven't wasted a thing.

Cheese wrap

Store cheese in foil, not plastic wrap. And try not to touch the cheese when you're slicing or grating. Better to wear food service gloves. It's the natural bacteria on our hands that cause cheese to turn green. Even your impeccably clean hands should never touch the cheese that goes back into the refrigerator.

Eggnog year-round

When buying eggnog during the holidays, buy it on sale or during a clearance sale. Simply freeze and you'll have eggnog in the summer while you celebrate Christmas in July.

Food and Cooking

Butter, sort of

If you like the taste of butter but need to restrict your intake, here's an easy way to cut down by half: Combine 1 cup of softened butter and 1 cup olive oil. Mix together. Store in a covered dish in the refrigerator. This mixture spreads nicely.

No more leftovers

For those that don't like leftovers or whose families simply won't eat leftovers, start making less food. Yes, less food. Not a lot less, but start by decreasing the amount of meat you cook. Start incrementally if you think it will be hard. By making slightly less you guarantee that everything will be eaten and your family will actually learn to eat less at meal times, which is healthier, too. This works best if you dish up everyone's plate before hand, instead of placing all the food on the table, family style.

DIY brown sugar

If you've run out of brown sugar or want to make your own, it's easy. To each cup of granulated sugar add 2 tablespoons of molasses. Mix well with a fork. Store in a tightly-sealed canister. Depending on prevailing prices this may be a more economical solution than purchasing brown sugar. Tastier, too.

Banana stash

Keep a large container in your freezer and add bananas as they become over-ripe. Just peel and add to the stash. Smash it down with a fork to make room for the next one. The blacker the banana the better the bread, so after you've accumulated enough frozen bananas thaw your bowl in the refrigerator for a few days, stirring every once in a while. You'll have really ripe banana goop, perfect for your bread recipe.

Hamburger meat stretcher

One pound of ground meat generally makes 3-4 medium size hamburger patties. If you add flour, milk, and an extra egg to your recipe, you can stretch your meat to 6-7 patties. It doesn't take a lot of flour and milk, but it does add extra volume so your meat goes further. Add your favorite seasonings and everyone will enjoy these tasty burgers.

Easy low-fat muffins

For low-fat muffins, take one box of cake mix (German Chocolate, Spice, or your favorite) and add one 15-ounce can of pumpkin. When mixing these two ingredients together they don't appear to blend well, but just continue to stir until the ingredients are well blended. Fill muffin cups about 2/3 full and bake at the required temperature on the cake mix box. These are easy and delicious, and will stay moist for days.

Fizzy Kool-Aid

Mix your favorite Kool-Aid with your sweetener of choice. Mix half Kool-Aid with half club soda. Similar to soda, but less and sugar and mystery additives.

Turkey leftovers

Package your turkey leftovers before you sit down for Thanksgiving dinner! Roast your turkey and make your gravy a few days before you plan to serve. Carve and set aside enough turkey and gravy for the big day. Then package all the leftovers into freezer containers. Now when you're in the mood for turkey leftovers your entrée is ready—all you just have to do is prepare the sides. Immediately freezing the leftovers ensures that you don't get tired of eating turkey for a week. You can even freeze the carcass to make soup at a later date, too.

Leftover tomato slices

When you have leftover slices of fresh tomatoes, put them in the freezer for later use in cooking. Frozen tomatoes will add moisture to leftover macaroni and cheese or other casseroles.

Roll 'em out

If your pie crusts stick to your bread board when trying to roll out, switch to your counter. Lightly moisten the counter with water. Tear off two sheets of plastic wrap large enough for the diameter of the pie crust. Place the ball of dough in the center, then tear off two more pieces of plastic wrap to cover the dough. Roll as usual to fit the pie plate. Remove the top layer of wrap, place pie plate on dough, and invert. You don't use as much flour, which causes pie crusts to be tough.

Chocolate syrup

Make your own chocolate syrup that's perfect as an ice cream topping or for making chocolate milk: Combine one cup unsweetened cocoa powder with two cups granulated sugar. Whisk to get rid of lumps. Add one cup cold water and 1/4 teaspoon salt. Bring to a boil over medium heat, stirring frequently until thick. Remove from heat, cool and add one tablespoon vanilla extract. Enjoy!

Cheap chicken

If you have a Wal-Mart Super Center near you, head to the service deli around 9:00 p.m. It's just before closing when they sell the hot deli foods and whole roasted chickens at half price. Call ahead to verify your store does this. Rotisserie chicken for $2.00 is a bargain especially when you consider that raw, frozen whole fryers can cost $4 or $5 from the meat department.

Root ginger

A little ginger goes a long way and you don't need much. When you buy a piece of ginger root there are two ways of making it last. Peel and cut it into small chunks and store in a screw-top jar with dry sherry. The ginger-flavored sherry will also be terrific in your recipes, too. Or you can bury the unused part of the ginger root in a pot of sand on your kitchen window sill. It will start to grow, but you can pull it up, cut off as much as you need and replant the remainder until next time.

Cheese flavoring

Instead of buying expensive cheeses for soup, stew or rice, just add a package of powdered cheese mix from the cheap boxes of macaroni and cheese. It gives soups and stews a nice cheesy flavor, and when added to the water when cooking rice it really makes for a nice side dish. When cooking with it be sure you have at least 1/4 cup of water or milk. The cheese packets are also great when making broccoli cheese soup—just add to the chicken broth. And sprinkled on popcorn makes is a tasty treat, too. Stock up when you come across specials on boxes of macaroni and cheese. There's no waste, either, since you can use the macaroni for any recipe that calls for noodles.

Oatmeal extender

When browning hamburger meat add 1/4 to 1/2 cup of dry oatmeal to 1 pound of meat. Stir until well incorporated and brown. Use this in any recipe that calls for ground beef. You and your family will be hard-pressed to detect this.

No-stale cookies

To keep homemade cookies soft and moist place one slice of white or whole wheat bread into the container with the cookies. Apply lid and wait a few hours. This even works if the cookies are a tad overdone but not burned. Once you try this, you'll do this for every batch.

Marinating meat

When packaging meat for the freezer put the marinade in a zip-type bag with the meat, then freeze. When you take the meat out to defrost it will marinate automatically.

Mold prevention

Regular table salt can extend the life of cheese and protect it from molding in the refrigerator. Take your cheese and wrap it in a cloth dampened with saltwater before refrigerating.

Salt adds lift

Add a pinch of salt when whipping cream. It helps the cream whip higher. This also works when beating egg whites, as they beat faster, higher and will firm up better.

Brown bag alternative

When cooking a turkey, use a brown paper bag instead of a roaster or browning bag. Slide the turkey in the bag with the spices of your choice, fold the top over and put it in the oven. Cook per instructions and length of time. After awhile you will be able to smell when it is cooked. You can still use the juices, and your turkey won't burn or be dry. And the best part? No basting.

Flavored coffee

Take 1/2 pound of whole coffee beans and add your favorite flavor extract or liqueur. Allow the beans to dry and the alcohol to evaporate. Grind and enjoy.

Fresh-looking apples

While cutting up apples for your favorite pie or dessert they can begin to turn brown. A solution of lemon and water works wonders in keeping apples freshly cut, but it's not recommended to submerge them in the solution. Instead, mix the lemon water in a spray bottle and spritz the apples as you're done preparing. By the time you're ready to assemble your ingredients your apples will look freshly cut.

Quick chill

To chill wine, champagne, beer or other drinks quickly, salt and ice will do the trick. Place the bottle in an ice bucket or other tall plastic container. Add a layer of ice on the bottom and sprinkle it with a few tablespoons of salt. Continue to layer salt and ice until it reaches the neck of the bottle. Then add enough water to bring it up to the level of the ice. After 10 to 12 minutes open and serve. You'll enjoy surprisingly cold beverages.

Sticky marshmallows

To prevent sticky marshmallows that always end up in the trash, transfer to a zip-type gallon freezer bag and add one tablespoon of powdered sugar. Shake really well. You will have fresh marshmallows for a long time providing the person opening the bag always seals it tightly.

Frozen soup cubes

When you make soup stock, freeze the stock in ice cube trays, then pop the cubes into a freezer bag. No more need to purchase canned stock.

Butter wrappers

When a recipe calls for using a "greased pan," use the butter wrappers to grease the pan. Extra wrappers may be kept in the freezer for later use.

Year-round fruit

Take advantage of all the yummy summer fruit, whether you grow your own or pick your own. Harvest and pick enough to freeze and you'll enjoy the "fruits" of your labor throughout the year.

Spice partners

Create a spice co-op with one or more of your friends and you'll never need to throw out old spices again. Whenever you buy anything new you split among your co-op. You'll save money and storage space, and you'll end up with a great spice collection, too.

Pie protectors

If you ever need to transport a pie but don't have a box, you can still protect it from getting crushed. Plastic holders for paper plates are great and they fit a nine-inch pie tin perfectly. Snap one on the top of your tin and you can even stack them up for easy transport.

Fruit-pops

Save the largest strawberries in the flat and make fruit-pops. Insert popsicle sticks into the fruit and freeze on cookie sheets. Bag them and store. Kids love these on hot days, and they are better for them than regular popsicles. Canned pineapple and fresh banana sections also work well as fruit-pops, but they don't keep as long.

Lemon harvest

Don't let those lemons spoil on the ground, juice them and freeze the juice in ice cube trays. Once frozen pop the cubes into zip-type bags and store in the freezer. This neat little trick can be used with oranges as well.

Veggie bags

Zip-type bags designed to store veggies were a bit hit for a time, but very expensive. They worked really well in prolonging the life of fruits and vegetables, but are no longer available (could it be because they were so expensive?!). But you can make your own veggie bags with ordinary zip-type bags. Place the bag on a cutting board and make a bunch of tiny holes all over with the tip of a sharp, pointed knife. Your fruits and veggies will last a lot longer stored in these bags.

DIY latte

Making your own lattes and coffee drinks not only saves money, but it gives you decision-making power over your ingredient and calorie intake. Purchase a fun travel cup and experiment with different brands of coffee drinks and latte mixes. By making your own drinks at home each morning you won't be tempted by the pastries or muffins at the local coffee store, either.

Meatloaf for meatballs

Besides using leftover meatloaf for sandwiches, cut the meatloaf into chunks and add it to spaghetti sauce for another meal. It's almost like having spaghetti with meatballs, but without all the work.

Save-ory soup

Try saving all your leftover meats and vegetables throughout the week to make a weekend pot of soup. Just add a few cans of diced tomatoes and maybe some chicken or beef broth to what you've collected. Simmer in a slow cooker for a while. You'll have a unique soup each weekend that doesn't require a lot of time in the kitchen.

Thermal carafes

Stop boiling water for tea all day long. Use a thermal coffee carafe to keep your tea hot for about 7 hours. This works really well with coffee, too, instead of keeping the burner of your coffee pot on all day.

Spray zone

To avoid a mess when using non-stick sprays, open the dishwasher door and place the pan on the door before spraying. Close the door and wash away the residue next time you run a full load. Just make sure your dishwasher is empty or has dirty dishes inside!

Pantry moths

When your pantry is invaded by those darned moths, you end up throwing away bag after bag of flour, cereal and crackers. Good news—there's a solution and it's cheap. Moths hate spearmint chewing gum. Open a package of gum, leaving the foil wrapper on the gum.

Place the stick of gum in canisters of flour or opened bags of cereal, etc. The gum will not affect the taste of the item and it sure keeps the moths out.

Onion odors

After cutting up onions, run cold water over your hands while rubbing them with a stainless steel spoon or utensil. This removes the odor from your hands. Also, if you refrigerate your onion before cutting it up, it will not burn your eyes.

Frozen cookie dough

Instead of buying expensive frozen or refrigerator ready-to-bake cookies, make your own. Here's a recipe that makes about 40 cookies: 1 package chocolate cake mix, 1 egg, 1 stick of melted butter, and 1 12-ounce bag of chocolate chips. Mix together all ingredients. Take tablespoons of dough and form into balls. On a cookie sheet, flatten the balls and place in the freezer for 1 hour. Then wrap the frozen dough balls in plastic wrap. The dough will last for at least three months. When you want to bake cookies, you can make 2 or 20. Let defrost for 10 minutes then bake for 9-11 minutes at 375 F.

Vegetable peelings

Save peelings from vegetables such as onions, carrots—anything that has a peel. Put them all in a freezer bag or bowl and store them in the freezer where they can be added to each time you peel a carrot or cut an onion. Add all the outside dry onion skins and celery trimmings, especially leaves. When cleaning out the refrigerator, add wilted carrots (unpeeled) and celery, removing any spoiled areas. Your freezer bag will grow quickly! To make a wonderful veggie broth just simmer all the frozen veggie discards with water for several hours, strain, discard the veggies to the compost. Freeze the broth in 1- or 2-cup, labeled portions and use for sauces, cooking rice, or other soups. The onion skins make an especially rich, colored broth.

Cooking spray

Instead of buying aerosol cooking sprays, purchase a reusable sprayer in which you can put any type of cooking oil. Try canola oil for frying and olive oil for roasting vegetables. There are many advantages to using your cooking oil of choice instead of whatever has been selected for the canned spray.

Fresh snacks

Keep snack foods and cereal fresh with a binder clip or clothespin. It really works and they're so much cheaper than special chip clips.

Fresh herbs

When storing your herbs in the refrigerator, wrap them in a damp tea towel and store in a plastic bag in the vegetable crisper. This keeps them fresh for days and they don't wilt at all as they would in a glass of water.

Cake tester

If you don't already have a metal cake tester make one out of the metal egg dippers in the Easter egg dying kits. Just straighten and use. It's great because it already has a loop for a handle.

Noodle pancakes

Saimin "pancakes" are inexpensive, healthy and easy to prepare. Boil two packages of ramen noodles and add at least one seasoning packet. While the noodles are cooking heat up a non-stick skillet with 1 tablespoon oil to medium-high heat. Drain noodles and add 2 beaten eggs and 1 tablespoon oyster sauce (optional) for flavor. Mix thoroughly. Pour noodle mixture in hot skillet, and spread evenly. When browned on one side, flip the 'pancake' over. Continue browning on the bottom side. This is a great starch side dish instead of rice or potatoes, or as a lunch entrée.

Upside down

Storing cottage cheese and sour cream upside down in your refrigerator after each use will prevent it from going bad as quickly. The cottage cheese will remain fresh long after the expiration date on the carton. This position allows a seal to form that keeps out oxygen.

Fast salad dressing

Empty jars of gourmet mustard and mayonnaise are great starters for salad dressing. Fill halfway with olive oil and vinegar of your choice, and shake well. Season to taste.

Snacks to-go

Turn party hats into snack holders. Cut off the elastic string and fill them with chips, cookies or crackers. These snack holders are easier to hold while standing than a plate.

Beef it up

Put your ground beef in a pan, but before you start cooking add a can of beef broth to the meat. Mix together until it looks like the beef won't hold any more. Cook through. This will enhance the flavor of the beef, and it makes it go farther, too. One pound of ground beef to one can of beef broth seems to work best.

Food and Cooking

Ground beef for less

Don't buy lean ground beef at high prices. Find a cheaper roast and have it ground. Select a lean top round roast or whatever is on sale and ask the butcher to trim and grind it. The roast may even be leaner than the ground beef you were going to buy.

No moldy cheese

Do you want to prevent mold from growing on cheese? Wrap the cheese tightly in plastic wrap along with a sugar cube and store it in the refrigerator. If your cheese is already moldy, simply wipe it off with a vinegar soaked paper towel. The cheese will then be edible, and the flavor won't be affected.

Raising dough

To encourage yeast doughs to rise, set the covered bowl or pan on top of a heating pad set on Medium heat. Prepare for a quick rise.

Summer cookie swap

Why wait till the holidays to do a cookie swap? Get together a few friends and ask them to bring their favorite cookies along with several copies of their recipe. You can lounge in the sun, eat cookies and swap recipes. You might just have some new ideas for this year's holiday baking, too.

Flour pest control

To rid yourself of those little bugs that get into your flour, put the flour in the freezer for a couple of days. The bugs will not be able to multiply, and your flour will still be perfectly safe to eat.

Clinging trick

Plastic wrap can be a nightmare when it sticks to things you don't want it to. If you keep your roll in the refrigerator it will be easier to manage and will quickly stick after you use it to wrap food and containers.

No-stick Krispie Treats

When making Krispie treats, rinse you hands with cold water before pressing the treats into the pan. The treats will stay in the pan, not on your hands.

Cheap cappuccino

To make a delicious, rich mocha cappuccino at home, fill a large travel mug with a heaping tablespoon of instant coffee and one packet of instant hot chocolate. Add hot water and top it off with a splash of low-fat milk. This costs a fraction of what you'd pay at a coffee shop and you can control the sugar and fat content according to your preferences.

Overripe bananas

Instead of throwing away bananas that are a little too ripe, peel and freeze them in a zip-type bag. They make "banana pops" and can be added to a smoothie for a wonderful creamy texture.

Lemon juice substitute

If you don't have lemon on hand, mix a little unsweetened powdered lemonade mix with water and use it as a substitute. A little packet goes a long way and keeps for a long time. You won't have to go on any spur-of-the-moment grocery runs when you are trying to finish your cooking.

Pith-free oranges

If you don't enjoy eating the orange pith (white stuff between the rind and the orange), first peel the orange. Then run the orange under cold water and rub it to remove all the left over pith. You'll have a clean and chilled orange to eat.

Freezer containers

Large family size yogurt containers make fantastic freezer ware, especially for homemade soup. Pour in your leftover soup, put the lid on top and place in the freezer. You can put it in the refrigerator to thaw before heating it up. Use individual yogurt cups to freeze small quantities of soup if you just want to eat a single serving.

Wine pourer tops

Buy wine pourers to use on liquid dishwashing detergent, cooking oil, vinegar and liquid hand soap. You will use less because the liquid will come out more slowly and you will be able to control the flow.

Cake decorating

To quickly and cheaply write on your next special occasion cake, use an empty, clean, squeeze-type mustard bottle. Just put icing in the container and write on your cake. If the icing doesn't come out easily, warm it gently by placing the container in a pan of hot water for a couple of minutes.

Lemon zest

Once you've squeezed the juice out of lemons, don't toss the rinds. Instead collect them in a bag in the freezer. When you need just a bit of lemon zest, pull out a rind and grate what you need.

Food and Cooking

Fix salty soup

If you put too much salt in your homemade soup, don't despair! Peel a potato and add it to the soup, allowing it to simmer briefly in the soup and absorb some of the salt. Remove before serving.

No stick garlic

If you have to chop garlic by hand and don't want it to stick to your hands, put a little drop of vegetable oil on the clove and then begin chopping. The garlic pieces won't stick to your skin or the knife.
Soft brown sugar To keep your brown sugar from hardening, slip part of an orange peel into the container and seal. Change the peel periodically.

Apple handles

If your kids enjoy peeled apples but have trouble handling them without making a sticky mess, insert corn-on-the-cob holders on each end of apple. Your kids will be able to eat up the apple without getting too messy.

Banana storage

Use a large cup hook under a cabinet to hang your bananas. It is cheaper than a "banana hanger" and still does the job quite well.

Birthday cake saver

If you dislike scraping wax drippings off your cake after the birthday person blows out the candles, place the birthday candles inside LifeSavers. The candies will catch the wax and save the top of the cake from candle puncture holes, too.

Bouquet of herbs

For fresh herbs, clip the ends of your parsley and other herbs and place in a small bud vase filled with water. Leave on the counter as you would a bouquet of flowers.

Boxed macaroni

If you like boxed macaroni and cheese, go for the store brand and stir in a slice or two of American cheese after making the macaroni according to instructions. The macaroni will come out creamy and rich Breadcrumbs Use the ends of bread loaves and any stale bread to make breadcrumbs. Put the pieces in a paper lunch sack and leave the bag in a cabinet for a week or so. Then put the bread through the food processor and store for use in recipes that call for breadcrumbs.

Breakfast to go

To make your own instant oatmeal, fill zip-type plastic bags with quick-

cooking oats, cinnamon or other spices and a tablespoon or two of trail mix or dried fruit. When you get to work dump the mix into a disposable cup, add artificial sweetener if desired, add hot water from the coffee machine, and pop it in the microwave for a few seconds.
Cake cutter Use dental floss to cut your cakes horizontally for filling. Just wrap a long piece of dental floss all the way around the cake, cross the ends and pull. No mess, straight cut and very few crumbs.
Cereal mixing Cut the cost of breakfast by mixing cheaper generic cereal into your usual brand. You can buy generic corn flakes and add it to a box of another type of cereal. Try mixing cereals together one bowl at a time until you find what best suits your tastes.

Cereal storage

Keep your cereal in clear plastic food storage containers to preserve freshness. Cut out the front of the box and put it inside the container so you can see at a glance which cereal is inside. Keep these box fronts and use them over and over.
Cheap cherries Maraschino cherries are expensive, so when you need only a decorative few for a pineapple upside-down cake just buy a can of fruit cocktail. It has enough of the bright red cherries for the cake, and you can eat the rest of the fruit.
Cheap flavors To make your own flavored coffee without springing for the higher cost of flavored coffee beans, sprinkle ground cinnamon or nutmeg in with the coffee grinds before brewing.

Cheese crumbling

To crumble a large amount of bleu cheese or goat cheese, grab a cooling rack and a paper towel. Place the cooling rack over the paper towel and carefully rub and push the cheese through the large grating in the rack. The cheese will be crumbled on the other side.

Chill the cheese

When you need to grate semi-hard cheese like jack or cheddar, pop it into the freezer for a half hour or so before shredding. This prevents the cheese from turning into a total mess on the back side of the grater. Chill and grate butter as well when a recipe calls for "dotting" the top of the casserole or pastry with butter.

Chopping tomatoes

Chopping canned tomatoes can be messy, so put the tomatoes in a bowl and use your kitchen shears to cut them as you let the bowl catch the juices.

Chopping walnuts

To chop walnuts or pecans quickly

and without creating a big mess on your counter, use a rolling pin. Place the nuts in a large plastic bag, seal and then roll the rolling pin over the nuts until they are well crushed.

Crazy funny cukes

Get the kids to help eat all those cucumbers. Slice one in half horizontally. Insert a small whole carrot in the middle where the seeds are. Make sure you press it in firmly, pushing it down so it it is snug in the middle. Using a sharp knife, slice the cucumber into disks, horizontally. Tell your kids these are "alien space saucers." Makes for a fun snack!

Cutting brownies

When you remove brownies from the pan, cut them with a pizza cutter. It zips right through. No muss. No fuss. And it makes it easier to cut them straight. This works well with most bar cookies, too.

De-fat stock

When removing the fat from homemade chicken stock, cover the container with plastic wrap, pressing it down so the wrap is directly touching the surface of the stock. Place in the refrigerator. The next day, peel off the plastic wrap and discard. The fat will come off with it.

Fizzy drinks

To keep the fizz in 2-liter bottles of soft drinks, simply put the lid on tightly and store the container upside down. The air cannot escape through the liquid, which causes the loss of carbonation.

Fresh veggies

Put a piece of paper towel or a napkin in your zip-type bags of vegetables. They absorb the condensation from the vegetables and keep the environment dry, which preserves the vegetables' refrigerator life. Change the paper when you notice it getting too damp.

Frosting saver

When you don't have a cake pan lid, insert a few toothpicks into the top of the cake before covering it with plastic wrap. It keeps the wrap from touching the cake.

Fun pancakes

Kids often enjoy having pancakes made in the shape of their initials, but it is nearly impossible to form the letters when pouring the batter from a pitcher or ladle. Instead, try using a large medicine dropper or turkey baster to dispense the batter into the hot pan. You'll have better control to make the shapes you want.

Gourmet ginger

Keep a large ginger root in the freezer in a zip-type bag. When a recipe calls for ginger, simply grate about 1 1/2 times the amount required right off of the ginger root with a fine hand-held grater. The ginger has the consistency of expensive ginger paste and the flavor is superior. Use fresh ginger in Asian marinades, salad dressings, pumpkin pie, and ginger cookies.

Grating garlic

Don't have a garlic press handy? To get that same pasty consistency without having to chop the garlic by hand, place a fork on the counter and firmly rub a peeled clove of garlic up and down the tines.

Hamburger buns

Save the ends of your bread to use as hamburger buns. Bread ends hold up better than inside pieces. The healthier the bread you buy, the healthier the bun.

Iced coffee

While your leftover coffee is still warm, add sugar and stir until it is dissolved. Store the coffee in a closed container in the refrigerator. When you are ready for some iced coffee, just pour it in your cup along with some ice cubes and add half-and-half.

Instant oatmeal

Buy a big container of instant oatmeal and add it into various recipes like pancakes, cookies and home-made breads to add more fiber and nutrition. Your family probably won't be able to tell the difference.

Juicing lemons

To get an abundant amount of lemon juice from a fresh lemon, place the lemon in a microwave oven for 25 seconds. Take it out and roll the lemon on the counter. Make a small cut in the lemon and squeeze. You'll get lots of fresh lemon juice.

Labeling leftover

If you like to label your plastic containers filled with leftovers, why waste time with felt-tipped markers and self-adhesive labels? Get a dry erase marker and write directly on the container. The ink can be wiped off easily with a wet paper towel.

Leftover dips

Leftover dips need never go to waste. Cheddar and salsa dip go well in macaroni and cheese or on broccoli. Salsa alone is good in spaghetti sauce and over chicken breast. Onion and garlic dips are good in mashed potatoes. All kinds of dips are good in vegetable casseroles. Lots of dips are good in salads. The dips add a lot of spice and flavor.

Lemon juice

You can buy lemons in the winter when they are cheap and freeze the juice in ice cube trays. One ice cube section equals about one tablespoon of juice.

Mystery marinade

Buy various salad dressings in bulk when they go on sale. When you accumulate enough varieties of dressings, make your own marinade and add to zip-type freezer bags along with the meat. They'll taste different every time, so you will never get bored.

Nachos in slow cooker

Put a baking bag (turkey size) in the slow cooker before adding the nacho cheese. This will keep the cheese from sticking or burning and makes for simple cleanup and storage of leftovers.

No mess deviled eggs

When you make deviled eggs, place the cooked egg yolks into a large zip-type bag, along with the rest of the filling ingredients. Smash the mixture with your hands to combine (kids love to help with this part because it feels funny). Then carefully snip the bottom corner off the zip-type bag and pipe the filling into the egg whites. Toss the bag, and your cleanup is complete.

No mess meatloaf

Mixing meatloaf ingredients is often a messy process. Instead of using your hands to combine the ingredients in a mixing bowl, put all the ingredients in a plastic zip-type bag. Push most of the air out of the bag, seal it and then knead the ingredients together until they are well-mixed.

Gooey ice cream

If you dislike opening your carton of ice cream to find a gooey film on the top, place a piece of wax paper directly on top of the ice cream before replacing the lid and putting it into the freezer. You can also just turn the ice cream carton on its head.

Nut substitution

When making chocolate chip cookies you can use broken pretzels as a substitute for nuts. The pretzels provide the crunch of nuts for a fraction of the cost and are a perfect alternative for those who are allergic to nuts.

Quick chop

When chopping herbs like basil, cilantro or parsley, use a pizza cutter instead of a knife. It cuts a large amount of herbs quickly.

Opening dates

When you buy something that is going to lose its pungency over time, such as herbs, spices and salad dressings, use a permanent marker to write the date you opened it on the lid. You will know how long the item has been in the pantry or the refrigerator.

Perfect cookies

If your cookies are spreading too much once they hit the hot oven here's what to do: Chill the cookie dough in the refrigerator before dropping it onto the sheet, and always allow the cookie sheet to cool between batches.

Pie protectors

If you ever need to transport a pie but don't have a box, pick up a plastic holder for paper plates from the dollar store. These fit a nine-inch pie tin perfectly! Place one on the top of your tin before transporting. Pre-buttered pasta When you cook pasta, add a teaspoon of margarine to the boiling water before you add the pasta. This helps the pasta not to stick together and become dried out when you drain the water. Plus it adds a little flavor.

Recipes to go

Store your recipes that are written on index cards in 4x6 plastic coated photo albums, which you can purchase at a dollar store or on clearance at a crafts store. Slip these albums easily in drawers or cabinets, and if you spill something on them while baking, just wipe it off. They are also small enough to toss into a purse or small bag to carry to the grocery store.

Rice cooker cleanup

To prevent rice from sticking to the bottom of your rice cooker once the rice is done, spray the inside with cooking spray before adding the rice and water for cooking.
Save the syrup After opening a can of fruit, save the juice syrup by freezing it in an ice cube tray. Add to your iced tea for extra sweetness and flavoring.

Shakes

You'll swear it's restaurant's chocolate shake: Soften 3 cups vanilla ice cream by placing it in the refrigerator for approximately one hour. Mix with 1 cup milk and 1/2 cup chocolate milk powdered mix in a blender. You'll get 4 servings of this delicious dessert.

Soften bread

If you have a baguette or a loaf of uncut bread that has gone stale, sprinkle the item with water until fairly damp. Pop into a hot oven for a few minutes until the bread is soft and hot.

Spinning dressing

Use your salad spinner to distribute dressing evenly over your salad. You'll use less dressing, and your salad will be nicely tossed.

Tidy cake

When baking a cake, you can skip the messy instruction that says to dust the greased pans with flour. Cut and place a round of wax paper in the bottom of each of the pans. Now grease the pans as normal. The finished cake will come out easily when inverted. Simply peel away the waxed paper.

Transport a cake

If you don't want to spend a lot on a fancy device for transporting cakes, just go to the dollar store and buy the biggest plastic bowl with a lid that you can find. Set the cake on the lid with a little frosting under the cake to hold it in place and then frost-now put the bowl over the cake and you have an airtight cover.

Veggie soup

If you over cook vegetables, turn them into soup. Purée the vegetables along with broth or milk, add some seasonings, and heat over the stove for delicious soup.

Yummy smoothie

To make a low-fat, low-calorie smoothie pop evaporated skim milk, fresh fruit and Splenda in the blender. This makes a delicious smoothie.

GIFTS

Gifts

Hospital gifts

When you visit a friend in the hospital, fill an inexpensive gift bag with a good toothbrush, soft Kleenex, a magazine and note cards.

Decoupage plate

Find a clear glass dish, colorful tissue paper, a photo, a sponge brush and decoupage medium. Cut the photo to fit the bottom circle on the back of the plate, brush decoupage medium or white glue on plate back, and place the photo face down on the glue Let dry. Coat entire backside of the plate with more medium, tear tissue paper into pieces, and stick the pieces onto the plate. Allow to dry and trim paper around the edges of the plate. Coat all with medium. Seal with spray sealer or varnish.

Quick gift wrap

Need a fast gift wrap? Use aluminum foil with a pretty bow.

Child's vegetable garden

Give your child a vegetable garden that he or she can care for. Find a spot in your yard where you can make raised beds and plant seeds. Decorate the garden with rocks and pinwheels. Wrap up a trowel and gardening gloves for your child to open, and then present the garden.

Suitable for framing

Give a box of assorted picture frames in all sizes and styles, along with a roll or two of film. This gift is easy to shop for all year long, and carries enough sentiment to be appropriate for any occasion.

Cookie dough

Prepare your favorite cookie dough, wrap it in colored plastic wrap, and freeze it. Wrap it up in a cookie jar along with the baking instructions. Double the recipe and make several gifts at once.

Gift in a jar

Choose one of your favorite cookie, brownie or cake recipes and buy the ingredients in bulk. Layer the dry ingredients for the recipe in a glass canning jar, screw on the lid and decorate the top with fabric or ribbons. Include mixing and baking instructions on the side of the jar and don't forget to include the recipe!

Free ribbons

Contact a local florist and see if they will save their ribbon scraps for you. Florists use high quality ribbons, and their scraps are still very usable in gift wrapping.

Greeting card gift box

Recycle greeting cards from all occasions by making tiny origami gift boxes with them. Look online for instructions on how to fold a box. Use the front of the card for the top of the box and the text or back of the card for the bottom of the box. Perfect for giving small jewelry items.

Ordering flowers

Instead of making a toll call to the area you want the flowers delivered, look up florists in the area on the Internet and see if they have a toll-free number listed—most do.

Decoration as gifts

Young adults and newlyweds usually do not have many Christmas decorations. Shop the after-Christmas sales and pick up lights and decorations—then wrap them up for a gift for next Christmas.

Affording holiday presents

Start saving for the holidays a little at a time. Stash $2 every day in a jar or savings account. By the time December comes, you will have almost $700 saved.

Wrapping paper envelopes

Collect old scraps of wrapping paper and lay them flat, white side up. Take apart an old junk mail envelope and trace it on the paper. Cut out the pattern, fold, and secure with glue or tape. Place blank sticky labels on the spots for the recipient's and return addresses. You have a lovely envelope for just pennies.

Gift card bonus

If you receive a gift card as a holiday bonus, save it for next year's gift shopping providing you've checked to make sure it is not subject to maintenance fees or has an expiration date. If it is a loadable card, you can add money to it throughout the year and save for your Christmas shopping.

Gift of stock

Teach kids about money management—give them the gift of stock. Some companies (like Disney) issue stock certificates that come with cartoon characters or pictures and can be framed and hung on a child's wall. Gift givers can request that the stock be issued in the receiver's name. When the child grows up, this gift can be sold to help with a college education, down payment on a house or other major purchases.

Tissue gift box

Facial tissue boxes can make inexpensive gift boxes. Cut off the top square, insert the gift, and then fill the rest of the box with colorful tissue paper.

Wedding gifts

If you are shopping from a couple's gift registry, search the retailer's outlets and online site for discounts before purchasing something from the main store. Sometimes you can find good deals on items you already know the couple will love. Always check for flaws when shopping in an outlet—before purchasing.

Coasters

Buy cheap wooden coasters from a hardware store and glue photos onto them. One photo per coaster looks best. Cut photos to size and spray coaster with a clear finish. Allow finish to dry and spray several more coats. Give to relatives and friends.

Bride's tool kit

Give a new bride-to-be a "tool kit" gift basket. Include a hammer, screwdrivers, an assortment of nails, a tape measure, a glue gun, and maybe a staple gun. Find these items at discount stores and flea markets and put them in a storage container. Now she's ready to decorate their new place.

Card display

Use a small easel set up on a coffee or end table to display a decorative or special homemade greeting card. You can admire the card and the giver will know it was appreciated.

Gift wrap storage

Ask a nearby flower shop for their shipping boxes for long stem roses. The boxes are the perfect length to store wrapping paper rolls, and you will be recycling boxes that usually get broken down and discarded.

Gift cards

Don't go out and spend your gift cards right away—save them for necessary purchases. When you need to buy something, check your gift card stash and purchase the item from one of those stores. You won't have to even tweak your monthly budget to do it. Caution: Make sure you know the details of your Gift Card. When does it expire, if ever? Is it subject to dormancy or maintenance fees?

Reusable gift boxes

Put gifts for children in clear plastic containers instead of cardboard gift boxes. Line the inside of the container with tissue paper so the kids can't see what's inside. When the present is taken out, the container can be used to store small toys in the house or car.

Secret codes

Use color-coded stars to mark holiday presents instead of buying gift tags. Each family member can have their own color of star, but keep it a secret until Christmas morning. Stars are cheaper than tags and will save you the trouble of writing names, too.

Recipe cards

Reuse holiday cards as recipe cards. Save your cards that have no writing on the backside of the picture portion. Then center an index card over the prettiest section, trace the rectangle and cut out the beautiful new recipe card. Write out one of your favorite recipes and give to a friend as a useful, personal gift.

Support local crafters

When you want to give a novelty gift, learn to make something yourself or find a local crafter to support. Visit about 10,000 of them at *www.etsy.com.* Handmade gifts are unique, offer the chance to own original art and that's something certain to be well-received.

Gift of appreciation

For a holiday gift, ask each family member to write down what they like most about each person in the family, using only one word or one short sentence. Compile a list so that each person has his/her own personal list of compliments from many sources. Use these lists as place markers at your holiday table.

Welcome mat

Ask your local carpet store for their sample carpet squares that they no longer need. Use fabric paint to write "welcome" on the squares, and then have children decorate them with their hand prints and footprints. Great gift for grandparents.

Homemade gift certificates

Use your computer to make gift certificates for a meal at your home or at a restaurant, a trip to the movies, or a batch of your recipient's favorite cookies. Tuck them inside a homemade card.

CD cookbook

Make a cookbook for your family

and close friends, and save on the cost of printing by putting the recipes onto a CD. Include family photos along with the recipes. Search the web for free templates for recipe pages.

Pocket calendar

For a college student or young adult who has recently moved out, buy a pocket calendar and record friends' and relatives' birthdays and anniversaries. You can also include little notes on holidays and days of special significance for the recipient, like graduations.

Gift bag savings

When buying gift bags, look in the craft section of your local discount store. Paper gift bags in the craft section can often be purchased for about a third of the cost of a similar bag in the gift wrap section.

Children's coin collection

Give a starter coin collection to a child. Go to a coin shop and purchase a coin folder, a roll of wheat pennies, a Mercury dime, Buffalo nickel, a penny from the early 20th century, a Walking Liberty Half Dollar and a coin collector's checklist. Put these items together in a gift bag. This keepsake is a great alternative to purchasing toys, which may quickly become outdated or forgotten.

Wrapping paper storage

Store wrapping paper in the legs of old pantyhose. This will prevent your paper from getting wrinkled and torn between uses, and you won't run the risk of ruining any of the paper by having to tape the rolls.

Gift baskets

Plan your holiday gift baskets in the summer. Come up with a theme for each basket based on your recipient's interests, such as cooking, home office, kitchen, auto, beauty, gardening or reading. Watch for sales and use coupons to purchase items for the baskets in the months leading up to December. When the holidays come, you will already have most of your baskets ready to go.

Neighbor gifts

Buy some inexpensive plastic plates with holiday themes and fill them with cookies for neighbors and colleagues. Wrap with holiday plastic wrap.

Birdfeeder

Take a few cups of birdseed and combine with a few tablespoons of cheap peanut butter. Mix well in a big bowl. Purchase some inexpensive cookie cutters and tie a loop of string to the top of each one. Then add the peanut butter mixture to the cutter, pressing it down tightly. Wrap up the cookie cutters in a cheap basket with a festive holiday napkin and write out these directions: *Take these nature nuggets and hang from the closest branch of a tree or bush. Enjoy the wildlife that comes to savor your treats.*

Holiday wrapping

When you have a large gift to wrap, look for paper holiday tablecloths. They are usually inexpensive and more durable than regular wrapping paper.

Mylar balloon wrapping

Use mylar balloons to wrap a small present. Sever the balloon's ribbon-tied base and cut along the seam so the two halves attach at the balloon's top. Either the pattern side or the reverse silver side will make flashy gift wrap.

Kids' birthday gifts

Birthday party gifts for your kid's friends can be expensive. So buy multiples of an inexpensive gift that is suitable for girls or boys of your child's age, such as blocks, puppets, bath toys or books. Wrap them at once and you will be ready for the parties. Make cards on the computer to save even more.

Postcards

Cut off the front of a note card you have received that does not have any writing on the opposite side. Put a postcard stamp in the top right corner, write a message on the left side and the address on the right, and send it off.

Gifts

If you have a home party business, save the free merchandise you receive and use it for gifts throughout the year. Kitchen items, candles and other household items make great graduation and wedding gifts.

Popcorn packaging

Instead of purchasing bubble wrap, use hot air popcorn to cushion items you are shipping. Popcorn is much cheaper and biodegradable.

Simmering Potpourri

For a holiday potpourri kit, get together some fresh oranges and apples, bay leaves, cloves, cinnamon sticks, tulle, ribbon, a small gift bag or tin and tissue paper. Line the bottom of the bag or tin with tissue paper and arrange fruit and bay leaves. Then cut out two squares of tulle. Put cloves and broken up cinnamon sticks on top of the tulle, bring the corners together and tie with ribbon. On a recipe card write: *Cut 1/2 of each fruit into four. Use one sachet of spices and one bay leaf and simmer in saucepan with water.*

Stocking exchange

Instead of a gift exchange, try doing a stocking exchange with your extended family. Have every family member draw a name and fill a stocking for that person. Set a spending limit and be creative. You can even reuse the stockings each year.

Gift of thoughtfulness

Put together a collection of objects that tangibly represent all the warm wishes you have for the recipient. Fill empty baby food jars with items like pennies for prosperity, Hershey's kisses for joy, bandages for health, fabric softener sheets for comfort, fortune cookies for hope, and super glue for strength. Decorate the outside of the jars with ribbon, glitter and paint. Include a card that explains the meaning for each jar.

Wrapping paper organizer

Organize wrapping paper and supplies in a suit bag. You can hang it in the closet to keep the rolls of paper upright. There will be plenty of room for tissue paper and ribbon as well.

Wrap it in a pillowcase

Wrap your gift in a homemade pillowcase. Buy a yard of a printed fabric and make it into a pillowcase with three simple seams. To wrap the present, either fold the fabric and fasten it with safety pins or gather it at the top and tie with a ribbon. This wrapping paper becomes part of the gift. If you use it for a baby shower present, the pillowcase can be for an older sibling.

Senior gifts

Seniors often appreciate practical presents, such as gift cards for groceries, hair care, gasoline, cable and the daily newspaper. They also often love to receive postage stamps.

Photos for the 'fridge

Take a piece of scrapbook paper and glue several pictures to the paper. Then laminate the paper, attach magnetic strips to the back of the paper and put on the refrigerator door. This is a great gift for grandparents.

Wedding photo album

Before the wedding purchase a roll of film and a small photo album that holds at least 36 photos. Arrive early to the wedding and very quietly begin taking candid photos. Make sure you get at least one picture of the bride and groom together after the ceremony. Then zoom to a nearby one-hour photo place to drop off the film. Pick up your pictures in an hour, put the photos into the album and give it to the bride and groom during the reception. Write inside the cover: *These may not be the best photos, but they're the first!*

Jar gift

Use iced tea jars to pack your holiday jar gifts and baked goods. Your recipients can make sun tea after they have enjoyed the gift inside. Shop for the jars during the summer to save money.

No gifts

If you would like to cut back and stop exchanging gifts with several people, send them a note a few months ahead of the holiday season. They will probably be very understanding and relieved not to have to exchange gifts anymore. If everyone knows ahead of time, there will be less opportunity for embarrassment or hurt feelings.

Alternative gift-giving

Find a charity that relates to your recipient's interests and make a donation in his or her honor. Send a card to let your recipient know what you have done, and include a simple tree ornament that represents the charity.

Family greeting card

To stay connected with family members who are living across the country, bring a greeting card to the next family get together. Ask everyone to sign the card or write a quick note. The recipient will hear from lots of family members all at once.

Memory lampshade

Instead of making a scrapbook of photos and newspaper clippings, decoupage them onto a lampshade. A trip down memory lane will be just a light switch away.

Wedding favors

Have some wedding pictures taken before the wedding. Develop the wallet photos, frame them, and set them by each placecard at the reception tables for the guests to take home.

Gifts

Pound gift exchange

Instead of purchasing new gifts for the adults in the family, have a pound gift exchange. Each adult draws a name and must give a pound of something—pennies, fudge, chicken feed—to their recipient. These gifts can be either meaningful or funny—or both!

Gift reminder

Don't forget where you stashed those bargain buys you bought for a distant birthday or the coming holiday season. Right after you purchase the gift, make note of its hiding place on your calendar on the month you will need the gift.

Rebate gifts

Save up the rebate and freebie items you collect throughout the year and use them as stocking stuffers or in gift baskets. Use the cash you get from rebates to save for holiday shopping, too.

Holiday mugs

Thrift stores have a great selection of inexpensive holiday mugs. They are usually in good condition. You can fill them with cocoa mix and a candy cane and give them as gifts.

Black and white photos

Copy a regular color photo on a color copier set to black and white setting and enlarged 200%. Frame in a black 8-by-10 frame with a white matte. The pictures look classy and make great gifts for family members.

Gift planner

Use a small expandable file folder to hold your holiday cash. Label each section with the name of a person you are buying for. In each section, keep a list of gift ideas for that person, the cash you plan to spend and receipts once the items are purchased. If the gift needs to be returned, you'll know exactly where the receipt is. You can use this folder all year round for birthdays and other events and to collect ideas for the next holiday season.

Card organizer

Organize your greeting cards in a small card box. Use index cards to make dividers for each month and place cards for birthdays and holidays between them. You can write the birthdays of your friends and family members on each divider card. You will be able to find your cards quickly and save them from being torn or bent.

Family gift baskets

Instead of buying individual presents for extended family, put together family gift baskets that everyone can enjoy together. Include games, crafts, mugs with hot chocolate, popcorn and video rental gift cards. You can set a price limit if you want to try this as a gift exchange.

Hospital gifts

If you visit someone in the hospital, bring a gift for both the patient and the spouse or relative who is staying with them there. Snacks, magazines, tea bags, an extra mug and warm slippers are all much appreciated.

Packaging hot chocolate

When you make your own hot chocolate mix, package it first in a plastic zip-type bag. Then place the bag on top of a square of fabric, gather up the edges of the fabric, and tie with a ribbon. This will be much lighter and inexpensive to ship than the mix wrapped in a mug or jar.

No more belated birthdays

If you are constantly forgetting birthdays, go online and make up free ecards for all your friends and family members at once. You can specify the dates that the cards will be sent, and have a notice sent to you when the card is opened.

All-purpose wrapping paper

Instead of buying seasonal prints, stick to wrapping paper with solid colors or generic patterns. You can select the appropriate colors for the occasion and use the paper all year round. To save more, buy plain paper in red, green, blue and silver at the after-Christmas sales.

Comical wrap

Use the comics section of the Sunday newspaper to wrap children's presents—it is colorful, entertaining for the kids and cheap.

Wrapping rack

Instead of purchasing an expensive wrapping paper rack, buy a shoe rack and fill with your rolls of paper, ribbons and tape dispensers.

Grandparent's gift

Give your grandparents the gift of a warm home by having their furnace cleaned and repaired in preparation for the coming winter months.

Usable wrapping paper

Wrap your gifts in items that can be used. For baby showers, wrap the gift in a crib sheet or receiving blanket and use diaper pins to secure. Bridal showers and wedding gifts can be wrapped in a tablecloth or set of towels. Finish with some ribbon to tie the whole presentation together.

Gift questionnaire

Type up a list of questions for your friends and family members to answer. Ask for things like their hobbies, favorite colors and interests. Answers to questions like "What do you have too much of?" and "What can you never have enough of?" are extremely helpful when shopping for gifts.

Postcard-a-month

Give an elderly relative the gift of communication. Make up postcards from index cards or the fronts of old greeting cards. Assign each family member a couple of dates to send a postcard to the relative and include a package of the blank cards. The grandparent or elderly relative will get regular mail updates from family members throughout the year.

Quick wrapping paper

Use your holiday wrapping paper all year round—simply flip the paper over to the white side and finish with a fancy bow and a ribbon.

Free stocking stuffers

Save the freebies, samples and coupons that you accumulate throughout the year while shopping online. You can even search the Internet for sites that offer freebies and giveaways. Use these items as holiday stocking stuffers.

Gift budget

Each year, take the time to make a gift budget. Write down all the gifts you plan to purchase for holidays, birthdays and special occasions and figure out how much money you need for them. Divide that amount by 12, and you will know the monthly amount you need to save to prepare for your gift-giving.

Address book for newlyweds

Newlyweds are blending their families and friends as well as their lives and personal possessions, so why not give them a newly updated address book? You can purchase a fancy one or decorate a plain one yourself. Guests can even sign the address book in place of a guest book.

Inspirational calendar

Make a personalized, inspirational calendar for your friends and family members. Collect 365 of your favorite quotes, scriptural references or words of wisdom. Design each day's page on your computer, printing several on each page. Purchase metal rings at an office supply store, punch holes in the calendar pages, and put the rings through the holes. You can include a special message on the recipient's birthday.

Surprise cookies for newlyweds

Be creative if you give money as a wedding gift—bake the bills into cookies! Wrap each bill in foil, bake into the cookies and package the cookies in a decorative cookie jar with the tag: *Marriage is a lot like a chocolate chip cookie, sometimes sweet, sometimes full of nuts, but always full of surprises!*

Discounted gift cards

If you want to purchase an item from a particular store, search online at sites like eBay for someone selling a gift card for that retailer at a discount.

Gift notebook

Keep track of the gifts you have given and plan to give. List gifts you have already given or purchased and make lists of gift ideas you have for friends and family members throughout the year. It will help jog your memory and think of new ideas.

Books for teachers

For the holidays, give your child's teacher a new book that he or she can read to the students. Books are often expensive, and your gift will benefit both the teacher and your child.

Handprint tiles

Have your kids make decorative tiles for relatives. Purchase inexpensive ceramic tiles and bake–on paint from a hobby store. Have your kids decorate the tile with their handprints, and bake the tile.

Picture frames

Personalize picture frames for an inexpensive, homemade gift. Pick up old frames from garage sales and thrift stores and use glue, glitter, buttons, fabric scraps, ribbons and paint to decorate the frames. It's a great activity to do with your kids.

Roll of dollars

If you include money in a birthday card, tape the dollar bills end to end and roll them up tightly. Kids will especially enjoy unrolling their long string of bills.

Gifts

Holiday gift of memories

Remind your grandparents or parents of your favorite memories with them. Send a postcard to them each week of December describing a memory or telling a story from your childhood. You could also include a small gift that represents the story. Coordinate with your siblings so that your parents or grandparents will receive multiple "memories" during the holiday season.

Teacher's umbrella

For a homemade class gift, purchase a solid colored umbrella and some fabric paint. Have students stamp their handprint onto the umbrella, and write each name underneath the handprint with a permanent marker. No more gloomy days, only sweet memories!

Vintage books

Check out second-hand bookstores and thrift stores for vintage books that you can give as gifts. You can often find vintage copies of children's books or old editions of classics. You may also find books that look brand-new, too.

Memory mug

Purchase a plain colored mug along with a ceramic marking pen. Have family, friends and co-workers sign the mug or write a short message. White mugs and black pens are an especially classy look. Great gift for someone who is moving away or graduating.

New baby kit

Purchase a photo storage box and fill it with baby supplies such as washcloths, wipes, rattles and lotions. The new mom will be able to use the supplies and keep the box for her baby photos.

Graduation photo frames

Graduates love to bring photos of their high school friends when they move out or start college. Find a picture of the graduate with his or her friends and have it nicely framed. Prom photos work well.

Mud pie mix

Give a child a mud pie kit. Fill a quart-sized zip-type bag with dirt and place it inside an empty cake mix box. Reseal the box and cover over the instructions with directions to "take outside and just add water." Pick up a plastic mixing bowl, spoon and pie pan from the thrift store to complete the kit, and wrap it in an old apron.

Gift of labor

Give elderly relatives or friends the

gift of your own labor. Wrap up some homemade certificates promising to help them paint a room, fix a squeaky door, clean a bathroom, and so on.

Gift wrap cover

To keep wrapping paper rolls from wrinkling, take a used cardboard roll and cut a slit length-wise down the roll. Slip this cover over your wrapping paper rolls to protect them in storage.

Hostess gift

When visiting, take pictures throughout your visit. When you return home have the pictures developed and place them in a small photo album with dates, names and places. Return this photo album to the person you visited along with a thank-you note. Make duplicate prints so you can keep one set for yourself.

Gift exchange give-and-take

For a lively gift exchange, ask each person to bring one inexpensive gift. Place the gifts in the center of the room and draw numbers to see who goes first. The person with number one chooses a gift and unwraps it. The next person can take the first gift or choose to unwrap another. If the gift is taken, the first person unwraps another gift. Continue until everyone has an unwrapped gift. A gift may only be taken twice—then it is frozen with the third recipient. At the end, the first person may choose to take anyone's present, perhaps even the frozen ones. You make the rules. Have fun!

Envelopes for free

The morning after a holiday, visit a discount store that carries greeting cards. The greeting card supplier is often there, changing the holiday greeting cards. Since they usually throw away the envelopes, ask if you can take some home. Use them when writing letters or when sorting coupons and your holiday shopping cash.

Gift wrap for free

When you purchase an item at a department or bookstore, ask for wrapping paper to wrap your gift. Sometimes large chain retailers will provide wrapping paper for free.

Birthday club

Save on the cost of birthday parties and start a birthday club with several other families. Each family picks a month and hosts a party for everyone whose birthday falls in that month. The point of birthday parties is to celebrate with others, so why not celebrate several at once?

Flowers

When sending flowers, choose a local florist rather than a more general online retailer or chain store. You oftentimes will get a better deal and undoubtedly better service. Even if you need flowers delivered long-distance, call a local florist close to the delivery point. Again, local provider, better service.

Fleece blanket

Make a no-sew blanket from polar fleece. Purchase two large rectangles (60 inches by 54 inches) of fleece and lay them on top of each other, wrong sides together. Cut away a five-inch square at each corner. Cut fringe into the fleece, about two inches wide and five inches deep, all the way around the edges. Double knot the fringe to finish.

History buff

Make your own scrapbook of local history. Visit the library and research a particular topic or time period for your local area. Copy articles and pictures and arrange them in a photo album or scrapbook. Your recipient will have a unique history book to peruse.

Limiting Christmas gifts

To discourage the "gimmes" in kids, limit the number of Christmas gifts to three as a symbolic way to remember the three gifts that Jesus received from the Magi. Kids will know what to expect and learn to whittle down their wish lists to the presents they want the most.

Coach gift

For a kid's coach, teacher or other leader, purchase an inexpensive director's chair with a solid color canvas back. Have each child sign his or her name on the canvas using a permanent marker. This makes a wonderful group gift.

Plant a tree

Contact a local environmental group and see if they have a volunteer reforestation project. Spend a Saturday planting trees in honor of a family member or friend. Take a picture of the trees and include it with a card telling the recipient what you have done.

Alternative greeting cards

Instead of purchasing a greeting card, buy your recipients a his or her favorite magazine. Inside the magazine cover, write your own personalized message. Magazines are often the same price as greeting cards.

Meals for the elderly

Give a homemade meal to an elderly relative who would normally not cook for him or herself. You can even make several dinners and freeze them, so the recipient can have a whole week's worth of home-cooked meals. Include paper plates and cups and plastic spoons so your relative won't have to do the dishes.

Shredded gift packaging

Use your personal paper shredder to make gift filling and Easter grass. Shred paper of different colors and use your scissors to curl it.

Share holiday memories

If your family is spread out and can't be together for the holidays, ask everyone to take pictures during their holiday activities and then send them to you along with a letter describing their holiday celebrations. Compile a CD from the letters and pictures and burn copies for each of the family members.

Bulk wrapping paper

Buy an industrial size roll of wrapping paper from a wholesaler and use for every occasion. These will typically last for years. Change the ribbons and bows to give different looks to your gifts. You can usually find wholesalers in the yellow pages.

Tissue recycle

To get the wrinkles out of tissue paper that has already been used, set your iron on a medium setting and press out the creases carefully.

Ribbon for cheap

Instead of buying expensive bows or ribbon, purchase raffia from the local craft store. Since it is a neutral color you can use it with most kinds of wrapping paper. It's also cheap.

Photos for grandparents

Buy bulk film from a mail order film developing company. After taking a roll of film, slip it into the return processing envelope and fill out the envelope with the grandparents' address. The photos will be sent directly to them.

Thank-you notes

Reuse extra birth announcements as thank-you notes for your child's birthday parties. Your friends and family members will be reminded how much your child has grown.

Gifts

Gift cache

Start a stash of generic gifts such as photo frames, gardening pots, decorative boxes, etc. that you buy on clearance. Whenever you need a last-minute gift for a teacher, coach or birthday party, go to your stash. You won't have to blow your gift budget.

Gift basket wrap

Instead of buying that expensive cellophane for gift baskets, wrap your baskets in tulle or netting that you purchase on clearance at a craft store. The fabric will be easier to manipulate as well.

Congrats!

For special anniversaries, birthdays or awards, you can contact your senator, congressperson and the President and receive a personal note of congratulation. These can be framed and presented as gifts. Either write or call and have names and dates ready.

Themed wreaths

Make a themed wreath for people on your holiday gift list. Consider each person's hobbies or interests and choose a theme. Collect odds and ends throughout the year that relate to the theme. In December purchase plain willow wreaths and decorate them with the objects, securing each item with hot glue. Finish with a matching ribbon.

Christmas card photo album

Save all the photos that come in each year's Christmas cards in a photo album. You will have a history of all your friends and families to look back on in years to come.

T-shirt blanket

Save your kid's old t-shirts and make them into a blanket. Cut the front patterns into squares, sew the squares together and add backing in your child's favorite color. Your child will have a comfy blanket that will bring back memories.

Candy bouquet

Gather some florist foam, long florist picks, green floral tape, colorful tissue paper and an assortment of hard candy or bite size candy bars. Wrap one end of the candy wrapper with the tape and attach it to the pick. Wrap the candy with tissue paper and insert the pick into the foam. Keep adding "flowers" until you have a bouquet.

Grans' advent calendar

Make a large advent calendar out of

felt with twenty-four pockets. Have all the grandkids create several small ornaments, cards, notes or other artwork—enough so there will be one gift for each day. Fill the calendar and send it to the grandparents to enjoy throughout December.

Photo pillows

Find an old, meaningful black and white photo and make it into an iron-on transfer at a print center. Iron the transfer onto muslin and sew the muslin into a decorative pillow.

Creative gifting

Collect a few small items related to the child's interests (small car, piece of ribbon, stuffed animal, etc.) and make up a story about the items. Record the story on a cassette tape or CD and send the items with the tape or CD to the child. This is a great way for long-distance grandparents to be involved in their grandchildren's lives.

Toddler bib

Trace the front half of a kid's artist smock onto kiddie fabric that has been folded pattern sides together. Cut out the shape and hand-sew matching or contrasting bias binding around the edges, slip-stitching the back to the fabric. Finish the necklines with bias binding in the same way, leaving a few inches of the binding as ties. These bibs are long enough to catch lap spills and wide enough to cover all of a toddler's shirt. They are also washable and durable. Mom's will love them.

Gift tag

Tear off a small square of foil and place it on table. Melt some wax and let it drop in a puddle on the foil. Quickly take a decorative button or stamp and press into the wax. Peel button or stamp off and let wax dry. Add some hot glue to the back and attach a ribbon. Then attach the ribbon to the gift. This can be an elegant tag for holiday gifts.

Charitable gift log

To keep track of your charitable donations for tax purposes keep a blank receipt form stored with items you are collecting for charity. When you bring the items to the collection site, get the receipt and a new form and start over. Your forms are filled out for tax time and you don't have to try and remember your donations.

Greeting cards recycled

If a card has a border design, cut it off, punch a hole and add a cord or ribbon for a bookmark. Cut small designs from cards and use them as gift tags. You can even recycle old cards as Christmas tree ornaments.

Grocery Shopping

Grocery Shopping

Angel Food Ministries

Check out Angel Food Ministries for inexpensive groceries. For $30 or less, you can buy a large box of food that can feed a family of four for a week. There is no qualifying or income threshold requirement. and you can purchase as many boxes of as you want. Search *www.angelfood ministries.com* for a host site near you.

Sales ads

Search through store ads, not just for items you need to purchase but also for items you have recently purchased at a higher price. Bring the sales ad and your receipt to the store and ask for a refund of the difference. Oftentimes the store will give it to you. For a fast checkout process, cut out the ad and tape it to the product along with any coupons you might have.

Grocery gift card

Budget for groceries by purchasing a reloadable gift card from your favorite grocery store. Put your weekly allotted grocery money on the card, and you will be sure never to overspend.

Grocery delivery

It may be worth your time to get your groceries delivered. Find an inexpensive service that will accept manufacturer's coupons as a way to off-set the cost of the groceries. Having someone else do your shopping will keep you from impulse buying, too.

Shop small

Many large grocery stores do not have the best prices. Check the smaller independent markets in your area and do some price comparisons. They may have fewer choices, but they may also have lower prices and shorter check-out lines. Many small markets also accept manufacturer's coupons.

Online groceries

If you are pressed for time, try ordering groceries online and having them delivered. The prices may not be as high as you think, and you can save your shopping lists from week to week. If you are able to cut back on your impulse buys as well, you could actually save money.

Flawed packaging

Many stores will give discounts on items with flawed or imperfect packaging. It never hurts to ask.

Double coupons

Shop at stores that accept double coupons. Wait for items to go on sale before cashing them in to save even more.

Coupon meals

Plan your menus around your coupons and the weekly grocery sales. Try to incorporate the items you already have on hand in your pantry as well. On your shopping list, write a C beside the items you have a coupon for so you will not forget to use them.

Coupon cash back

When you use coupons, ask the cashier for the total before deducting the coupon savings and write a check for the larger amount. Use the cash back to save for a family night or holiday shopping.

Coupons online

Did you know that you can download and print manufacturer's coupons on your home computer and use them at the supermarket? Do an Internet search for sites that provide these coupons. Also, check your supermarket's web page for special offers not advertised in the newspaper or at the store.

Restaurant supply houses

You can buy items in bulk for rock bottom prices at restaurant supply stores. These stores usually are happy to sell to the public and don't charge a membership fee. Check out their selection of quality cooking gadgets as well.

Monthly shopping

When you buy groceries on sale stock up on a month's worth. Make use of your freezer and pantry space to save both time and money. If you're single, you may be able to shop for several months at a time.

Coupon reminder

When using manufacturer's coupons, it is easy to forget the store where you were going to use them. Write the store's initials on the corner of each coupon as a reminder.

Coupon clippers unite

Talk with a few friends and exchange your product preferences. When you clip coupons, you can keep an eye out for your friends' products. Meet regularly to exchange your coupons. You can even make a weekly party out of it.

Grocery Shopping

Menu planning for groceries

If you prepare weekly menus, list the ingredients you need to purchase on the side of the menu. Then simply take this menu to the grocery store. Organize your menus in a notebook so you can reuse them periodically.

Only food

Only buy food items in grocery stores. Pet food, paper products, cleaning supplies and toiletries at the supermarket are generally more expensive than the same products at discount stores, except when on a special sale.

Grocery list

Instead of keeping your grocery list somewhere in the kitchen, keep it in your purse or wallet—then you'll never go to the store without it.

Soda savings

Individual soft drinks are usually more expensive than the liter containers, especially at convenience stores. Grab the liter containers and save.

Shopping strategy

When making your grocery list prepare it according to the aisles you go through in the store. It will save you a lot of time.

Protect your purse

Use the child safety strap on the shopping cart to secure your purse while shopping. Wrap the strap around the handles several times, and it will be hard for a purse-snatcher to grab.

Find coupons

Before completing the checkout process when you are shopping online, find the website's customer service number. Call and ask where you can find online coupons for their products. They are usually more than willing to tell you.

Charitable shopping

When you pick up a sale item or a loss leader at the grocery store, get an extra to donate to charity. You can stay within your budget and help others at the same time.

Shelf tricks

Most retailers set their shelves with the largest size of a brand-name product to the right of a display. Generics are to the left of that and then the smaller sizes of the brand-name to the left of the generics. This is because most shoppers are right-handed. Not watching what you grab can be a costly gotcha.

Expired coupons

Some supermarkets will accept expired coupons. If not and you cannot bear to throw them away, send them to a military family overseas. Commissaries on foreign soil accept expired coupons.

Product praise

When you purchase a product, call the toll free consumer hotline on the back of the package. Tell the rep either what you liked or what you didn't like about the product. Either way, the rep will usually send you money-saving coupons. You can save a lot just by giving a little feedback!

Warehouse club savings

Save on the cost of a warehouse club membership—go in on it with a friend, if the club does not prohibit shared memberships. Usually stores will issue two cards per membership, so you can each take one.

Ready-made grocery list

Save several grocery receipts over the course of a few weeks. Then prepare a list of all the items you regularly buy at the supermarket. Make two columns: one for the item name and one for a check mark indicating if you have a coupon. Leave room at the bottom to write in additional items. Each week, print out the same list and highlight or circle the items you need.

Loss leader tracker

Keep track of the sales and loss leader prices for items you frequently purchase. You will often notice that a pattern appears, and you can anticipate when these items will next be available at dirt-cheap prices.

Bakery goods

Search for a bakery thrift shop in your area. Purchase dates for these products are usually the current date or the day before. You can save a lot on specialty items and breads.

Coupon album

Organize your coupons in a small photo album. You can organize the coupons by store or category and can easily flip through it to find the ones you want. The album will fit neatly into a purse or small bag.

Reusable grocery bags

Purchase some inexpensive canvas

or cotton bags at your local whole foods market. Use these instead of paper or plastic bags and the store may give you a small discount. You will also be recycling.

Price comparison notebook

When grocery shopping, it is sometimes difficult to tell if you have found a good deal or a good advertisement. To track the everyday prices of items you frequently purchase, use a pocket-size address book to record the cost, unit size and store name. The next time you want to evaluate an advertised price, check your notebook.

Recipes for loss leaders

If you found a great deal on a product you don't have a recipe for, search the Internet for recipes. Sites like *www.allrecipes.com* allow you to search recipes by ingredients.

Certificate savings

If you buy gift certificates at your supermarket, you sometimes get a 5% discount on large purchases. Pool your money with a few friends so you can purchase the amount needed for the discount.

Shopping plan

On your next visit to the grocery store pick up one of their floor plans. Make several copies and use one each week to create your grocery list, marking the items on the aisles where they are located. You will know exactly what to get when you walk through each aisle.

Food co-ops

Many food cooperatives offer discounts for members who volunteer. You can save a lot on groceries by volunteering a little bit of your time every week.

Coupon Mom

Search for sales in your area and coupons for your favorite products at *www.couponmom.com*. You can sort and print the ones you want.

Online groceries

Before purchasing groceries online, run a quick online search for any discount codes for your particular store or product.

Coupons at the ready

If you use a coupon organizer, make sure you pull out the ones you need and slip them into an envelope before going into the store. This will save you time in the checkout line, since you won't be digging around to find them.

Grocery Game

Check out The Grocery Game at *www.thegrocerygame.com*. They will help you track manufacturer's coupons and match them up with sales so you can have double the savings.

Buy one, get one free

When you see a buy one, get one free deal at your supermarket, try to wait until the end of the sale when the store is sold out of the item. You can get a rain check and then purchase the item at the reduced price anytime you want.

Family outing

Make grocery shopping a family event. Pass out lists for items you need, along with coupons and directives to each family member to track down the items on their list. You will teach your family about saving while spending time together.

Cart trial run

When going to the grocery store, park near a cart and push that cart to the entrance of the store. That way you can give the cart a "trial run" to find out if it has any wobbly wheels. You'll also be helping out the courtesy clerks, who won't have to return that cart.

Coupons with the list

If you have trouble remembering to give the cashier your coupons, write your grocery list on an inexpensive, white envelope and slip the coupons inside. You'll already have them in hand when you hit the check-out line.

Grocery bingo

Before making your meal plan for the week, check all of your cupboards, the garden and the freezer to see exactly what you already have. Then try to plan your meals around these items and tick each one off the list as you incorporate it into a meal. You get a "bingo" when every item is ticked off or every meal is based on what you have on hand.

Grocery hauler

If you find it difficult to carry all your groceries at once and end up making numerous trips from the car to the house, buy a trash can with wheels and load your groceries into it. You can just wheel it right into the kitchen.

Grocery Shopping

No cart shopping

Here's a tip for how to get out of a grocery store without spending a lot of money when all you really need are just a few things. Don't use a cart. If you limit yourself to what you can carry, you will spend less but still get what you need.

Ultimate sales insert

If you often spend Sunday afternoon paging through the week's sales inserts for your favorite stores, check out *www.sundaysaver.com.* This site has handy links to all weekly sales and specials for hundreds of stores like Kohls, Wal-Mart, Old Navy, Walgreens, Home Depot and Amazon. You can page through the catalogs using your mouse.

Carry load

A quick and easy way to reduce the amount you spend at the grocery store when you stop in for "only milk and bread," is to not grab a cart or basket. If you buy only as much as you can carry you will not be so prone to buying other things on a whim.

HEALTH AND BEAUTY

Health and Beauty

Earring organizer

Keeping track of your many pairs of earrings can be difficult. Purchase a couple of cheap ice cube trays and sort your earrings into the separate compartments. The trays can be stacked on top of each other and will fit in most dresser drawers.

Jewelry holder

Organize your jewelry in a bead organizer to keep it from getting tangled.

Metal allergy

If the metal of your cheap earrings irritates your ears, put a tiny dab of antibiotic ointment (like Neosporin) on the end of the earring before inserting it into the ear lobe. This eases any discomfort.

Hair rid

If you use products on your hair, after time you'll experience a build-up that needs to be removed. And brace yourself for the cost of the commercial product that does that. Instead, do what many hair professionals recommend: Pour shampoo into your palm and stir in enough baking soda to make a thick paste. Shampoo as normal and rinse well. Follow with a good conditioner. The baking soda is abrasive enough to clean the shaft without damaging it. You are going to love this.

New earrings for sore ears

Cheap earrings are often made of metals that irritate sensitive ears. If you still want to wear your inexpensive earrings, pick up some sterling silver earring hooks from the craft store and switch out the cheap metal hooks for the silver ones. Use a pair of needle nose pliers to help maneuver the tiny metal pieces.

Earring storage

Store your earrings in 28-day pill containers. The compartments are large enough to hold one pair of small earrings each.

Storing necklaces

Slip each of your fine chained necklaces through an individual drinking straw and close the clasp. You can pile the straws in your jewelry box and prevent your necklaces from getting tangled. Cut the straws shorter for chain bracelets.

Jewelry care

Take your jewelry to a local jeweler

to have it cleaned and inspected for loose gem stones or weak clasps. Most jewelers will do this and not charge you at all if you only have one or two pieces. The bonus is that you will learn if your ring or pendant has weakened prongs and you're about to suffer a tragic loss.

Necklace storage

Buy a suction cup hook for your bathroom mirror and hang your necklaces on it. You can easily find your necklaces and they won't tangle.

Ring remover

Squirt a bit of Windex on your finger and gently slip the ring off. This often works even when your fingers are swollen in the summertime.

Family haircuts

Buy a haircut kit and learn how to cut your family's hair. These kits usually come with an instructional DVD or video as well as all the necessary tools. You can save a lot over the course of the year. If you have young boys, you can also simply invest in a hair clipper.

Bang trim

Most salons have a separate price for a simple bang trim that is a fraction of the cost of a whole haircut. If you are growing your hair out, you can save money by just asking for a bang trim.

Cheap haircut

Save money by visiting your local beauty college for haircuts, hair coloring or other services. The prices are much lower there than at most beauty salons. Just allow a little extra time for the services.

Cutting bangs

To give a child's bangs a straight cut, put a strip of adhesive tape across the child's forehead at the level you want to cut the hair. Then cut the bangs along the tape edge. The tape removes easily afterwards.

Straight cut

If you only want a straight haircut or a little trim, go to a barber instead of a hair dresser. Barbers usually charge much less.

Hair care

To remove shampoo build-up and add shine to your hair, mix four parts water with one part white vinegar and wet your hair down with this. Let stand a couple minutes then proceed to wash as usual. Do this twice a month for shiny, healthy hair.

Health and Beauty

Hairspray remover

To remove hairspray build-up in your hair, squeeze one lemon into a bottle of cheap V05 shampoo. Your hair will have a wonderful shine again.

Home job

If you have shorter hair and use packages of hair dye to simply touch up your roots, try mixing only half of the hair dye solution. Save the unused portion of the dyes in their respective containers for future use. Your hair dye will go twice as far. Note: Never mix and then attempt to store hair color solution.

DIY color

Go to a local beauty supply store, pick up your favorite hair dye and some instructions and learn how to color your hair yourself. You won't have to spend as much on salon visits.

Forget it

Why color your hair? You can save a lot of money by letting your hair go back to its natural color. To get past the "growing out" stage, have it highlighted.

Stay-put strip

To help metal barrettes stay in place, put a little hot glue on the sides of the barrette. Once cooled, the glue acts as a soft gripper strip that will hold the hair without pulling it.

Soft and static-free

To reduce static, work a small amount of fabric softener into your hair. It will leave your hair softer as well.

Hair towel

To make your own twist towel for wet hair, sew two hand towels together, long end to short end. Put the sewn corner on your head and wrap the flaps around your hair to make a turban. Tuck in the towel ends at the back.

Natural hair care

Try rinsing dark hair with tea, coffee or rosemary water to add luster and shine. Light hair does well with chamomile. Mayonnaise makes a wonderful hair conditioner.

Hairbrush

Buy your natural wood bristle hairbrushes at a pet shop. Brushes sold there are equal in quality, work just as well on humans and are considerably cheaper than those in beauty salons or beauty supply stores.

Minty treat

Add one drop of peppermint essential oil for every two ounces of shampoo in your bottle and shake well. The peppermint will give your hair a wonderful smell and get rid of dandruff flakes.

Hot roller traction

To keep hot rollers in place, slip off the outside covers of Velcro rollers and put them over the hot rollers. The Velcro will grab the hair and hold it in place while it is curling.

Conditioner pump

Store your hair conditioner in a pump-type soap dispenser. You will never squirt out too much.

Headband it

If your headband keeps slipping, try sticking some soft adhesive Velcro pieces on the inside of the band. No more slipping! You can find Velcro pieces at the craft store.

Blower clean-out

Use an old toothbrush or razor brush to gently sweep the lint away from the screen on the side of the blow-dryer. This will help prevent fires and keep your blow-dryer working well.

Dandruff help

Use Listerine Antiseptic in your hair as a rinse after you shampoo to get rid of dandruff flakes. It will leave your hair shiny and smelling great, too.

Gray away

Save yourself the cost of frequent trips to the salon to color gray roots by using waterproof mascara on the roots in just the areas that are visible. You can delay a dye job by a couple of weeks.

Revitalize hair

Buy two different brands of shampoo and switch brands once every two weeks. You will keep your hair from getting used to one kind of shampoo, and you can keep buying the brands you like.

Upside down

When you think you have finished off an aerosol can of hairspray, turn the can upside down and spray it again. There is usually enough left for a few more sprays.

Oily hair

To freshen oily hair, sprinkle a little baby powder on the roots and brush it through the hair. It will leave the hair looking fresh and just washed. This tip works best on lighter colors of hair.

Kool colors

For a temporary hair dye, find an unsweetened powdered drink mix (like Kool-Aid) in the color of your choice and mix with enough conditioner to highlight or completely cover hair. Blue is an interesting choice, but only if you're a teenager. Or wish to teach one a lesson. Apply to hair, let sit for 45 minutes and rinse out.

Redheads only

For shiny hair, mix two egg yolks with a capful of rum and work into your wet hair. Add a bit of cider vinegar to the rinse water to remove every trace of the mixture.

Cheap shampoo caution

If you color or perm your hair, cheap shampoos can strip your hair of its treatments or weaken a curl. Choose your shampoos with care.

Hair static

To get rid of hair static, keep a piece of a dryer sheet in your purse. When your hair gets static cling, lightly stroke the ends of your hair with the dryer sheet. The sheet lasts for many uses and smells great.

Headband holder

Install a small towel rod on your closet wall and hang your headbands on it. You can select the one you want at a glance, and they won't get bent as they might when stored in a drawer.

Sharing soaps

Save all the shampoos, conditioners and lotions you collect from hotels when traveling. You can donate these toiletries to the Salvation Army or another charity and help someone out.

Cheap hairspray

Buy your hairspray by the gallon from a beauty supply store. The price per ounce is substantially less than it is at a regular retailer, and a gallon will last you for years. Pour some into a small size pump and refill as needed.

No-tangle spray

Make your own hair detangler spray by putting a drop of conditioner into a spray bottle and filling the bottle with water. Spritz on a bit before styling your hair.

Hot roller clip

If you can't find a hot roller clip, use a jaw clip to hold your roller in place. Jaw clips are spring-loaded and have interlocking fingers.

Spa baths at home

Try adding 3 tablespoons of honey, 1/2 cup of Epsom salts or a tea bag to your bath as a home spa treatment. Oatmeal, processed in a blender, works well to sooth itchy, dry skin. One-half cup powdered milk when added to a warm bath will relieve dry or flaky skin. Does that sound too weird? You'd be surprised to learn that the best spas in the world use natural products like these in their spa treatments. It's their best-kept secret!

Dry skin solution

To sooth dry skin, fill a spray bottle with baby oil and spritz on after your shower. You won't even have to rub it in.

Vanilla bath oil

Combine 1 cup sunflower oil, 1/2 cup castile soap, 1 tablespoon vanilla extract and 1/4 cup honey in a small bowl and mix until well-blended. Pour into an empty storage container and add 1/4 cup to your bath. Shake mixture well before using.

Unscented hand soap

If you suffer from scent allergies, fill your hand soap dispensers with unscented baby shampoo. Baby shampoo is cheaper than most unscented hand soaps and is very gentle. A little goes a long way.

Sore feet

If you need to wrap a sore foot, knee or ankle, try using vet wrap. It is used to wrap legs of animals, but works equally well on humans. And here's the good part: Sold as a veterinary product vet wrap is a lot cheaper than traditional elastic bandages sold in drug stores. Look for vet wrap in a pet store or buy it directly from a veterinarian.

Face mask

Mix 1 tablespoon powdered milk, 1/2 teaspoon of milk and one drop of honey into a paste. Smooth over entire face and let dry for ten minutes. Rinse with cold water. Your face will feel smooth and radiant.

Body powder

Use cornstarch as an inexpensive body powder after you shower. You can even spray it with your favorite perfume or add a drop of essential oil for a scent. Cornstarch works as a baby powder as well—just avoid using scents that would irritate a child.

Oily skin help

To reduce shine on oily skin, cut cheap coffee filters into small pieces and blot on your face to take away the oil. Keep the filters in an old business card holder in your purse.

Eye luggage

Apply Visine under your eyes to get rid of under-eye bags and swelling. Simply dab it on with a cotton ball.

Hand scrub

Take off all your rings and put 1/2 teaspoon of Vaseline in your palm along with 1/2 teaspoon of sugar. Rub your hands together for a minute, making sure to rub the backs of your hands as well as between your fingers. Rinse with warm water and soap and finish up with your favorite hand lotion. You will marvel at your soft, smooth hands. Works well on elbows and feet, too.

Steam facial

Fill a pot with water and bring to a boil. Set the pot on top of a potholder on the kitchen table, put your face over the pot, and drape a large towel over your head and the pot. You can add a drop of peppermint oil, a lemon slice or an herbal tea bag to the pot if you would like a scent. Allow the steam to work on your skin for ten minutes. (You can pull up the towel to allow some steam to escape if you get too hot.) Then wash and rinse your face. This will revitalize your skin and your sinuses!

Dry skin prevention

To avoid dry skin and the need for expensive lotions, use soap sparingly during showers instead of doing a total body sudsing. To maximize the effects of lotion, be sure to apply it right after gently patting dry.

Lotion stretcher

Mix your expensive scented lotions in equal amounts with a cheaper unscented brand. Just mix the amount you need in your hand whenever you put on lotion.

Dry skin scrub

Mix a tablespoon of cornmeal, olive oil, honey and lemon juice together and store in the refrigerator. Apply to dry heels, elbows and knees, let the oil have time to absorb, and then shower. Your skin will feel soft and clean.

Tub back rest

Purchase an inexpensive baby bath sponge and use it as a back rest when you take a bath. These sponges are large enough for your entire back, they stick to the tub, and they stay warm as long as your water does. Throw the sponge in the washer now and then to freshen.

Foot soak

Cut up two oranges and put them in a bucket of warm water. Soak your feet for ten minutes, then let your feet drip dry. Mix vegetable oil with sea salt in a cup or container and rub over feet for about five minutes. Rinse. Your feet should feel smoother and softer.

Powder-puff

Can't find a powder-puff? Dust on powder with a round terrycloth car wax applicator. Wax applicators are durable, washable and inexpensive.

Homemade bath gel

Mix 3/4 cup boiling water with one packet of knox gelatin until it is dissolved, then add bubble bath. Allow to cool and use as bath gel. Put in a decorative bottle and add plastic toys or jewelry inside the bottle to decorate.

To the last bit

When you are unable to squeeze any more cream or salve from a tube, put on the cap and run the tube under hot water for a few sections. The contents should then flow freely.

Bubble bath

Try using Suave Chamomile shampoo as a bubble bath. It is inexpensive, has a great scent and makes wonderful bubbles. Just use a small amount for a bath full of bubbles.

Massages

Check out the rates at the local massage schools in your area. Students are supervised by professionals, charge low rates and aren't allowed to accept tips.

Soothe dry feet

Before you go to bed, coat the bottom of your feet with Vaseline and slip on a pair of socks. By morning your feet will feel smooth again.

Bath for dry skin

Add one cup of apple cider vinegar to your bath water to keep your skin soft and smooth. You won't smell like vinegar when you get out.

Shower soap dispensers

Install a soap dispenser on your

shower wall with separate containers for shampoo and conditioner. Whenever you come home with shampoos or conditioners from hotels, add them to the dispenser. You can put a hand lotion pump on the bathroom counter for hotel lotions, too.

Soap stretcher

Unwrap bars of soap as soon as you get them home and let them dry out for a day or two. They will harden and last a lot longer in the shower.

Salt scrub

Mix Epsom salts with either almond oil or baby oil until the mixture is like wet snow. You can add other scented oils to the mixture if you wish and use sea salt in place of Epsom salts. Rub on body during a hot shower for smooth skin.

Soothe dry hands

Mix one tablespoon of olive oil or vegetable oil with one tablespoon of salt. Massage on hands for a few minutes and rinse with warm water. Pat dry. Your hands will be soft and smooth.

Paraffin wax treatment

You were so thrilled to get your very own melted wax machine—just like the one at the day spa. Then you discovered how expensive it is to buy the paraffin refills, so your machine sits on the shelf. Well, it's time to get it down. You can make your own refills by simply purchasing a block of paraffin wax from the grocery store. You'll find it with the home canning supplies. Melt the wax in the machine and add a few drops of scented oil or food coloring if you wish. Wrap your feet in plastic grocery sacks after dipping in the wax.

Beauty chill

Put your beauty items in the refrigerator. Under-eye and aloe vera gels are more soothing and refreshing when cool. Chilled lipstick lasts longer, too.

Exfoliator

Oatmeal makes a great exfoliator and can be used as a facial mask as well.

Yogurt facials

Yogurt is a great natural facial cleanser. Apply to face, leave on for several minutes and then wash it off. You can experiment with different flavors. Mix yogurt with honey for a facial mask.

Facial scrub

Mix a small amount of baking soda

with water or your liquid face cleanser to make a paste. Apply paste to your wet face, gently scrub and rinse. The paste is very mild and non-irritating and exfoliates your skin so it is smooth and glowing. Use this facial scrub a few times a month.

Astringent

For a natural facial astringent, mix one part apple cider vinegar to eight parts water and apply to skin. This will soothe redness.

Moisturizers

Use olive oil, butter, or soy margarine as a natural skin moisturizer.

Blemishes

Put a couple of drops of Visine on a blemish to get the red out. It shrinks the blood vessels just under the skin and takes away the redness. It also helps to dry out the blemish.

Zap a blemish

Apply tea tree oil to a blemish using a cotton tip. The oil helps dry up the spot and doubles as an antiseptic to prevent infection. A dab of honey also works well as a natural healer.

Blemish fix

Put a dab of toothpaste on a blemish and let it sit overnight. The toothpaste will dry out the blemish and shrink it.

Exfoliant

For a cheap exfoliant for face and body, buy a packet of powdered rice bran from the health food store. Put a small amount of the bran in the palm of your hand, add water and rub over your skin. It will leave your skin feeling smooth.

Shower gel

Try using shampoo in place of your shower gel. Shampoo is often cheaper than shower gel and is still milder than bar soap.

Zit blitz

Mix a drop of lotion with a drop of maximum strength benzyl peroxide cream and apply to acne. The mixture will clear up the blemishes and leave your skin feeling soft. Note: benzyl peroxide creams can bleach material such as towels and pillow cases, so use with care.

Eyeliner

Use your mascara as an eyeliner. Dip your eyeliner brush in the mascara tube and use it as a liquid eyeliner. You can achieve the "penciled" eyeliner look by smudging the mascara a little bit.

Sharpening eyeliner pencils

To keep an eyeliner pencil from breaking while being sharpened, place the pencil in the freezer about thirty minutes before sharpening. Let the eyeliner return to room temperature before using.

Base coat

Your makeup will go on more smoothly if you first apply a light lotion to your face and let it dry for five to ten minutes. The lotion will work best if it is applied right after you shower or wash your face. Use a dab of lotion to rub out eyeliner or lipliner mistakes as well.

Makeup cover-up

Put a kitchen apron over your clothes before applying your make-up. You will keep falling powder from getting on your clothes and smearing.

Foundation color fix

If you have a foundation that is too dark for your skin, mix it with your moisturizer until it is the desired color. Now you can put on both in one easy step.

Facial powder

Stretch your facial powder by buying a darker color and mixing it with regular baby powder until it is the desired color. Baby powder is much cheaper than facial powder.

Stretch your lipstick

Don't let all that lipstick in the bottom of the tube go to waste. Purchase a couple of lip brushes and use them to reach the lipstick that remains at the bottom of the tube.

Change lipstick colors

To darken a bright red lipstick, apply a very small quantity of brown or dark green eye shadow to your lips after putting on the lipstick. The color will be darker and will last longer, too.

Homemade lip gloss

Combine the remainder of a lipstick with Vaseline and microwave on Low for 10 to 20 seconds. Mix and store in small jar or tin. This lip gloss gives your lips a sheer color and also acts as a Chapstick.

Lip wrinkle cream

Carmex works as well as specialty lip creams to reduce the appearance of lip wrinkles, and it is a lot cheaper.

Eye makeup

If you are allergic to eyeliner or just want to save a little money, get an eyeliner brush, dip it in water and apply a dark shade of eye shadow to your eyelids. eye shadow is usually cheaper than eyeliner and achieves the same effect.

Eye shadow blush

Find a pretty pink or berry shade of inexpensive eye shadow and use it as a blush. Just brush it on gently with a makeup brush. You can use the eye shadow on your eyes as well—and you will always know your colors are coordinated.

Eyebrow brush

When replacing mascara, wash and save your old mascara wand and use it as an eyebrow brush. The stiff little bristles are great for brushing brows into shape.

Makeup remover pads

Cut your round makeup remover pads in half to make them go farther. Usually you only use half the pad anyway.

Curling eyelashes

Heat an eyelash curler with a blow-dryer for several seconds. Test it with your finger to make sure the metal is not too hot; then use the eyelash curler on your eyelashes, holding it on the lashes for about five to ten seconds. Heat an old clean toothbrush for several seconds with the blow-dryer and use it to separate the eyelashes.

Numb the brows and lobes

Put some over-the-counter oral anesthetic solution on your eyebrows five minutes before you pluck them. This will prevent the pain. Apply some to children's ear lobes before they get their ears pierced as well.

Compact sponge

When your compact powder is ready to be replaced do not replace the sponge applicator. You can use the same sponge for several powder refills before you need to replace it. This way you will be able to use the powder that would have just soaked into a new sponge.

Cosmetic storage

Save the cap from an aerosol container and use it to store lipsticks, eye pencils and mascara. You can see lipstick colors at a glance.

Makeup secrets

Several makeup companies with department store brands also have drugstore brands. For instance L'Oreal makes both Lancôme and Maybelline. Often times these companies use the same technology to make the different brands of make-up—so try out the drugstore versions and see if you like them. Drugstore brands are a lot less expensive.

Compact photo holder

When you finish a mirrored compact, clean out the powder tray and cut a photograph to fit in the tray. Glue the photo in place and keep in your purse. You will see a loved one's face every time you check your hair and makeup.

Cuticle cream

Pick up a large bottle of mineral oil from the drugstore and use it as a cuticle cream. Transfer a small amount to a travel size container for easy application.

Nail polish removal

Use old nylons dabbed in nail polish remover to get rid of fingernail polish. You will not need to use as much remover solution, and you can forgo the messy cotton balls that end up sticking to your fingers.

Quick nail drying

For a quick dry for your manicure, fill your sink with cold water and add about five to ten ice cubes. Dip your newly painted nails into the water for ten seconds; then blow on them with your blow-dryer on a cool setting for another five to ten seconds. Your nails will be dry in less than thirty seconds!

Clean yellow fingernails

Sometimes nails turn yellow when they are painted with polish for several weeks. To get rid of the yellow tint, apply lemon juice to the nails using a cotton ball. Let the lemon juice set for a few minutes, rinse and repeat as necessary.

Nail polish storage

Store your nail polish bottles upside down to keep the polish from thickening. Make sure their lids are securely closed before flipping over. Five or six bottles will fit comfortably in an empty plastic margarine container.

Quick nail file

If your nail has a snag and you don't have a nail file on hand, find a matchbook and use the striking strip as a file.

French manicure

Do your own French manicures.

Cut a piece of tape into strips and wrap a strip around each of your fingernails, leaving a little space at the tips of your nails for painting. Paint the white polish on your nail tips and allow polish to dry before removing the tape. Finish with clear polish over the nail.

Shave with conditioner

Try shaving your legs using an inexpensive bottle of hair conditioner in place of shaving cream. Conditioner is cheaper and will leave your legs feeling soft and smooth.

Razor storage

Keep disposable razors from getting dull too quickly by storing them blade down in a cup of light canola oil. After use, rinse razors well before returning them to the oil.

Shaver saver

Instead of shaving your face over the sink, try shaving in the shower. You can use the suds from your shampoo as lather and save on the cost of shaving cream. The shampoo will help keep your razor blade from rusting, too.

Aftershave stretcher

Mix expensive colognes or aftershaves with witch hazel to make them last longer. The witch hazel also works as an astringent.

Shaving legs

When you shave your legs in the shower, first wash them with a mesh loofah to remove dry skin and then apply baby oil. You won't have to keep applying soap or shaving cream, and the oil will help your razor last longer.

Antiperspirant

Use Winsor & Newton #45 Oil Color zinc white for an antiperspirant. Squeeze a dab on each forefinger and then paint the underside of each arm.

Deodorant

Use cornstarch and baking soda as a deodorant. Keep them in separate containers with separate powderpuffs and first apply the cornstarch, then the baking soda.

Deodorant

Stop wearing deodorant. Instead just use a good deodorant soap every day.

Perfume applicator

If you have a perfume bottle without a sprayer top, put it in an empty roll-on deodorant container. To remove the roller ball, put the deodorant container in the microwave for a few seconds and then pop out the ball. Pour in the perfume and replace the ball.

Toothpaste clip

Use a chip clip or a binder clip to hold the rolled end of the toothpaste tube. It will save you having to squeeze the end of the tube every time you need some toothpaste.

Toothpaste saver

If your kids squeeze too much toothpaste onto their toothbrushes, attach a cake decorating tool where the cap goes. Pick a tool with a slender hole. Kids will love the design it makes when squirting, but it will be difficult for them to squeeze out a huge amount.

Sanitize toothbrush

After you have had a cold or the flu, put your toothbrush in the dishwasher's silverware holder and run it through a cycle. The high temperature wash will sterilize your toothbrush.

Baking soda toothpaste

If you use baking soda for brushing your teeth, don't dip your toothbrush in the box of soda. Fill an old salt shaker with the powder and apply it to your brush. You can also just pour the soda into your hand and then dip your wet brush in the powder.

Empty the toothpaste tube

When you think you can't get one more bit of toothpaste from the tube, put on the cap and gently roll over it with a rolling pin. You can now use the last of the toothpaste.

Toothache relief

Make a paste of water and ground cloves on a patch of gauze and apply it to the sore area in your mouth. The cloves will ease the pain of the toothache.

Free toothbrush

Your dentist will often offer you a free toothbrush when you come in for a cleaning. If you have your teeth cleaned every six months, you won't have to buy toothbrushes very often.

Stop grinding your teeth

Try wearing a sports mouth guard at night if you have the habit of grinding your teeth. Mouth guards are cheaper than most teeth grinding guards.

Teeth cleaning

Invest in a dental scraping device and remove plaque from your teeth after you have brushed and flossed. These instruments are usually inexpensive and easy to use.

Sunglasses

Instead of buying prescription sunglasses, pick up a pair of shades that you can clip on and remove from your prescription glasses. These "sun clips" are available at most optical stores.

Glasses frames

Shop for glasses frames at thrift stores. Often they have a basket of used prescription glasses, which will normally have quality frames. Take your frames to the optical center and only pay the price of the lenses.

Eyeglass repair

If a screw in your eyeglasses comes loose, apply a tiny drop of fingernail glue to the top and bottom of the screw before inserting it back into the glasses frames. The glue should hold the screw in place and still allow you to bend the arms of the glasses.

Contact case

Put a large dot of red nail polish on the right eye side of your contact lenses case. If you can't see well enough without your contacts to identify the "L" and "R" marks on the case, you will know the red dot is on the compartment with your right eye's lens.

Cheap gym membership

See if your community center has any weights or exercise equipment available for public use. Often the fee to use the equipment is much less than a gym membership.

Paid exercise

Cancel your gym membership and get a delivery route. Call up your local newspaper and ask if they need someone to deliver flyers. You will be paid to take long walks a couple of times a week.

Hula-Hoop fitness

Instead of investing in expensive exercise equipment, try using a Hula-Hoop for thirty minutes every day while you watch television. This is exercise equipment that certainly won't break the bank and will still keep you in shape.

Sports equipment

Check out your local thrift store before you invest in any brand-new sports equipment. Thrift stores often carry tennis rackets, bike helmets, rollerblades, balls and fishing gear that are still in good shape. Families with active kids can save a lot by hitting the thrift stores before the sporting goods retailers.

Exercise balls

Save on the cost of a yoga or exercise ball. Go to the toy section of a discount store and purchase a giant bouncy ball.

Homemade dumbbells

Purchase two one-gallon juice containers with substantial handles. When you finish drinking the juice, wash out the containers and fill them with equal amounts of water. You can increase the amount of water to increase the weight.

Gym showering

Use the shower at the gym after you work out. You might end up saving a lot on your home's water and gas bill.

Drinking water

To remind yourself to drink water, keep track of the number of glasses of water you drink throughout the day. Group several magnets on one side of the refrigerator door, and move a magnet to the other side every time you return to get another glass of water.

Sunburn relief

To relieve burning from a minor sunburn, put some apple cider vinegar on large gauze pads and wipe the burned area. Note: Always consult your doctor before treating severe burns. Or dampen several regular (not herbal) tea bags and place them on the burned area. The tannic acid will pull the heat and pain from the burn in about twenty minutes.

Ease sunburn pain

Ease a minor sunburn by applying mayonnaise and allowing it to sit for fifteen to twenty minutes. Rinse with cool water.

Sunburn relief

To ease the pain of a minor sunburn, apply milk of magnesia to the burn and stand in front of a fan for a few minutes.

Upset stomach

A small piece of peppermint can often calm an upset stomach or morning sickness.

Soothing puffy eyes

If the skin around your eyes is red

and puffy in the morning, rub your eyelids and the area underneath your eyes with hemorrhoid cream (not ointment). Leave on for a few minutes, and wash off before applying makeup.

Stomach acid

To relieve stomach acid reflux, squeeze the juice from a half of a lemon into a mug. Drop in the used half as well. Pour boiling water into the mug and steep. Drink warm after every meal and before bed.

Peroxide spray bottle

Keep a spray nozzle on your peroxide bottle. You can simply spray peroxide on scrapes and scratches for a quick fix.

Cold sore remedy

Apply a bit of liquid antacid to cold sores using a cotton swab. The antacid will heal the sore.

Splinter removal

To reduce pain while you are trying to remove a splinter, spray the area with a dab of sunburn relief spray. The topical anesthetic will numb the area and reduce the pain.

Chapped lips

To treat dry or chapped lips, apply a little Crisco around the lips and mouth. Crisco is safe for kids to swallow, so you won't have to worry about them licking their lips. Try using it on red runny noses as well.

Insect repellent

Rub all of your exposed skin with a dryer sheet to keep insects away. You won't even have to worry about getting spray in your child's eyes.

Mosquito repellent

Pat rubbing alcohol on your exposed skin (not your face) and let it air dry. The alcohol will keep the mosquitoes away and won't dry out your skin very much.

Insect repellent

Pick up a bottle of wheat germ oil as well as tea tree, Citronella and Pennyroyal essential oils from the health food store. Fill a two-ounce bottle 3/4 full of wheat germ oil and add five to ten drops of each essential oil. Shake well and apply to skin. The Vitamin E in the wheat germ oil is also great for your skin.

Mosquito repellent

To keep mosquitoes from collecting in enclosed areas put moth crystals (not mothballs) in a cotton bag or sock and hang in the enclosed area.

When the crystals evaporate, refill.

Insect sting relief

To relieve the pain from an insect sting, soak a cotton ball in ammonia and apply it to the area of the sting. Ammonia is cheap and works quickly. Note: Do not use on serious bites or if allergic to an insect sting.

Poison ivy relief

If you have been exposed to poison ivy, bathe with a bar of Fels Naptha soap, making sure not to miss any spots. The sooner you do this after being exposed, the less you will feel the effects of the poison ivy.

Heating pad

Fill a clean sock with uncooked oats and tie the end. Put in the gas oven for a few minutes to warm up the sock, then use the sock as a heating pad to soothe sore body parts. You can also fill the sock with rice and heat it in the microwave for several minutes.

Stop bleeding

To stop the bleeding of minor cuts, sprinkle ground black pepper on the cut and let sit for a few minutes. The blood will clot quickly. Rinse the pepper off the cut and dress it.

Sty prevention

If you suffer from frequent sties, wash your eyelids daily with tear-free baby shampoo to prevent any reoccurrence.

Baby rash

Try putting olive oil on a persistent diaper rash. It is much cheaper than other creams and usually clears up the rash in a day or so.

Prevent spreading illness

To prevent the spread of colds and the flu in the family or among roommates, put your toothbrushes in different places and clean them weekly by pouring hydrogen peroxide on them. To prevent mixing up your pillow with your spouse's, use contrasting pillowcases so you will always remember which one is yours. Immediately put tissue in a paper bag or the trash can so the germs won't have time to spread to a counter or table.

Cold pack

Keep a zip-type bag half filled with unpopped popcorn in the freezer and use it as a cold pack for injuries. The frozen popcorn conforms to the area of the injury and stays cold for a long time. It also keeps its shape after thawing. Mark the bag with a permanent marker so everyone knows it's a cold pack.

Cold pack

A small bag of frozen peas works well as a cold pack. The bag conforms to the injured area and stays cold for awhile. Put back in the freezer when finished and use again.

Ice packs

Make your own ice packs. Mix one part alcohol and two parts water in a large zip-type bag and put the bag in the freezer. The alcohol will keep the water from completely freezing. Apply pack to an injured area and it will conform to the spot.

Count your meds

Always count your pills after you pick up a prescription. Sometimes the pharmacy will make a mistake, and it will end up costing you money if you don't check.

Leg cramps

Try drinking tonic water on a regular basis to alleviate leg cramps. Cramps are sometimes the result of decreased levels of quinine in the body, and tonic water provides the necessary quinine.

Bee sting relief

To relieve the pain of a bee sting, wet an aspirin or Tylenol tablet and rub it onto the sting area. The pain will start to ease immediately.

Bunion treatment

To prevent foot bunions, take a rubber band and hook it over your two big toes. Keeping your heels together, fan your feet apart stretching the rubber band. Repeat ten times every day.

Cold sore remedy

As soon as you feel a cold sore coming on, press an ice cube wrapped in a clean rag or paper towel against the sore area. Keep the ice there for about fifteen minutes, until the area is numb. If you catch the cold sore early enough, this will prevent inflammation and spreading.

Soothing itching

Fill an old, clean nylon stocking with 1 cup of oatmeal and tie both ends of the stocking securely. Sit in a warm bath, wet the stocking and pat the stocking over itchy areas.

Hospital visits

If you have a close family member

in the hospital and visit him or her daily, ask the hospital's family services department whether they will give you a special rate on a parking permit. They may have recommendations for inexpensive hotels and meals in the area as well.

Med remind

If you take medications more than once a day, turn the bottle upside down after you take your first dose. When you take your second, turn it right side up. You can always look at the bottle if you can't recall if you have already taken a dose that day.

Drug samples

When your doctor writes you a prescription, ask if samples of that medication first. You may not need to get a prescription refill for awhile, and you will save a lot on the cost of the drug. But best of all, you'll have a few days' worth of medication—plenty of time to discover if you are allergic to it. Unfortunately, if you've already forked out a lot of money to purchase only to discover you cannot tolerate it, you will have to eat the cost of the prescription.

Hospital stays

Avoid excessive hospital expenses by bringing your own supply of pain killer that you take for fever, pain and headaches. Some hospitals charge large amounts for small bottles of these over-the-counter medications. Your doctor will have to approve this little move, but it's worth the effort.

Medication information

Enter all the names of your medications on a blank business card and carry it in your wallet. You will have the information if you need to fill out medical forms or if something happens and you are unable to advise the doctors of your medications.

Caretaker information

When caring for an elderly relative, keep a list of his or her current medications, dates of medical tests and hospitalizations, any surgery procedures, and his or her living will on hand. This information can come in handy when filling out medical forms or speaking with a physician.

Hospital BYO

If you know you will be in the hospital for several days, bring along your own combs, brush, toothpaste and toothbrush. Sometimes hospitals will charge large amounts for these simple toiletries.

Medical supplies

Before you purchase a back brace or other medical supply from the hospital, check out the prices at a medical supply store. You may be able to get a better price at the store.

Prescription co-pays

Pill dosage matters when determining the co-pays for some health insurance plans. It may be cheaper to get more pills in a lower dosage than fewer pills of a higher dosage. Make sure you always check your individual plan. And check with your doctor to make sure you can split pills.

Mosquito bite relief

If you have a mosquito bite that itches, just rub your deodorant on it and instantly the itching stops! You'll have to reapply after showering.

Nail repair

Don't you hate when you break a nail or smudge the polish just after a manicure? To avoid making a mess out of the other nine nails during the repair, simply cut the tip off the end of the appropriate finger on a thin latex glove. Wear both gloves while applying nail polish remover and cotton balls and the other nine fingertips are protected during the repair job. The gloves also work great for doing a pedicure without ruining a manicure.

Pretty dated

When you purchase new cosmetics, mark the date of first use on the container. Certain items like mascara should be replaced after three months to avoid problems with bacteria.

Pushpin hangers

If your necklace chains keep getting tangled in drawers and boxes, put a pushpin on the wall in the bathroom near the sink or in your dressing room. Line up three or four and hang your necklaces there to keep them from tangling.

Quick earring fix

Lost an earring back and still at work? Cut a piece of rubber band or a piece of the eraser from the end of a pencil and slip it on the back.

Smaller is better

Purchase the smallest contact lens holders for your contacts. The larger ones are free, but you will end up wasting solution filling up the holders. Smaller holders will save you money over time.

Soften cuticles

When your cuticles are looking rough and you don't have any cuticle cream handy, just rub on a bit of Chapstick lip balm. It works great to lubricate the skin.

To the last drop

When you're down to almost no toothpaste, cut the tube in half with scissors—there's a lot more toothpaste that can be scraped out.

Untangle necklaces

To untangle a fine chain or a delicate necklace, put a drop of baby oil on a piece of wax paper and set the necklace chain in the oil for a minute or two. Then use two straight pins to work at the knot gently, which will soon be undone.

Washcloth ice pack

When you need an ice pack for your face, take a washcloth, wet it, fold it length-wise into thirds and place it in a small plastic bag. Then place it in the freezer. In just a short time your freezer pack will be ready for your face. When it is no longer needed you have your washcloth back.

Watch batteries

What a pain to haul all your watches to the repair store just to get the batteries replaced. And new batteries aren't cheap, either. So next time make sure to pull out all the stems on watches you are not currently wearing. It's a simple trick to save battery life.

Home

Home

Humidifier scent

Mix a small amount of liquid potpourri with the water to be used in your humidifier. The potpourri will add a pleasant fragrance to the air and help keep the filter free from hard water residue and mildew.

Window screens

Wash your window screens periodically to keep your windows clean. Rain will often wash dirt from screens right onto the glass. In cold climates, wash your screens and put them away for the winter to allow more sunlight and heat to come through the window. You will have clean screens to install in the spring.

Window film

Instead of paying more for cooling units or air conditioning, keep the heat out of your home by putting low-E window film on your windows that get the most sun.

Attention quilters

Save used dryer sheets for your paper-pieced quilt projects. They are transparent enough for tracing the pattern and do not add much bulk to your finished work. And they smell nice, too.

Tire traction on ice

Sprinkle natural, clay-based kitty litter on your driveway to provide traction for your car's tires during icy conditions. Put litter on your walkways as well to prevent visitors from slipping. Carry the litter in your car in case you need it in a parking lot.

Labeling fuse box

If the switches are mislabeled in your fuse box, plug in a small electric radio to an outlet in a room. Turn up the volume so you can hear the music in the room with the fuse box. Then flip all the switches until the music stops. Label the fuse for that room and repeat the procedure for all the rooms in your house.

Heating savings

Save on winter heating bills by lowering the house thermostat at night and using an electric blanket. Save on the purchase of the blanket by using the twin size on any bed except a king size. A twin blanket is large enough to heat the top of a double or queen size bed.

Extend film life

Store camera film in the refrigerator. Film can last up to a year beyond the expiration date when refrigerated. (But if the film has already expired, forget it.)

Extra heat

The heat from the dryer exhaust is incredible. This is a very simple heating technique. With some inexpensive venting material from the hardware store you can direct your dryer heat back inside your home. Or direct the heat into the garage during the winter to keep pets and plants warm. You'll want to make sure you cover the end of the vent hose with something to filter any flying lint. The warmth and moisture help during the winter months when the air can be so dry. Check with the home improvement center to see if your clothes dryer might be a candidate for redirecting its heat into your living areas.

Taping trick

The best way to never lose the end of the tape on a roll is to stick a dime to the tape at the very end.

Fire starter

Melt the discarded wax from old candles in a double boiler on the stove top. Tear out pages of magazines, roll them up and dip both ends in the melted wax. Let them harden on aluminum foil. Store by your fireplace and use two or three to start a fire. Cardboard paper towel rolls dipped in wax are also effective as fire starters.

Repel insects from houseplants

To keep insects away from your houseplants, insert one clove of garlic into the soil of each planter, about 1/4 inch below the soil. Water as usual. The bugs will relocate and stay away.

Shoo fly

To get rid of flies around the garbage can, thoroughly wash the garbage can and put a few moth balls in the bottom of the can. Replenish the moth balls after every weekly garbage pickup.

Send the ants marching

To keep ants away, spread a thin line of salt across any entry where ants are entering. Ants will not cross a line of salt.

Mice repellent

Purchase a bottle of mint extract at a health food store. Soak cotton balls in the extract and place them in drawers and cabinets to keep mice away. Your house will smell great, too!

Get rid of ants

To get rid of ants, mix half a package of yeast and some honey together on a plate and leave it out on your counter. The ants will flock to it, eat the solution and die.

Painting pickup

When painting, line the roller paint tray with heavy-duty aluminum foil. When finished, simply pull the foil together and throw it away. You will never have to clean a paint tray again.

Matching your paint

When painting a room also paint a paper plate. It can be cut to fit in your purse or pocket so you can easily match fabric for window treatments, pillows or other accessories while shopping. Keep the plate in your files for future reference as well.

Oops! paint

Ask to see the "oops! paint" selection at your local home improvement store. Most stores have a collection of paints that did not match the color that the original customer wanted, and this paint is sold at low prices. Their mistake is your gain.

Flower food

Add 1/4 cup of hydrogen peroxide to your cut flowers' water. Change the water once a week, adding the same amount of peroxide and making sure there are no leaves below the water line. Your flowers will last for weeks.

Homemade curtain rods

Purchase a wooden dowel and decorative finials at a craft store, and pick up dowel screws and hardware to hang a curtain rod. Drill a hole in each dowel and insert the dowel screws. Screw the wood finials on each side of the dowel, mount hardware, and hang your curtains on your new curtain rod.

Pillow covers

Make your old silk pajama pants into neck roll pillow covers. Cut the legs so that they will cover the pillow with several inches of material left on either end. Tie both sides with a ribbon.

Gently rented

Call your local furniture and appliance rental store and see if they have returned items that they will sell to you. They will be used, but also inexpensive. The store may even deliver.

Budget bookends

Go to the home improvement store and pick up a pair of glass blocks to use as bookends. They are heavy enough to hold the books and small enough to fit on a shelf. Because they are clear, they will go with any décor.

Customized ceiling fan

Buy a can of spray paint in the color that matches your décor. Remove the blades from the fan with a screwdriver and paint them. Your colorful fan will brighten up the room.

Luminaria

To make a reusable luminaria, put sand in the bottom of an empty mayonnaise or canning jar and add a small tea light.

Keep candles in place

To keep candles from tilting in their holders, wrap a small piece of double sided tape around the base of the candle before inserting it into the holder.

Trimming candles

Use a pair of fingernail clippers to trim the wicks of your narrow jar candles. They are easier to maneuver than a pair of scissors. Candle wicks should be trimmed to 1/4 inch.

Bathroom candles

Instead of buying deodorizers for the bathroom, use scented candles. Large quality candles will effectively eliminate odors and last a long time.

Rug mats

Buy a roll of rubber shelving (stocked with the shelf paper) and cut it to fit under your rug. It will be cheaper than buying a rug mat and it works just as well.

Homemade headboard

Ask your local fencing company if they have any scrap fencing material you can purchase. Sand the boards, paint them, and lay them out vertically in a stair step pattern so that the boards become gradually taller towards the middle. Nail them together and use as a headboard. Use leftover boards to make matching night stands.

Cup of fragrance

For an inexpensive home fragrance, add a little water and a tea bag to a ceramic potpourri pot and light the candle underneath. It is easy to clean up and change the scent.

Address box

Instead of an address book, make

an address box. Buy a package of index cards and a card box. Fill out index cards with your friends' and family members' addresses, phone numbers and birthdays and organize them in the dividers that come with the card box. If someone's information changes, you can simply fill out a new card.

Sewing cleanup

Keep a foam drink insulator by the sewing machine and use it to hold discarded threads. The threads will stick to the foam and save you the trouble of picking them up off the floor later. You can also stick sewing pins in the foam.

Curtain rod change

Thicker curtain rods are very popular but the rods themselves can be quite expensive. To achieve the look for less, use pipe insulators. They are made of foam and come with a hole in the middle. Simply cut the insulator to the width of your window, insert it in the curtain hem and gather the curtain as you wish. You can then insert your plain old skinny curtain rod through the hole in the center and hang your curtains as usual.

Slash your electric bill

Get aggressive with your power bill by cutting your electricity consumption. Replace your standard light bulbs with energy efficient compact fluorescent light bulbs. Put your microwave and entertainment center on power strips and switch off the strips when the machines are not in use. Line dry your clothes in the summer (and the winter if you live in a dry climate).

Kid's room borders

Create your own customized borders for your kid's bedroom. Find several rolls of borders and cut out your kid's favorite characters. Measure the walls, plan a design, lay out the pieces and apply to the walls. You can mix and match characters for a unique layout.

Don't forget the laundry

Place a baby monitor in your laundry room and carry the hand-held monitor around with you as you continue with your housework. When the washer or dryer turns off, you will hear it on the monitor and be able to immediately transfer your clothes to the dryer or remove your clothes promptly for folding.

Fix those squeaks

Try using your spray-on body lotion as a lubricant to fix squeaky doors, rocking chair springs and door keyholes. The oil base in the product will help the metal glide smoothly again.

Light timers

If your kids (or you) constantly forget to turn off the bathroom and laundry room lights, install mechanical time switches in those rooms. These switches will keep the lights on for anywhere from 15 minutes to several hours before switching off, depending on your settings. One easy installation could lower your electric bill significantly.

Long life to batteries

If a battery goes out in a flashlight or a remote control just when you need it, take out the battery and rub the terminal with a pencil eraser. This will extend your battery life for a little longer until you can pick up some new batteries.

Cheap packing material

Save your Styrofoam egg cartons and use the bumpy side to cushion fragile items when mailing packages. The cartons don't weigh much and are easy to store if you nest them inside each other.

Stencil trial

If you just can't decide whether you'll like a particular stamp or stencil on your wall, use it on a piece of plastic wrap and hold it up to the wall. You'll know exactly what the stencil will look like—and may prevent a decorating goof.

Fresh cut flowers

When you get your flowers home, cut off the ends of the stems, arrange them in a vase and add a pinch or two of salt to the water. Just a little bit of salt will keep your flowers fresher for longer.

Pinecone fire starter

To make a pinecone fire starter, melt paraffin wax in a coffee can placed in a pan of water on the stove. Add cinnamon, nutmeg or other scents to the paraffin as well as colored wax or drops of oil if you wish. Tie a piece of candlewick or string to the top of a dried pinecone and dip pinecone into the paraffin. Allow paraffin to harden and dip again, allowing paraffin to harden after each dip. Place pinecones under logs before starting a fire.

Fix fraying towels

When your bath towels begin to wear and fray on the sides, trim off the edges and purchase marked-down yarn that coordinates with the towels and bathroom décor. Crochet the yarn along the long sides of the towels, using a small steel hook to get through the thick cloth of the towel. Now you won't be embarrassed to let your guests use your old towels.

All-natural air freshener

Fill a spray bottle with water and ten drops of your favorite essential oil. Twist on the top and shake before using on sheets, mattresses, carpet, etc. This solution will not stain material and is safe for kids and pets.

Night-light bulbs

Pick up white holiday bulbs at after-Christmas sales and use them as refill bulbs for your night-lights. The refill bulbs in the light bulb section are much more expensive, and they are practically the same product!

Drip-proof your candles

Cheap candles often look good but drip all over the place. To prevent drips, soak new candles in a strong salt solution for a few hours. Allow to air dry well, without rinsing. Now the candles will burn but not drip.

Sock-a-ladder

When you bring a ladder into the house from out of doors or the garage, protect your carpet by putting old socks on the feet of the ladder. Make sure someone holds the ladder for you to steady it.

Furnace checkup

Get your gas furnace cleaned and checked every year and you won't have to worry about emergency repair jobs during a cold snap.

Incredible uses for dish soap

Not only does Dawn dishwashing detergent do a great job with dishes, it is also a great and safe pesticide, a lubricant for jammed drawers and a flea dip for dogs! Save a lot of cash by using the detergent instead of other higher-priced products.

Firewood cover

Use an old shower curtain to cover firewood to protect it from rain and snow. It is easier to maneuver than a tarp. Hold down the curtain with some large rocks.

Address labels at the ready

Cheap address labels are infinitely useful. Put them in the front covers of your books before loaning them out and on rolls of film before sending them in to be developed.

Stick a label inside the battery compartment door of your camera. On forms that only require a name and address, just add a label. Carry a few in your wallet or purse in case you need one.

Dollars saves hundreds

Invest in new intake hoses for your washing machine yearly. Spending a couple of dollars on hoses could save you hundreds of dollars in repairs and water damage if your washer's hoses rupture during a cycle.

Bathroom water bucket

Keep a large bucket in the bathroom. When you are running the water for a bath or shower, let it fall into the bucket instead of down the drain. Use the water in the bucket to flush the toilet. You will save tremendously on your water bill.

Packing for a move

Pack your fragile items and dishes in white tissue paper that you can buy cheaply from the dollar store. The tissue paper goes a long way and does not dirty the objects as newspaper does. You can reuse it in gift wrapping after you unpack.

Long-lasting candles

Put new candles in the freezer overnight before you start burning them. The candles will burn longer.

Drying flowers

Use plain, cheap clay-based kitty litter to dry all roses and other flowers. Put a layer of kitty litter in the bottom of a box lined with paper towels. Place your flowers in the litter so they aren't touching each other and gently cover them with the extra litter. In about seven to ten days, they will be dried and ready for use in crafts or projects. You can spray them with a cheap, super-hold hairspray to protect them and give their petals a slight sheen. The litter is reusable, too.

No couch potatoes here

It is hard to change the TV channels while running on a treadmill. So place a strip of Velcro on your treadmill and the matching side on the back of your remote control. Then you can easily surf the channels without breaking your stride.

Clothespins to the rescue

Wooden, spring-loaded clothespins have an infinite number of uses. When storing winter gloves and mittens for the summer, use one to clip the two gloves together. Clothespins close potato chip bags and frozen vegetable bags. Add two clothespins to an ordinary wire coat hanger to hang up a skirt. Hang up children's artwork with clothespins. And of course, you can always use clothespins to hang your laundry out to dry in warm weather.

Remove carpet indentations

If you place an ice cube in an indentation in the carpet and leave it there until it is completely melted and dry, the indentation will disappear like magic. It won't leave any marks on your carpet either.

Piano-sitter

Often a job transfer or temporary move will mean that a family's piano has to go into storage. Why shouldn't it find a home with you? Tell friends (and ask your local Realtor) to be on the lookout for someone who needs a temporary home for their piano. You may be caretaker for a year or several years, or may even get permanent custody of one.

Fabric scrapbooking

Fabric scraps make a neat addition to your scrapbook pages. Use them as accents or to mat your photos. They give your pages some variety.

Keep a spare

Make a list of all nonperishable, essential items you need in your home—things that would mean a special trip to the store if you ever ran out. Then make a point to always keep at least one spare in your own home stockpile. Toilet paper, pantyhose, feminine products, dry pet food, ink cartridges and paper for your printer, essential school supplies, and an emergency $20 bill all come in handy. If you stock up when they're on sale, you'll save even more.

No pressure

Many washing machines have water shut-offs just like those under sinks and other plumbing. When you're away from home, flip the lever or turn off the water pressure (depending on the type of shut-off you have). That way you won't risk a hose blowing and causing a flood. It's a good idea to routinely replace hoses to avoid such an unfortunate occurrence.

Easy potpourri

Peel an orange and put the peels on your stove to dry. Once the peels are thoroughly dry, mix them with a stick or two of cinnamon (broken in pieces) and several cloves. For fragrance, empty the potpourri into a small pot full of water on the stove and simmer, adding water as needed. This makes a great Christmas gift, too.

Free packing material

Forget Styrofoam peanuts, paper shreds or bubble wrap. Plastic grocery bags are perfect packing material. Just wad them up and stuff them in and around the item in the box. One more great way to use those free bags.

Buying a mattress

If you are in the market for a new mattress, consider buying a floor model. Mattress stores switch out their floor models about once every three months and will usually be willing to sell one to you for half price if you ask. The beds are usually covered in protective plastic and have only been "tested" for a few minutes by a few customers—especially in stores with low traffic.

Watering houseplants

Use an empty wine bottle to water your houseplants. The long neck on the bottle lets you guide the water into the pot without dripping. Just make sure you wash out the wine before using.

Ant plugs

If ants are entering your house through the electrical sockets, pick up some of the plastic plugs that are used to prevent babies from touching open sockets. Cover all the open sockets that the ants appear to be using.

Sliding door insulation

Your home can lose a lot of heat through the large glass windows on sliding doors. Purchase several sheets of Styrofoam insulation board from a home improvement store and lay them between the curtain and the glass doors during the night. It will help you cut down on your heating bill.

Vacuum air freshener

To inexpensively freshen the air in your house each time you vacuum, simply place a cheap car air freshener inside your vacuum where the bag is, near the exhaust vent. Every time you vacuum, you will freshen your house. Fresheners usually last for three to four months.

Touch-up paint container

The plastic cartons that coffee is often packaged in make great paint containers. The molded handle makes them easy to hold and carry up and down ladders when you are doing a paint touch-up job. They will also keep paint fresh until the project is done!

Home

Refrigerator care

If the power goes out for awhile or you have to unplug your refrigerator for a move, make sure you leave the door cracked open. If not, it will mold due to the moisture inside. If you didn't read this tip in time and your refrigerator has already molded, first clean it thoroughly with a solution of one part bleach to ten parts water. Then pull apart pages of a newspaper, loosely crumple them and place them in the refrigerator to absorb the smell. Try to fill the refrigerator to capacity with the newspaper and change daily until the odors are dissolved. Now you don't have to buy a new refrigerator or freezer.

More light, less energy

For more light in a basement or garage (where you usually don't have the lights on for long) buy some two-bulb adapters that screw into the ceramic light sockets. They are sold at many discount stores. Once the adapter is installed, you can then put two 75-watt or higher bulbs in them and double your light output. If you are really skilled, install a double adapter in a table lamp and make it twice as bright (this will require removing the harp and perhaps turning the lamp switch slightly before replacing the harp).

Making a bed

To save yourself from having to check that a sheet has the same amount hanging over both sides of the bed, simply sew a little one or two stitch marker in the middle of the sheet. When you make the bed put the little stitch in the center of the bed. Use thread that is a different color than the sheet. The stitch is so small that it won't distract from the design or color of the sheets.

Don't lose your film

Nothing can be more disappointing than sending in your film for processing and having it lost along with your special memories. To prevent this from happening, keep a 3x5 file card in your camera case with your name, address and phone number on it in bold letters. Each time you load a new roll of film, snap a close-up photo of that identification card so that the film processor will have a record of the film's owner.

Art for cheap

Wait until after New Year's Day to get closeout prices on calendars with big splashy prints by wonderful artists. Keep them stored flat until you find the perfect frame at a thrift shop or discount store. Find matting to match at a craft store or hobby store. You can fill your walls with wonderful works that only cost you a few dollars.

Microwave potpourri

If you would rather not leave a burning candle unattended, but would still like a fragrance that fills a room, mix liquid potpourri with water in a thermal coffee mug and microwave it for about a minute. Place the mugs in the rooms you want to freshen, and the mug will disperse fragrance and stay warm for a long time. When the mug cools down, it's easy to pop back into the microwave and reheat.

Pillow plump

When a favorite pillow either becomes too lumpy and uncomfortable or too flat, there exists a remedy: Fill the pillow with the feathers of an old down coat.

Kerosene heaters

Purchase a kerosene heater to help with the heating bills. Two of these can heat a 4,000 square foot home for a third of the cost of natural gas heat.

Cheap carpeting

For inexpensive carpeting in places like a carport or a college dorm room, buy matching carpet samples for a dollar or two per rectangle, and tape them to the floor at the corners with carpet tape. The rectangles remove easily when you no longer want them.

Buffet space

When entertaining, increase your counter space when serving buffet-style by placing a finished board over the kitchen sinks. An old shelf or large cutting board works well.

Window treatments

For an elegant window treatment, purchase a curtain rod with nice finials at either end along with some heavy fabric that matches your paint and furniture. Then simply swag the material over the curtain rod yourself, letting the ends puddle on the floor. You don't even have to hem or sew. It is also easy to clean and inexpensive to change.

Mattress shopping

It is often difficult to do price comparisons for mattresses among different retailers because many mattress companies use different colored covers and model numbers to avoid consumer comparisons. So try shopping at warehouses such as Sam's and Costco, which offer quality mattresses at much lower prices than department stores.

Home

Driveway sealing

Use a 12-inch paint roller at the end of a broom handle to apply your driveway sealer. Fluffy rollers are best for rough surfaces. The sealer will go on more smoothly and evenly with a roller than with squeegees or brushes. And the job takes about half the time!

Simple wall decorations

To add beauty to apartments where the landlord will not allow permanent decorating or seasonal touches, cut patterns of whatever you like out of material, soak in liquid starch and place on the wall. You will need to wipe with a towel when applying. When you are ready to remove the material, just pull. The material comes right off the wall!

Closet curtain

If your kids are constantly pulling their closet doors off the tracks, save yourself some hassle and replace the doors with a shower curtain. Purchase a shower tension rod that will fit inside the closet along with shower curtain rings and let the kids pick out a shower curtain they like. The curtain becomes part of the décor, and it is easy for kids to move.

Burner covers

Use the lids from popcorn tins as burner covers for your stove top. You can even decorate or paint them—just remember to remove them when you turn on the stove. Use the popcorn canister as a small trash can.

Unwanted candles

Have you ever purchased a scented candle that you thought smelled heavenly, only to bring it home, light it, and find that its smell isn't really what you had in mind? Next time you are considering purchasing a new scent, buy the tiny votive version first and try it out in your home. If you like it after a few days, you can go back and get the larger version. If not, you won't feel badly about tossing it. You will save money and won't have candles you dislike stacking up in your cupboards.

Ant repellent

Sprinkle coffee grounds outside your house, especially under windows and doors, and the ants that have been invading your home will soon be gone.

Save couch cushions

If your couch cushions are starting

to look ratty but the couch's back and arms are still in good shape, purchase an inexpensive throw blanket that coordinates with your couch. Pick up some sheet fasteners/suspenders, too. Fold the throw in half, and spread it lengthwise across your cushions. Secure the throw on the underside of the cushions by stretching the sheet fasteners from front to back. You can also place a fastener in between the cushions to tighten up slack, making it appear each cushion is separately upholstered. Wrap the remaining cloth around the couch edge and tuck it into one of the fasteners on the back. You won't have to adjust the throw much, even after months of use.

Natural curtain rod

Use grape vine branches in place of curtain rods. They will give your windows a natural look, and you can probably get them for free.

Throw pillows

Make throw pillows from cloth table napkins. Sew or glue two napkins right sides together, leaving a hole for stuffing. Flip the napkins right side out, stuff and close the hole. You can create a gathered, softer look by wrapping a rubber band tightly around each corner before flipping the pillow right side out.

Buy used crafts

To try your hand at a new craft, buy an unfinished one at a garage sale. The seller will more than likely explain this project to you to make the sale. For 50 cents to a dollar, you have an opportunity to discover a new talent or hobby.

Save electricity

To save electricity and add moisture to your home or apartment in the winter, just use your dishwasher. When the dishwasher has run all its rinse cycles, immediately open the door and turn the knob to "off." You will save on the electricity used to operate the heater in the bottom of the machine. The moisture coming out of the dishwasher will make the air easier to breathe in your home, and the heat from the hot water will allow the dishes to air dry.

Mirror messages

Buy a dry-erase marker or two and use them on the bathroom mirror to write notes and reminders to your family members. After all, the bathroom is the one place everyone checks into in the morning or night. Wipe off marker with a tissue, dark towel or rag and periodically clean with glass cleaner. If someone uses a permanent marker by mistake, a little rubbing alcohol will remove it.

Home

Futon no-slip pad

If the mattress on your futon constantly slips, making for a sloppy look and uncomfortable seating, purchase several no-slip shelf liners and position them between the futon frame and mattress. You won't have to adjust it again for a long time.

Slipcovers in place

An easy way to keep slipcovers from shifting too much is to purchase an inexpensive package of pipe insulation. You can find it at home improvement stores, and it is usually priced cheaply. Simply cut the insulation tubes to fit between your cushions and furniture backs.

Reuse your glasses

If your dishwasher is constantly running because your family members get a new glass every time they want a drink, buy a package of multicolored rubber bands. Assign each family member a color and instruct them to put a band on their glass so they won't forget which one is theirs. Now everyone can reuse their glass throughout the day and you can run your dishwasher less.

Pool chemicals

If you have a swimming pool, don't pay the big prices for pool chemicals at the pool supply store. Buy all you need at the supermarket or warehouse club. Baking soda will increase pH levels in the water and laundry borax is a great pH buffer.

Pest control

To help control pests and keep them from moving in, buy a large bag of cedar animal bedding shavings and sprinkle them all around your foundation and in all flower beds about once every three months. The shavings break down into mulch, but the oils in the cedar will last two to three months and repel pests.

Painting drop cloths

Recycle your discarded vinyl flannel-backed tablecloths as drop cloths for painting. Lay them flannel side up on the floor. All your spills and mishaps will be absorbed by the flannel and the paint will not seep through the vinyl, saving your floor from paint stains. No more stepping into wet paint puddles and tracking the paint through the house. When painting is finished, hang the cloth outside to dry and hose or sponge off vinyl side if necessary. These drop cloths last for years and can be used many times.

Building supplies

If you need building supplies for some outdoor or indoor remodeling, keep an eye out for building sites that are wrapping up their work. Developers often end up with extra materials which will simply be thrown away because it costs more to store them than to toss them. You may be able pick up bricks, lumber, windows, fixtures, and landscape plants and trees if you simply ask if you can take home some items. The builders will probably be grateful.

Valuables inventory

Create an inventory of your valuables. Go room by room writing down the make, model and price of each item you own. Include the original receipt with the information if you still have it. A photograph or video of each item would also be helpful. Make several copies of this information and store them in different locations, e.g. your house, a relative's house, a safe-deposit box, etc. This will prove extremely valuable in the event of theft or fire.

Get rid of ants

Mix equal parts of borax and sugar. Put spoonfuls into small containers such as bottles or jar lids or yogurt cups, and tuck them into the back corners of cupboards and any other places where you find ants. Those ants will soon be gone.

Recycled magnets

Before you throw away old shower curtain liners, cut out the magnets at the bottom. Then hot glue a decoration (like a shell) on one side and use the magnets to hold notes on your refrigerator.

Make guests feel welcome

Hang an over-the-door shoe organizer on the door of your guest room. Fill each of the different clear pockets with items the guests can use during their stay. A map of the local area, sun lotion, soaps, shampoos, note cards, a good paperback book (with a note saying to take it with them if they haven't finished), candies, a flashlight, a variety of medications and personal items, a couple of stamps and some postcards from the surrounding area are all appreciated items. Most of these little items are free or very inexpensive.

New furniture from old

If you are shopping for inexpensive furniture at a flea market or thrift store, always consider if you could make what you find into something better to fit your needs. For instance, a set of bathroom cabinets and drawers could become a set of nightstands if you pulled them apart and made new tops for them. Get creative and see what you can come up with.

Fitted sheets

If you upgrade from a full to a queen-size bed, you can still use your full-size flat sheets. Just pick up some sheet garters and put them on the full-size flat sheets. You won't have to buy a complete sheet set.

Recycle empty vases

Instead of throwing away those empty vases and baskets that your flowers came in, call your local florist and ask them if they will take back the containers and baskets. They may throw in some fresh flowers for your trouble.

Card table repair

When your old card table needs a lift, try taking the top off and measuring it for a new top cover of your choice. You can purchase material for a new cover at the fabric store and recover the table yourself. Paint the metal on the table in a color to match the new fabric, and you have a new table.

Inexpensive curtains

If you have a large window and do not want to spend a great deal of money for curtains, simply purchase two cotton lace shower curtains. Then go to your local hardware store and buy a piece of copper pipe measured for your window and some finial pieces to match. Stop off at the office supply store and pick up some binder rings. Loop your binder rings through the top of the shower curtain, mount the curtain rod and hang the curtains.

Wall borders

Those self-stick removable borders can be expensive and often don't adhere well to the wall. So put them up with thumbtacks. Buy some borders on clearance with a solid color along the edge. Match that solid color with some craft paint and use it to paint the heads of the tacks. When the tacks are dry, insert them along the border edge, one about every two feet. No one will be able to see them, and your borders will stay in place.

Upholstery care

To strengthen your upholstered furniture, dot common Elmer's white glue along the seams, smear it and allow it to dry. It will add extra strength to those areas where wear and tear are the greatest. Do test in a hidden area to make sure the glue dries invisible. If you get a tear on the backside of a piece of furniture, an upholsterer can sometimes remove and repair the visible tear—but you'll have to place the chair or sofa against the wall after that.

Disaster bag

Put your precious family photos and financial records inside a trash bag, along with your name and phone number. Place the bag in the closet. If a tornado, flood or other disaster strikes your house, your important papers and photos will have a better chance of surviving. And if they get swept away from your home, people will be able to contact you if they are found.

Mouse stopper

You can save money on mouse traps and poison if you stuff steel wool, available in hardware stores, in the holes around the plumbing pipes under the sinks in your bathrooms and kitchen. The mice are repelled by the steel wool and won't come in your house.

Save money on repairs

If you are purchasing expensive remodeling materials like windows, get a few estimates for local companies before you settle on a supplier and a price. Sometimes a company will offer to beat a price if they see that they could lose your business to their competition. They may throw in extras in the bargain as well.

Repel ants with lemon

If you have ants in your home, wipe their trails down with a sponge soaked in fresh lemon juice. Wipe your counters and baseboards with it, too. Ants hate lemon juice and won't cross it. Baby powder and cinnamon are also good to use outdoors on ant trails when you don't want to use pesticides. Just sprinkle liberally.

China finds

That favorite china in need of rejuvenation? If you are shocked at the department store prices for replacement pieces, check out thrift stores and websites that sell used products. Goodwill has a website (*www.goodwill.org*) where you can shop for china and collector's items across the country. You might even get lucky and find a piece at a garage sale.

Hanging window toppers

Need a cheap way to hang a window topper? Hammer in some nails along the top of the window, hang your window topper on them, and cover the nail heads with button covers.

Bathroom decorating

It doesn't have to cost a lot to decorate your bathroom. If the shower curtain that you have your heart set on is outside of your budget, see if you can find a similar pattern in a vinyl tablecloth. Use a grommet set to punch holes along one side and slip rings through the holes. Hang as a shower curtain with a curtain liner on the other side. Save your empty glass jars for bath oil and fill them with water that you have tinted with food coloring that complements the shower curtain. Display these bottles on your bathroom counter along with some sea shells.

Strengthen houseplants

Because houseplants lean toward the sun, they tend to get lopsided if they remain in one place. Get in the habit of turning your plants every few weeks—whenever you notice that they are beginning to bend too much. Your plants may end up being stronger and healthier as a result.

Avoid shipping costs

When shopping online, have your order shipped to the closest retail store in your area for you to pick up. Many online stores will then waive the shipping cost.

Shower timer

To help your family save on water and electricity, have everyone commit to cutting down their shower times. Make it into a game by putting a kitchen timer in the bathroom and setting it for a certain amount of time for each shower. It may bring out the competitive spirit in your family as everyone tries to beat the clock. Use a timer to monitor your time online and the time you spend on cleaning or some other unpleasant task, too.

Cheap baking soda

If you use a lot of baking soda around the house for cleaning, purchase it at your local pool supply store. They may have cheaper prices and you can buy it in bulk.

Plant exchange

Instead of buying new houseplants, get together with friends and exchange "slips" from plants. It's an inexpensive way to add beauty to your home.

Photo art

When you go on vacation, make

sure to take several landscape shots of beautiful scenery. When you get home, select a few, enlarge and put them in inexpensive frames from the discount store. Look through your friends' and co-workers' vacation photos as well, and ask them if you could make a few copies of their best landscape shots. You'll end up with some exotic wall art.

Summer air conditioning

To save on the cost of running your central air conditioning during the night, buy a window unit for your bedroom. You will save a lot on your utility bill.

Half a log

If you like to use those fire starter logs when building a fire, try cutting them in half to make them go farther. You can usually get a fire started just as well with half a log.

Linens storage

Store your sheet sets inside the matching pillow cases for tidy stacking in the linen closet. No more searching for the flat sheet that matches the fitted one you want to use.

Dump it

If you currently pay for trash pick up, consider taking your own trash and recyclables to the dump. Many dumps will take both. To make sure the trash doesn't mess the back of your car, double bag everything or use quality trash bags. You may need to invest in another trash can as well, but the savings over time will be worth it.

Thread pickup

If you sew a lot, you may have trouble with threads getting wrapped around the rotating brush of your vacuum cleaner. Next time, before you vacuum, brush over the carpet in your sewing room with a lint brush. The brush will sweep the threads into one pile, which you can pick up and discard. Your vacuum will thank you.

Bookmark momentos

Save those used theater and sports tickets! They make great bookmarks for the family. You will be reminded of a fun memory every time you close or open your book.

Fruit fly catcher

Fill a small dish with 1 inch of apple cider vinegar and 1 to 2 drops of dish soap. Cover tightly with plastic wrap and cut a few small holes for entry. Cider attracts the fruit flies, and soap kills them.

Home

Photo swatch

If you are redecorating and forgot to save a swatch from your couch, take a photo of the fabric on your digital camera. You can play with the lighting and the colors on your computer until the printed version matches the actual fabric perfectly. Then take the photo to the store so you will know whether a color or pattern will match your current furniture.

Clearance mattresses

At some large furniture stores, they have a section of clearance mattresses that are mismatched with the box springs. You may be able to buy high quality mattresses and box springs at huge savings—the mattress and box springs will just be two different models.

Tilting candles

Do you have candles tilting to one side in your candle holders? Wrap a rubber band around the end of the candle and push it into the holder. It acts as a seal and keeps the candle from tipping over.

Clearance houseplants

Did you know that many gardening shops have a clearance section? Check out the plants and see if you can find some you like. You might save a lot.

Candle decorating

Buy votive candles on sale and arrange them inside assorted glass containers that you purchase from thrift stores and garage sales. You can make some beautiful groupings by putting a small glass holder inside a larger one, or filling a container with glass marbles before adding the candle. Place candles on top of a mirror to increase the effect.

Keeping ants away

Once a year the dreaded lines of ants appear on your kitchen counter, floor and anywhere else they might find a tasty morsel. So get in the habit of washing your floors and counters with lemon Ajax dishwashing detergent. Ants hate the stuff and will stay away.

Drying flowers and vines

When you need to rush dry flowers or grapevines for wreaths or swags, just lay them in the back of a van or station wagon on a hot day. The vehicle will heat up in the sun and dry the plants quickly. You can also wrap a wire around the coat hooks on either side of the car and hang dry some of the plants.

Fresh smell

To get rid of the musty smell that old houses can have, hide a dryer sheet in every room and closet. The air in your house will be freshened.

Votive jars

Baby food jars make great votive holders. You can paint them to make them look especially pretty.

Holiday placemats

Pick up some clear contact paper and inexpensive holiday themed fabric. Cover the fabric with the contact paper, then cut out your favorite placemat shape. Instant wipe-off placemats. You can even pick up extra fabric, cut out a few squares and hem some napkins to match.

Help for squeaks

Use Pam, the non-stick cooking spray, to oil squeaking doors and sticky drawers. You won't have to oil them again for awhile.

Round sandbox

Ask a local tire dealer if you can have an old tractor tire. Purchase some sand, place the tire in the backyard, and fill the tire with sand. Kids love to play in a round sandbox that is fun to climb on, too.

Stop puddles

To keep water from getting on your floor while taking a shower, buy a long strip of Velcro with the adhesive on the back. Attach one side of the velcro strip to the top edge of shower curtain liner, then mark where the strip will meet the wall and make a slash with your pencil. Attach the second Velcro piece to the wall over the mark. You will never have to pull your shower curtain liner against the wall again.

Lint fire starter

Save the lint from your clothes dryer in a can and use it as a fire starter when grilling or building a fire in the fireplace. It certainly beats the smell of starter fluid and is a good way to reuse the dryer lint.

Goofed up paint

When using "goof" paint (the mis-mixed paint sold at a discount price) combine two gallons together to ensure that you will have enough to completely paint your room. This way you will not run out of a color that you can't match. Any leftover paint can be mixed with another gallon to extend it and so on. Just be sure to mix semi-gloss with semi-gloss.

Ant tea

Put mint tea bags inside the baseboard of your heating unit to keep ants away. You will be spared an ant invasion and have a faintly minty aroma every time you use your heating system.

Keep drains clean

To keep drains clean, try pouring plain old chlorine bleach down the sink and bathtub drain weekly—about 1 quart for the sink and 1/2 to 1 full gallon for the tub. It's a whole lot cheaper than drain cleaners, and much cheaper and easier than calling a plumber.

Extra curtain rod

Hang an extra shower curtain rod on the inside of the shower stall (about an inch away from the wall) to hang wet towels, washcloths, hand-washed clothes, or an overly-wet bath mat. It won't interfere with bathing if you put it high enough, and it will come in handy for all of your drip-drying needs.

Reduce carpet static

To reduce the amount of static in your carpet combine one capful of liquid fabric softener and two cups of water in a spray bottle. Lightly mist the carpet when static becomes a problem in your home. (Do not saturate your carpet—you just need a little bit.)

Get rid of fleas

To get rid of fleas with a natural solution, liquefy some orange peels, grapefruit peels, 1 tablespoon rosemary (fresh is better, but dried will do) and 1 pint of water in your blender. Then put mixture in a pot and heat it on low for 15 to 20 minutes. Strain liquid so you can put it in a spray bottle. Spray on pets and rub well into their coats. Also spray in their favorite napping areas and carpeting. Avoid getting it in your pet's eyes.

Long life for flowers

To make your garden flowers last longer after cutting, try these tips: Always cut the stem at approximately a 90 degree angle and use a very sharp knife for a clean cut. Paring knives work well. Clean all the leaves from the stem that might touch the water, as they can cause bacteria to grow in the water. Use very warm water immediately after cutting and re-cut your stems every three days.

Shop the classifieds

Always check the classifieds for great deals on furniture. The Sunday paper for a large metropolitan area is the best place to look.

Alternative paper towels

Use cloth diapers for cleaning

around your house. They are sturdy, washable and absorbent. You can save a lot of money by not buying paper towels.

Flea away

If you have a flea problem outside your house this will keep them away from your doors. Find a myrtle bush, pull off some small branches and hang them up to dry. When dry, place them around the doors.

Save on toilet paper

Kids sometimes go through toilet paper way too fast because they like rolling it off. So before you put on a new roll, press down hard on it so the roll is oval shaped. It will not roll as easily and your kids will likely use less tissue.

Scrapbook pictures

Save on your photography bills by collecting all the free brochures for the area where you are vacationing. Cut out the pictures of the places you've seen and add these to the family pictures you've taken. Now you have quality landscape photos of the places you've been at no expense to you.

Fancy dinners at home

If you find you spend too much eating out, make dining-in like eating out. Go to a thrift store and pick up some new tablecloths, placemats or napkins. You might even find a cheap set of dishes. Set up a pretty table for supper and your family will feel like honored guests in their own home. You can reuse these items and save on the cost of eating out.

Recycled road maps

Reuse your old road maps as shelf liners for drawers and pantry shelves. They fold easily and will remind you of the fun places you've been.

Wasp spray

Dilute liquid dishwashing detergent in water and put it in a spray bottle. Use it to spray wasps and fire ants.

Striped walls

If you want to give your walls a new look with some stripes, use a water soluble pen to mark off the lines for the stripes on your wall before taping them for painting. The pen always washes off in water, whereas pencil can sometimes be stubborn and take a lot of scrubbing to remove.

Watering houseplants

Use a turkey baster to water your houseplants. You will be able to measure the amount of water each plant gets and you can direct the flow of water easily so it does not spill. Carry a jug of water around with the baster for quick refills.

Stop the ants

Make your own ant killer. Take a baby food jar and fill it up halfway with syrup or molasses. Then sprinkle some yeast on top of it. The ants will eat the mixture and die.

Wine glass charms

If you lose an earring, make wine charms. Take its mate, wrap it around the stem of a wine glass and secure. You can be sure there won't be a duplicate!

Discount seating

Instead of buying chairs for your rectangular kitchen table, why not use benches instead? Benches are easier to clean, especially if you have kids. You can buy the materials to build and stain a pair at a home improvement store. Now all you need to get is two chairs for the ends of the table.

Home fragrance

If you are using up scented candles way too quickly, invest in an electric potpourri pot. Fill the pot with water and a few drops of essential oil, throw in an old unscented candle and turn it on. The wax will hold the scent, so you can reheat it multiple times.

Paintings on loan

For young couples who are just starting out, finding nice artwork to hang on the walls is difficult. Head to your local library and ask if they loan out their framed paintings to patrons. The pictures are usually either works by local artists or framed prints by more recognizable artists. For a few months, you can fill in areas of your home with loaners while you look for more permanent pieces. Check to see if your public library offers the same service.

New duvet for comforter

If your comforter is looking a little worn on the outside, instead of throwing it out get a duvet cover for it. You can spend a lot on an expensive one at the department store, or you can make your own by sewing two matching flat sheets together on three sides and attaching some Velcro to the open side. You can even make a few and rotate them for a new look every few months.

Fabric shower curtain

If you buy a white fabric shower

curtain and liner, you won't ever have to inhale nasty fumes as you try to clean off the mildew and grime. You can simply throw the curtain into the washer with your white towels and some bleach, and it will come out as good as new. These fabric curtains will last for years.

Cheap shelf paper

Go to any store that sells wallpaper and check out their bargain bins. Sometimes you can find a double roll for around $5 that will paper all of your cabinets. You'll probably have enough left over to replace any paper that may get water or chemical stains over time. Much less expensive than the $2.50 to $3.00 a roll for contact paper, which usually only covers two to three small cabinets.

Need a humidifier?

The air inside your home can get very dry when your heat is on full blast during the winter months. For a cheap humidifier, fill your slow cooker with water and plug it in on a low setting. The water in the slow cooker will last a great deal longer than in a humidifier, too.

Dye, dye, dye

Did you know you can dye curtains, bed ruffles, bed pillows, couch pillows and more? Pick up some Rit Dye at the supermarket or discount store and change the color scheme of your rooms from season to season or year to year. This is a great way to fix up items you pick up at yard sales as well. Cotton items work the best.

Shining up houseplants

Instead of using expensive houseplant shiner products, a dab of mayonnaise on a soft rag will clean and shine up flat-leafed houseplants in a jiffy. Note: Do not use this on plants with fuzzy leaves, such as African violets.

Bed accessories

When you purchase a new quilt or comforter, you don't have to buy all the matching pillows from the store—you can make your own. Buy an extra flat sheet or two that coordinates with your bed's colors and use the material to make pillows, lampshades and curtains. You will have a lovely matching bed for a fraction of the cost of the ready-made items.

Alternative curtain rod

Instead of purchasing curtain rods, go to your local home improvement store and buy an untreated wooden closet rod cut to the size you need, along with a pair of unfinished wooden end caps and brackets. Stain the wood so it will match your other furniture. Everything matches, and you've spent hardly anything at all!

Dresser decorating

If you buy an old dresser at a garage sale, you can "dress" it up with some paint and leftover scraps of wallpaper. Sand and paint the dresser, then cut out designs from the wallpaper and glue them to the dresser. Add a clear coat of finish over the paper so the pieces will not come loose. Kids especially will love this new, personalized dresser.

Broken light bulb removal

To remove a light bulb that has broken at the base, first unplug the lamp or turn off power to the light source. Now take a potato, cut it in half, press it firmly into the broken bulb and then twist to remove. If you don't have a potato, try a bar of soap. Before putting in a new bulb, rub a thin layer of Vaseline on the base of the new bulb for easy removal in the future.

No-skid tablecloths

No-skid mats that are sold to go under rugs can be used under a tablecloth to keep it from slipping. You can cut it to size.

Towel rugs

Make your old towels into a beautiful soft rug for your bathroom. Cut the towels into 1- or 2-inch strips and sew the ends of the strips together to make three long strips. Then sew the ends of the three strips together at one end and braid them. Coil the braid, lightly tacking the pieces together with a few stitches every couple of inches until the rug is as big as you would like it. These rugs are washable and durable. Make them to match your bathroom décor!

Paint storage trick

To store leftover paint, transfer the remaining amount to a one-gallon glass pickle jar that has a metal sealable lid. Put some plastic wrap on the top of the jar before replacing the cap to make a good seal. You can easily see the paint's color at a glance and quickly mix the paint by giving the jar a good shake.

Scratch pads

Use the blank side of printed pages from your printer to use as scratch paper. You can cut the pieces to a smaller size and stack them by the phone or on your desk.

No-spill gardening

When watering small houseplants and cut flowers, take an empty water bottle with the pop-up sports top, fill it with tap water, replace the cap, and pull up the spout. You can gently spurt water into the pot or vase over and over and never spill a drop on your table or yourself.

411 on flatware

When buying stainless steel flatware, check the bottom for the numbers 18/8 or 18/10. The top number stands for the percentage of chromium and the bottom number is the percentage of nickel. A higher content of nickel makes the stainless steel stronger and more resistant to heat, not to mention shinier.

Air bag packaging

As a substitute for bubble wrap or packing material, gather some zip-type baggies and a plastic straw. Insert the end of the straw into the bag and seal the bag the rest of the way. Blow up the bag with the straw; then quickly remove the straw and seal the bag. Fill up your package with as many "air bags" as you need.

Back to cloth

Replace paper napkins with cloth that can be laundered and re-used. It's good for the environment and adds a touch of elegance to the dinner table.

Cheap calls

Check out the dollar store to purchase a phone card. Sometimes they have some good deals on international and long distance rates.

Cheap notepads

Reuse desk calendars as notepads. If you tear off a few months' worth of days at a time and flip them over, you've got a great source of scrap paper.

Cheap Sachet

When spray perfume bottles get to the point where the long tube cannot reach the liquid, remove the top and soak cotton balls in the remaining fragrance. Then place them in a corner of your clothing drawers so they are not touching any of the garments. Your clothes will have a pleasant scent that you already know you love.

Cut flowers

When your cut flowers begin to droop, give them a second life by cutting the stems off near the blossoms and floating them in a bowl with warm water into which you have mixed a crushed half of an aspirin tablet.

Earrings for pushpins

If you wear earrings, you probably have lots of loner ones floating around that have lost their mate. So use them as pushpins for your bulletin board. The mismatched earrings will give your board a decorative look.

Fabric storage

It is easy for bolts of fabric to get creased or wrinkled when they are folded in a bag or box. Save your cardboard rolls for wrapping paper and roll your pieces of fabric around them. You can secure them with a ribbon or a safety pin.

Fix-it book

Organize all of your instruction manuals and warranties for electronics and appliances in a three-ring binder with clear sheet protectors. Whenever an appliance has a problem, you can easily find the information you need to fix it yourself or call customer service.

Floor plan

If you like to rearrange your furniture from time to time you can save a lot of wasted effort by drawing a floor plan of your house and pictures of your furniture drawn to scale. This way you will at least be able to see if things will fit in the new location before moving them.

Fragrant mail

Use the cologne sampler strips found in magazines to perfume your stationery. Just place opened pieces behind your sheets of paper, cards and envelopes. Do not allow the strips to touch the surfaces on which you will write, as the alcohol content is just enough to make it difficult for the ink to adhere.

Freshen curtains

To freshen your fabric curtains and remove pet hair, take them down and stick them in the dryer for ten to fifteen minutes on the "Air Fluff" setting. Remove the curtains promptly and hang them up immediately to prevent them from wrinkling. Clean out any pet hair from the dryer lint trap.

Hanging curtains

After just hanging new curtains insert a butter knife in the hem to add weigh and straighten out the edges if needed.

Homemade towels

Go to the fabric store and purchase terry cloth in a color you like. Then hem or zigzag a stitch along the edges, and you have your own custom-made towels.

Label removal

To remove labels or stickers from soft plastics, pour a little vegetable oil on the sticker and let sit for 15-20 minutes. Then rub sticker gently with your finger and wash in soapy water. The sticker comes right off.

Lasting calendars

Recycle a favorite calendar from year to year by printing a free calendar from the Internet and taping it over the old one. Do this every month and you'll get to enjoy your calendar's graphics for many years.

Light bulb efficiency

Compact fluorescent lights (CFLs) are rated differently than regular incandescent light bulbs. Here's a quick tip for how to determine the size wattage you need to replace your incandescent bulbs: Divide the wattage of the incandescent bulb by four. For example, a 100-watt incandescent bulb should be replaced with a 25-watt CFL.

Lighting candles

If you don't have extra long matches, try lighting a piece of spaghetti. It will burn for a while and allow you to light multiple candles.

Like a glove

While cooking, keep a small plastic baggie near the telephone. If someone calls while you have both hands messy, you can put your hand in the bag and then pick up the phone.

Long-distance cards

If your phone has memory and speed dialing, you can program it to dial all those numbers on your prepaid long-distance calling card. Just put the toll-free number into one memory space and the card number into another. Press the first speed dial to start the call and the second when you hear the prompt to input the card number.

Nail removal

When removing nails from a wall with the back of a hammer, it is often hard to avoid scuff marks on the wall. Try placing a dry, clean sponge between the hammer end and the wall as you pull out the nail. The sponge, and not your wall, will take most of the pressure from the hammer.

Home

New drapes

When selecting new draperies (whether you buy them or make them yourself), make sure they are lined. Lining helps to insulate the window, keeping the cold air out or in (depending on if it is winter or summer) and protects the drapery fabric from sun damage.

No-burn candles

You can have a wonderful home fragrance without burning a candle. Just set a jar candle on your range top next to the oven vent. The heat melts the candle and sends the wonderful scent all through the house. And the best part? The candle never burns away.

Organize linens

Binder clips are a great way to organize not just your papers, but your linens, too. Clip together folded and matched napkins and placemats in your linen closet for quick retrieval.

Packing noodles

Have too many foam noodles lying around in the garage? Use them as packing material for your packages. A serrated knife cuts through them well, and they hold items in your box stable until they arrive at their destination.

Paint can lids

Punch a few small holes in the lip of the paint can so that excess paint doesn't collect in the rim. The holes allow the paint to fall back in the can. Putting the lid back won't be nearly as messy anymore.

Paint cleanup

Make painting cleanup easier with these tricks: Instead of using old sheets or buying drop cloths to cover the furniture, use clear plastic dry-cleaning bags. When torn across the top and down one side, these expand to cover most furniture pieces, kitchen cabinets, bathroom fixtures and countertops. Rubbing alcohol works well to remove those "oops" paint splatters from the tub, toilet and even marble countertops.

Picture perfect

Use a digital camera when you go to the home improvement store for help. You can take pictures of furniture or fixtures to match paint and other decorating supplies. If you need a specific replacement fixture for a pipe or drain, take a picture of your current fixture so the salesperson can help you find what you need. Always measure the fixtures for dimensions as well.

Placemat coasters

Give your old plastic placemats a new life by making them into coasters. Take pinking shears and cut the placemats into squares. Keep them handy on your coffee or end tables to use anytime.

Polishing brass

To polish tarnished brass, take half a lemon and dip it in some salt. Rub the lemon on the brass. Rinse brass and then polish with a soft cloth.

Pot of noodles

If you need some foam to fill in the bottom of a large flower pot, cut up a large swimming noodle with your knife or scissors and place the pieces in the bottom of the pot. Now the pot is not completely filled with dirt, it doesn't weigh as much and it's great for drainage.

Protecting plants from pets

If your pets are getting into your potted plants and digging, try covering the dirt on top with rocks or pebbles. The water will still get through to the soil and your pets will probably be less interested in messing with the pot.

Chair cushions

The padded seat cushions on kitchen chairs tend to slide everywhere, especially when kids are sitting on them. Attach small pieces of Velcro to both the chairs and the cushions so the cushions will stay in place.

Quick fix

If you can never find the correction fluid when you need it, use the borders from the self-adhesive stamps and mailing labels to cover mistakes and make corrections. They are already cut into small sizes, and in several shapes.

Quick wall fix

Your walls are probably filled with little holes from previously hung pictures. To make them less visible, grab the correction tape and rub it over the holes—soon you won't be able to see them anymore.

Safe, not sorry

If you are considering having a security system installed in your home, you will be happy to know that most insurance companies give homeowners a credit for having a security system. Although you will have to pay for the unit and monthly monitoring, you may still come out ahead. Call your insurance provider and ask.

Sanding for painting

If you need to do some minor wall repair or spot painting, use emery boards to "sand" small areas where you have patched or where you are going to paint. A large pack of these nail files can be found at the dollar store.

Sleeping sheet

When your large-size fitted sheet loses its elasticity or your flat sheet gets too tired for regular use, fold it in half and stitch up the bottom and side, leaving the top open. Then you have a sheet sack that is great for camping on warm nights when a sleeping bag is too hot.

Strong and cheap

Fishing line is marvelous for hanging and holding things. It is practically invisible as well as inexpensive. Use it to suspend pots from trees or wreaths in front of mirrors. They will appear to be floating on air.

Watering houseplants

Drop an ice cube or two into potted plants to water them. The ice melts slowly, and the soil absorbs the water before the water can create a puddle or drip out of the pot.

Hot water

If you have an electric water heater but do not wish to install a timer, simply throw the breaker off when you do not need large amounts of hot water. The tank is insulated and keeps the water hot for 12 to 18 hours unless large amounts are removed for washing clothes or taking showers. Of course you have to remember to turn the breaker on, but if you are consistent this tactic will result in reduced utility bills.

Cut water usage

Add a water aerator to your sink faucets that do not already have such a device. This will cut your water use in half. These can be purchased at any home improvement store and the home department of many other stores. You can save up to 100 gallons per year per faucet.

Energy savings

Change the bearings in your air conditioner to the low friction variety and you can save a substantial amount on your utility bill.

KITCHEN TRICKS

Kitchen Tricks

Cast iron pan care

Always use hot water to clean cast iron cookware, unless seasoning the pan. To keep your cast iron cookware from rusting after washing place the pan on top of the stove and heat until completely dry. As added protection, store your pans in the oven if you have a gas stove with a pilot light.

Fast defrost

Use a blow-dryer to make a quick job of defrosting your freezer. Just aim the dryer at a patch of frost for a few seconds until it begins to melt slightly, then use a plastic pancake spatula to pry it loose. Pick up the large chunks of frost as they fall, to avoid large puddles to clean up later. When all the frost has been removed wipe down the sides with a weak water and bleach solution (1/2 teaspoon bleach to one quart water). Dry well and you're ready to replace the frozen foods.

Small knife caddy

A toothbrush holder makes a dandy caddy for transporting a small paring knife.

Better beater scraper

Scrape the batter from the mixer beaters with a fork. It quick and easy because the fork scrapes both sides of the beater's tines at the same time.

Leftover sweets

Those last few baked treats can that have turned a bit hard don't need to land in the trash. They're still perfectly edible, they just need a new purpose. Drop them into the bowl of your food processor and give them a whirl. You'll end up with perfect crumbs for topping ice cream or other desserts. If you have enough, substitute for the graham cracker crumbs when making the bottom layer or "crust" of a dessert recipe.

Cleaner copper

A thin layer of ketchup smeared over copper cleans it quite well without any scrubbing. Just let it sit for about 5 minutes before rinsing. This is much cheaper than commercial copper cleaner and easier too, as the cleaners require scrubbing.

Line with foil

It sounds so simple, but it's not always that easy. But here's a way to make lining any pan with foil a cinch. Turn the pan to be lined over and lay a piece of foil over it molding it to the exact shape of the pan. Now turn the pan right side up and set the perfectly-molded foil into it. Perfect fit every time.

Soap stretch

Dishwashing liquid is so thick and concentrated, you can mix it 50/50 with water. Continue using the same amount as before. You'll find the diluted option works just as well, probably because we use too much of the concentrate. Provided the label on the soap container does not say "Do not mix with bleach," you can add a couple of teaspoons of bleach to add a disinfecting feature to your liquid dishwashing soap.

Stainless steel sinks

To make your stainless steel sinks shine, polish with a small amount of baby oil.

Leftover wine

Don't throw out the last of the wine. Instead freeze it in an ice cube tray. Now you have just the right amount for a future recipe.

Almost empty reminder

When you notice you're running low on dishwashing detergent or other items you use regularly, let that be the signal to watch for a coupon so you can replenish. Don't wait until you are out or you'll end up having to pay full price. A quick call to that product's customer service toll-free number (find it right on the package) may land you a few coupons in the mail. Simply tell them how much you enjoy their product.

Easy off caps

In time sticky items like honey and syrup will crystallize at the top of the container, making it difficult to remove the lid. Coat the top of the container with nonstick spray and the bottle will open with ease every time.

Sticky wrap

If your kitchen's plastic wrap is always getting stuck to itself and then pulling off unevenly, keep the wrap in the freezer. It will roll off perfectly without sticking to itself. Within a matter of seconds it will stick to its intended surface.

Sink liner

Even if you have a garbage disposal you may opt not to put lots of potato peels or other vegetable trimmings through it. But if you peel into the sink as many do, that means you have to fish it all out, which can be messy. Try this: Line the sink with several layers of newspaper. Now start your peeling. Once done, simply fold over the paper and place the whole thing in the trash, or dump the debris into the compost heap. Easy, quick and effective.

Big ice

Fill muffin tins with water and freeze. Pop the big cubes out and store in a large plastic bag in the freezer. You need only one of these big ice cubes to cool a drink. And they last a long time.

Sanitary straws

Flexible drinking straws always seem to come in a plastic bag or box that opens at the top. This represents a sanitation problem if every member of the family reaches in to get a straw. It's impossible not to touch the top of all the straws. Here's a solution: Empty the entire box of drinking straws into a gallon-size food storage bag, placing the straws horizontally in the bag. Now when you reach in to get one, you are not touching the drinking end, but rather grabbing one from the middle.

Garlic slicer

The cheese plane you keep in the kitchen drawer does a fine job on cheese. And it works great on garlic, too. Instead of pulling the plane across the garlic as you would a block of cheese, stand the plane on its front tip, then draw the garlic across the blade. Makes perfectly thin slices of garlic every time.

Cabinet shelf liner

Instead of typical shelf paper, use peel-and-stick floor tile to line your kitchen shelves. They are simple to cut with utility scissors and clean up easily with a damp cloth. And when they're on sale, peel-and-stick vinyl floor tiles are quite cheap.

More than a cake tester

A metal cake tester can easily fill in for other objects in the kitchen. Use it to test the doneness of vegetables. Easily skewer a pickle from deep inside a jar. The diameter of the cake tester is so small, it is likely just the right size to unclog the holes in the top of a salt or cheese shaker.

Bag o' trash

Store the roll of kitchen trash bags in the bottom of the trash can under the bag you are using. The next time you bag the trash pull it out, tie and toss. Then just reach down to pull out a new clean bag. Using this trick you always have a fresh, clean bag at your fingertips ready to go. No more having to go somewhere else to find the bag replacement.

Easy cleanup

One way to get sticky substances out of measuring cups and spoons is to spray a little cooking spray into the measuring container. Now measure out the sticky substances like honey and molasses. This allows the ingredients to slide right out. It works wonders.

Stains and plastic ware

Spray your Tupperware or other plastic storage containers with non-stick cooking spray before pouring in tomato-based sauces. No more red stains.

Easy shelf-paper removal

Adhesive shelf paper can be very difficult to remove the longer it sits on a shelf. In anticipation of wanting to remove it someday, do this: Cut a piece of waxed paper that is one inch smaller on all sides than the pieces of shelf paper you are about to lay down on the shelf. Position the wax paper in the center so that the edges of the adhesive-backed paper comes in direct contact with the shelf on all four sides. Now the shelf paper will adhere nicely, but will also come up easily when that time comes.

Stop the roll around

Get your rolling pin out of the drawer or cupboard and up onto the wall. You'll always know where it is and gain valuable drawer or cupboard space in the process. Measure the distance between the handles of the rolling pin. Now mount two inexpensive wooden curtain rod holders to match this width. Simply suspend the rolling pin as you would a curtain rod.

Unequal colors

When you are in the market for a new appliance keep in mind that the price will vary according to which finish you select. For example, stainless steel is typically the most expensive option, while surprisingly black is often the cheapest. Check the prices before you settle on your color scheme.

Quick vacuum seal

If you don't have a drinking straw handy to suck the air out of a zip-type bag, try this: Submerge the opened bag almost to the top into a basin of water, but not so far that water spills in. Now drop the items into the bag. You'll notice that the pressure of the water forces the air out of the bag. Zip it closed, remove from the water and dry the outside of the bag.

Putty knife trick

In an ideal world no one would have food stuck to the kitchen floor. And while you wait for that to happen, keep a clean putty knife with your kitchen tools. Use it to clean up dried-on food from your kitchen floor. Easy, fast and very effective.

Stretch the detergent

Instead of filling both detergent cups in your automatic dishwasher, try filling the one you do not close with baking soda instead—but only if you do not have a water softening unit installed. In that case, adding too much baking soda could create an adverse chemical reaction that could result in permanently etched glassware.

Refrigerator odor

Used coffee grinds can absorb even the worst of refrigerator odors. Simply take out the used coffee filter with the coffee grinds in it and place it in your refrigerator in an open container. Just replace the coffee grinds each time you finishing brewing up a pot of coffee.

Save the fridge

To reduce the times the refrigerator is opened during the hot summer months, store bottles of chilled water and snacks in your ice chest. Freeze water in milk cartons to keep the ice chest chilled. Keeping this right by the refrigerator will cut down on refrigerator "shopping" by little ones, and your refrigerator will not have to work so hard.

Quick dish cleanup

Keep a spray bottle filled with a very weak solution of water and dishwashing detergent (about 1 tablespoon to two cups of water) right by the sink. As you have large items or other kitchen utensils that cannot go into the dishwasher, simply give them a spray, a quick swish and a good rinse to cut down on counter clutter.

Smells good

Remove the dryer sheet from the dryer after use and put it in the bottom of the trash can. Then put in your trash bag. The dryer sheet seems to absorb the odors.

Jam-free

Don't you hate it when you try to pull open the drawer where you keep boxes of foil, plastic wrap, parchment and waxed paper and the tops catch, causing a major drawer jam? You can easily fix this problem if when returning the box to the drawer you simply turn it top side down. Now the drawer will glide open every time with no obstructions.

Drawer space

Take the boxes of plastic sandwich bags, rolls of aluminum foil, plastic wrap and wax paper out of the drawer and stand them upright in the perfectly shaped compartments of an empty beer or soda six-pack container. This takes up less space in a cabinet than the same items placed in a drawer.

Tidy stovetop

Splatters from a hot pan can make a mess of the other burners on the stovetop. You can prevent this if you simply have a baking or cookie sheet upside down over the burners not in use. Splatters hit the tray, not the burners. Just pop the tray into the dishwasher, and your stovetop stays much cleaner.

Free measuring devices

The small scoops that come with baby formula measure exactly one tablespoon. Don't throw them away. They make perfect measuring devices for coffee, grits and other dry food pantry items. And the lid that comes with liquid laundry detergent measures several increments that are handy for measuring rice, flour, sugar and so on. You'll find dozens of uses once you start thinking about it.

More efficient dishwasher

If your dishwasher seems to be losing effectiveness, check the water inlet valve. There's a little screen in there that could be clogged. It's easy to clean. Turn off the power, then go to *www.repairclinic.com*, find your appliance and follow the directions for removal of this small part. Once removed, unscrew the part of the valve closest to the water source to reveal the debris screen. The screen is easily pulled out and cleaned with a toothbrush. Reverse the steps to complete the project. Cleaning may be all that's needed. If, however, this valve has failed, it's easy to order a replacement and install it yourself.

Septic care

If you have a septic tank, put one tablespoon of yeast down the kitchen drain once a month to keep your tank clear and functioning properly. This will reduce the frequency of your service calls to have it pumped out.

Mini cutting board

The lid from an empty Cool Whip container makes a great cutting board. The plastic won't harm your knife, and it's the perfect size for cutting a tomato, onion or pepper. The lip around the edge catches any juices, and the lids are dishwasher-safe. When they get nasty-looking just throw them out.

Cheaper kitchen towels

Buy kitchen towels in the automotive section of your department store or at an automotive specialty store. A typical price is about $5 per dozen. These towels don't shed, they wash well and last a long time. They're great in the kitchen and for cleaning around the house.

Bar mops

Instead of paying upwards of three dollars each for kitchen towels that don't last long, buy "bar mops." These are square kitchen towels available at restaurant supply stores and from time to time at warehouse discount clubs. They cost less than a dollar each, are more absorbent than regular kitchen towels and hold up well during repeated washing and drying.

Refrigerator odors and mold

If your refrigerator quits or you have to unplug it for a move or repair, make sure you leave the door slightly ajar. If not, mold will form due to moisture inside. If yours does develop mold and you cannot get the smell out, do this. First clean the inside of both the freezer and refrigerator with a weak bleach solution (1 part bleach to 10 parts water). Next crumple enough newspaper to fill the refrigerator and freezer compartments. Change daily until the odors disappear.

Sharpening scissors

It is very frustrating when scissors become dull and seem as if they are of no use anymore. But don't give up on them. Fold a large piece of aluminum foil a few times so you have a substantial thickness. Cut through it with those dull scissors. Repeat four or five times. The result is razor-sharp, like-new scissors!

Smelly garbage disposal

Most garbage disposals stink from time to time. You can buy little packets of mystery cleaner to deodorize your disposal but they cost money. But did you know that your dishwasher most likely drains into your disposal as well? Every time you run your dishwasher, simply run the disposal while the dishwasher is draining its pre-wash and wash cycle. The dishwasher detergent will clean the disposal, too.

Easy dish soap dispenser

To maximize your dish soap and

slow its consumption, purchase a bottle pour top (the kind found on liquor bottles that bartenders use) for about $2 at any store that sells kitchen gadgets. Fill a wine bottle (or other decorative container with a narrow neck) with your dish-washing liquid. Apply the pour top. Now you can dispense just a small amount of detergent at a time—the correct amount to do the job. The decanter looks great on the counter, too.

Flatware in the dishwasher

When loading up the dishwasher separate the spoons, forks, and knives in their own compartments so when you put them away—no sorting. Saves time and effort.

Single drink blender

You know those drink blender machines that whip up your milk shake right in the glass? Forget them! Just get out your hand-held kitchen mixer and attach only one of the beaters. It fits into into th e glass and you can whiz away. Easier cleanup, too.

Paper and plastic, please

When asked, "Paper or plastic?" at the supermarket, ask for both—ask for your purchases to be double-bagged, first in plastic then placed into paper. You will have a much sturdier situation as you transport and unload the groceries. As a bonus you will have a nice variety of bags for trash at home.

Fill as you go

When washing dishes start with just a little water. Wash the small items first and run the rinse water into the wash water. By the time you wash the larger items you will have enough water and you haven't wasted any during rinsing.

Water ready

Wash two-liter plastic soft drink bottles and fill with water, leaving at least 1 inch headroom. Apply cap. Store in the freezer. Now you have fresh water in case of a power outage. And if you leave the door closed, the freezer will remain very cold for a long time without power if it is packed with many of these bottles of frozen water.

Drain maintenance

For slow drains, use this drain cleaner once a week to keep drains fresh and clog-free: 1/2 to 1 cup baking soda, 1 cup white vinegar, 1 gallon boiling water, 1/2 used lemon. Pour baking soda down drain/disposal, followed by vinegar. Allow the mixture to foam for several minutes before flushing the drain with boiling water.

Pie crisp

When taking pie from the oven, do not put it on a flat surface or a table or counter to cool but on a high wire rack. The air under the rack helps to keep the crust crisp.

Sweet not sour

To sweeten cream that has turned sour, add 1/4 teaspoon baking soda to 1 quart of cream.

Bun re-heat

To reheat rolls or muffins, put them on an aluminum baking sheet and cover them tightly with an aluminum cake pan. Set into a moderate oven for about 10 minutes. They will look and taste just like freshly-baked rolls.

Eggs uncracked

When cooking eggs wet the shells thoroughly with cold water before placing them into the boiling water. This will keep them from cracking.

Half onion

After cutting an onion in half, spread a little butter on the half left over and it will keep fresh and will not mold.

Flaky trick

To make a flaky pie crust, use cream instead of water.

Pie vent

When you make a double-crust pie, put a piece of macaroni upright through the top crust to create a vent. Now the juice will boil up through that vent and will not run out into the oven.

Clean pot

Before scalding milk, rinse out the saucepan with a little hot water. This will prevent the milk from sticking to the bottom of the pan.

Pizza cutter for everything

Pizza cutters can be used for so many more things than just slicing up pizza. They're great on finger foods, sandwiches, pancakes, toast, lunch meats—anything that needs to be bite-sized. And you might even find time to use it to cut your pizza, too.

Odor-free hands

After chopping garlic the best way

to get the odor from your hands is to soap up your hands and rub them on your kitchen spigot. Stainless steel removes the odor. They sell stainless steel stones for this very purpose, but why spend the money?

Bag organizer

Organize the plastic grocery bags you are collecting under your sink by placing them into an empty tissue box. When you need a bag, you can just pull one out like you would a tissue.

Boiling pot help

If your pot is about to boil over (even after you have turned down the burner), throw a couple of metal spoons into the pot. The metal will absorb some of the heat and prevent your meal from spilling all over the stove.

Bowl caps

If you have bowls or kitchen equipment that you stack inside each other in the cabinet and rarely use, you know that dust often settles inside them. To prevent this from happening, simply take a shower cap and stretch it over the top of the bowls. The cap will protect your bowls from dust.

Burnt-on food

When you burn anything in your pan while cooking, just put about a cup of water in it, return it to the burner and let it boil about five minutes. The burnt food will come out with a little scrubbing.

Cheap produce bags

Grocery stores will sometimes sell customers their produce bags for a very low price, and a roll lasts forever. You can use them for your produce, sandwiches and cheese. Twisting them several times at the top will keep the produce inside fresh.

Cleaning Tupperware

To clean stained Tupperware, use baking soda. The plastic will look brand-new when you are finished.

Disposable cutting board

Chop vegetables and meat on paper plates. It's cleaner than a chopping board and you can throw it away when you are done.

Freshen plastic container

If you have plastic food containers that retain a smell, even after being washed, stuff several wadded up pieces of newspaper inside and seal the container overnight. The newspaper will absorb most of the odor by morning.

Hand wash prep

If you squirt some dish soap on the sink divider before you clean chicken or deal with another messy item, you can wash your hands with that squirt of soap without messing up and possibly cross-contaminating the soap dispenser.

Hang a recipe

When following a recipe from a magazine that you are reluctant to cut, take a hanger and two clothespins and clip the open magazine to the hanger. Hang from your kitchen cabinet doorknobs or handles. You can read the recipe as needed without dropping ingredients on the paper or wasting counter space.

In the bag

Use the empty bag inside the cereal box for crushing graham crackers, soda crackers or dried bread to make crusts and crumbs. These bags are much more durable than plastic storage bags and they are virtually free.

Knife safety

Loose knives in the silverware drawer can be a safety hazard. Take a paper towel roll, flatten, and staple one end closed. Slip your knives into this homemade sheath. No more cut fingers.

Laminate recipe

To laminate recipes that you clip from the newspaper and magazines, lay the clipping on the sticky side of a piece of clear packing tape that is twice the length of the clip. Then fold the tape over so both sides are covered. The tape is usually just the right size for the column.

Now and later

When you are measuring the dry ingredients for a recipe like cookies or muffins, grab a plastic container or bag. Measure out another single or double batch into the container, label it, and put it in the cupboard or 'fridge. You'll cut the prep time for the next baking venture.

Open a jar

Can't get that lid off a tightly sealed jar? Try using your mouse pad to grasp and turn the lid. Works like a charm.

Pepper grinder

If you have one, you can use the old fashioned hand crank coffee grinders on your pepper, too. You can mix whatever blend of pepper you wish and play with how coarse you want the grind. Then when cooking just crank a few times, open the drawer and sprinkle.

Pie mat

Instead of using waxed paper for rolling out a pie crust, try a silicone mat or two. The crust won't stick to the mats and it only takes a quick rinse to clean them off.

Spatter guards

Buy coffee filters at the dollar store and use them as spatter guards for food heating in the microwave. They will help the food warm more quickly as well.

Spice organizer

If a drawer organizer for spices is a little out of your price range, purchase some non-skid fabric and place it in the drawer you were intending to use for spices. The spices will stay lined up and barely move when you open the drawer.

LAUNDRY

Laundry

Fabric softener savings

Keep a container on your dryer—an empty tissue box works well—to hold used fabric softener dryer sheets. When you have a stash, toss three used sheets into a load to be dried instead of one new sheet.

Coat cleanup

Try spraying stains on your winter coat with oven cleaner and allow to dry overnight. This is a tried and true trick used in some used clothing stores to get coats ready for sale.

Unshrink wool

Mix a solution of one gallon lukewarm water and two tablespoons baby shampoo. Soak the garment for about ten minutes. Now the important part: Don't rinse! Simply blot out all the excess water with a dry towel and very gently lay it flat on a fresh towel. Reshape slowly and carefully stretch it back to its original size. Dry out of direct sunlight or heat. This tip comes from the Wool Bureau who verifies this technique will work provided the fibers have not become permanently damaged.

Fill first

When filling the washing machine, add the detergent first, let the water fill and then add the clothes. Adding the detergent first allows the soap to dissolve and distribute well and also helps to prevent overloading the washer since it is hard to shove too many clothes into a tub full of water.

Yellow out

Vintage linens, doilies and other textiles pieces that have turned yellow may be restored back to bright white by following this procedure: First soak the item in lemon juice. Ring it out well, then lay flat or hang the items in the bright sunshine for a full day. Launder as usual.

Laundry soap (liquid)

You really can save a lot by making your own laundry detergent. In a saucepan mix 1/3 bar Fels Naptha Laundry bar soap, grated, with 2 cups of water and simmer until soap is dissolved. Add 1/2 cup borax and 1/2 cup super washing soda, stirring until it dissolves. Remove from heat. In a 2-gallon household bucket add 2 quarts of very hot water to the soap mixture. Stir until well mixed. Top off bucket with cold water and stir until mixed well. Let it sit for 24 hours before using. Use about 1/2 to one cup per load. This recipe multiplies well, but you'll need a 5-gallon bucket. This is a non-sudsing detergent. If you need suds to prove it is "working" this is probably not your detergent. But at about 2 cents a load this is going to be a big money saver. All of the ingredients required to make your own laundry detergent are available in some supermarkets. Or online at *www.soapsgonebuy.com.*

Laundry soap (powdered)

1 cup grated Fels Naptha Laundry bar soap, 1/2 cup washing soda and 1/2 cup borax. Mix and store in airtight container or bag. For light loads, use 2 tablespoons. For heavy loads, use 3 tablespoons.

Pre-treating

Keep a container of laundry pretreatment by each family member's clothes hamper with a new rule that all stains must be treated before landing in the hamper. Getting to a stain early is key to its removal so this will help out immeasurably in making sure that happens.

Washing machine saver

Never set the washing time for longer than 10 minutes. Most laundry detergents have done all the work they are going to do by then; the rest of the time your clothes are just agitating in the dirty water. It may not seem like much, but when you multiply these couple of minutes by the hundreds of loads of wash being done in the typical household, limiting the wash time will save on electricity and wear and tear on the appliance.

Odor rid

Instead of fabric softener, pour 1/2 cup of white vinegar into your washing machine's compartment designed for liquid softener (or the refillable Downy ball). Don't worry, your laundry will not coming out smelling like salad dressing. White vinegar counteracts detergent and does a great job of releasing the soap residue when it is released during the rinse cycle. Additionally, another natural property of vinegar is that it removes tell-tale odors—the kind of odors that often remain even after washing with detergent.

Crayon stains

If you have kids you probably have problems with crayon stains—the worst being those from crayons that have melted in the dryer and taken up permanent residence on otherwise perfectly good clothes. To remove these stains, saturate the spot with WD-40, working it into the stain with your fingers. Once the WD-40 has begun to break down the petroleum base of the crayon, apply concentrated detergent to remove the stain and then place the garment through another wash cycle. It works like a charm.

Laundry savings

Keep a piggy bank close to the laundry area. As you find coins and currency in the wash, feed the pig. If your family members are particularly careless, by the time you need a new washer and dryer you could have a nice down payment with your newfound source of savings.

Stain remover standby

If you run out of stain remover, try this: Apply liquid laundry detergent to the stain. Sprinkle with powder laundry detergent. Scrub area with a brush. Launder as usual. This is a bit time consuming, but usually quite effective.

Annoying tags

Tags at the neck of a garment can be quite an irritant for the wearer. But removing them eliminates much-needed laundry information. Here's the solution: Remove the tag then sew it to an inside pocket or hem. You may have to play hide and seek but you won't run the risk of unfortunate shrinkage.

Blood stains

Hydrogen peroxide poured through the blood stain on kitchen linens, clothes and other fabrics will remove most, if not all, of the stain. Follow with your favorite stain remover and wash as usual. Caution: Hydrogen peroxide can act like bleach so be sure to test in an inconspicuous place first.

Pitch out

Here's a quick and easy solution for wood pitch that gets on clothes, shoes or hands: automotive hand cleaner. Just rub a glob into the pitch. Or if you do not have that particular item in the garage, grab a can of WD-40. Either one will make quick work of that pitchy mess. Follow with soap and water or in the case of clothes, launder as usual.

Laundry sense

Not every garment needs to be laundered after each wearing. To keep track you need to know how many times an item has been worn. Here's a great way to do that: Keep a stash of rubber bands in a convenient place in or near the closet. At the end of the day if you determine an item is not yet ready for the wash, hang it up and slip a rubber band over the hanger hook. This tells you how many times that item has been worn. Now you have the information you need to determine when an item is destined for the laundry or dry cleaner.

Cleaning Old Glory

If you fly a U.S. flag at home and it's getting a little dirty, you can possibly get it dry-cleaned free. Many, if not most, dry cleaners in the U.S. will clean any American flag for no charge.

Laundry fresh

Place a fabric softener sheet in the bottom of your laundry hamper. This will keep the area smelling fresh until those dirty clothes can get to the washer.

Quick dry

Want your clothes to dry in half the time? Toss one or two clean dry bath towels with each load.

Stretch the softener

Cut a new sponge into several pieces. Place them in a small container that has a lid. Add one capful of liquid fabric softener and two cups of water. Cover. Each time you dry your clothes drop in one of the small sponges (squeezed well so it is not dripping) into the dryer. Softener will last through many more loads of drying and your clothes will still be soft and static-free.

Better bleaching

Wait 5-6 minutes after the clothes start agitating before adding bleach. Bleach can destroy detergent enzymes if added immediately. Waiting gives the enzymes time to attach to soil in fabrics.

Long live your clothes

Before washing your clothes turn them inside out. This transfers the wear and tear of the agitation and tumbling to the inside of the fabric so clothes stay looking new longer.

Brrrr!

Use cold water for laundry that is only lightly soiled. Heating the water is the major cost in washing clothes. Switch to cold water washes and save. As long as your laundry isn't heavily soiled, cold water is just fine. And you can expect to save about $1.50 a load, depending on your specific conditions.

Floor mats

Take all floor mats out of the car and load them into a triple loader at the coin-operated laundry. Wash in warm water, cold rinse cycle and remove before the spin cycle. Lay flat to air dry.

Re-blacken

If black clothing is beginning to turn brown, restore black color by adding coffee to the wash water.

Coke out

To release grease stains from clothes, dump the contents of a can of Coca-Cola in the wash cycle.

No more lost socks

Give each family member a lingerie bag of a different color with this instruction: All dirty socks go into your own bag. When it's full—but not stuffed—zip it closed and toss it into the hamper. On wash day, just drop the bags into the washer and dryer and send them back to their owners. No more sock orphans. And even better: You'll never have to sort socks again.

Washer maintenance

Do not overload your washing machine. The money you'll save using less water, detergent and electricity is minuscule compared to the cost of having your washer repaired. Overloading will actually cause parts to break over time. Having your washing machine working properly for many years will save more money than washing fewer loads.

Towel assignments

To make sure everyone in the family sticks with the same bath towel, attach a wooden clothespin to each person's towel on which you've written or painted his or her name. Having everyone stick with their towel for several days reduces the need to launder more frequently than necessary.

Baseball cap laundry

To wash a baseball cap so it comes out just like new, set in on the top rack of your dishwasher. Add detergent as usual and run it through a regular cycle, removing it before it goes into the heat cycle. Remove the cap and set it on a large coffee can or other item that will allow it to air dry while maintaining its shape. Once dry it will look like new.

No fuss delicates

Think you have to take that sheer voile blouse, beaded top, fringed silk shawl, or lace-trimmed dress to the cleaners? Think again! You can clean these at home by simply tying the articles in a cotton pillow case, knotting it closed, and washing in cold water on regular cycle. Beads, sequins, buttons and delicate laces will not fall to pieces, and garments can be restored by steam ironing or steaming in the shower.

Not just for hair

Cheap hairspray is a great spot remover, especially for ink and other tough stains. Just spray it on, allow to saturate, then wash as usual.

High-rise solution

If you live in a high-rise apartment with the laundry in the basement, get rid of that heavy laundry basket. Replace it with a new trash can that comes with wheels and a lid. It will hold a lot of clothes and travels well in an elevator.

Ironing on hold

At the end of the summer, pre-spot and launder your washables, but don't iron them. Put them in your out-of-season closet and forget them until the next year. After being stored for six months or so you'll probably want to launder them again to refresh them. Then you can iron them for the summer.

Line-drying

If you are partial to line-drying your laundry but wish the dried clothes were softer, do this: Once dry, toss them in the dryer with a dryer sheet for about 10 minutes. You'll have soft, line-dried laundry.

Set color

To prevent dark and bright colors from bleeding and fading prematurely, perform this treatment before items are washed for the first time: Fill the washer with cold water and add 2 cups of table salt. Agitate so the salt can dissolve, then turn the machine off. Add the new colored items and allow to soak for about 3 hours. Complete the cycle, followed by a complete rinse. Now the colors are set and will stay bright and dark much longer.

Red clay stains

You can get red clay out of white pants by adding Cascade automatic dishwasher powder with your regular laundry detergent. Add about 1/2 cup to your normal wash. Takes out even old stains and even greasy, oily ones, too.

Laundry stroller

Don't throw away your old baby stroller if you like to hang laundry on a clothesline. Either set the laundry basket in the stroller or just put all the wet things in without a basket, depending on the configuration of your stroller. Just push it along and the job will be much easier.

Hang-up space

If your laundry area is configured in such a way that opposing walls are fairly close together, put up a tension shower rod. You'll have the perfect place to hang clothes immediately as they come out of the dryer.

Wash rayon

Rayon can be washed right in your washing machine. No more trips to the dry cleaner. Simply wash your rayons in cold water, hang to dry and steam iron on "rayon" setting to restore to pristine condition.

Chewing gum challenge

Here's a quick way to get stuck-on chewing gum out of washables. Wash them using your regular detergent plus two heaping capfuls of liquid laundry detergent added to the wash cycle. The gum will just slide off.

Remove mildew stains

To remove mildew stains from clothes and linens, do this: Moisten stained spots with a mixture of lemon juice and salt, and then spread the item in the sun for natural bleaching. Follow with normal laundering.

Rust stains on washables

Rust is one of the trickiest stains to remove but this simple solution defies the idea that it is impossible: Rub a paste of equal parts salt and vinegar into the stain; let stand for 30 minutes then launder as usual.

Save on dry time

Your clothes dryer requires a lot of energy—whether it runs on gas or electricity. To cut down on running time do this: Before you take your clothes out of the washer, spin them 2 or 3 extra times. You will be amazed at how much more water comes out of the clothes. Now your clothes will dry faster and you will save money.

Spot cleaning

Got a spot on a dry-clean-only garment? Don't panic. Clean that spot with a baby wipe. You'll be amazed how quickly it comes up. Just allow the garment to air dry and you'll save yourself and your wallet a trip to the dry cleaner.

Screen clean

To wash a wool sweater without destroying its shape and size, lay it flat on a clean window screen and position it over the sink or tub. Baby shampoo is a great cold water wash for wool. Pour this through the sweater so the water drains into the sink (or tub) below. Follow with clear rinse water. No need to wring or squeeze. Simple allow it to air dry in place.

Three-way sort

Set up three baskets for your dirty laundry. One for colors, one for whites and one for spots. Now you know which items need to be spot-treated before landing in the washing machine.

Luggage carrier

You know those fold-up wheels you use to carry luggage when you travel? Keep them in the laundry room. Now when you want to hang up a load of clothes on the clothesline, just wheel it out and save your back. Wet clothes can be very heavy.

On the go

Hand sanitizer makes a dandy spot remover in a pinch. Keep some in your handbag and you'll always be ready to treat a stain.

Yet another spotter

Original blue Dawn dishwashing liquid gets just about any kind of spot out of washables. Keep a small squeeze bottle in the laundry room so it's always handy.

Zip your zippers

Close all zippers before washing to prevent the teeth from snagging other garments in that load.

Measure well

Instead of using the measuring device included with the laundry detergent, use a real 1/3 cup measure—the amount suggested for a normal size load of medium soiled clothes. Use the device that comes with the product and you'll likely use more detergent than necessary.

Mildew stains

If your clothes or linens develop a mildew stain, spray with Tilex Stain and Mildew Remover and launder right away. Stains will be gone, and clothes will be saved.

Four times longer

Cut dryer sheets into fourths. Use one strip per dryer load. You'll see that is sufficient to soften the whole load. And your box of dryer sheets will last four times as long.

Laundry

Easier ironing

To make your ironing more efficient, remove the cover from your ironing board and wrap the top with aluminum foil, then replace the fabric cover. Now the heat and steam will be reflected back to the garment as you iron, and your wrinkles will disappear much more quickly.

Stinky laundry

To remove even the nastiest organic odors and stains left behind by puppies, kittens, babies, seniors—you name it—add a cup of baking soda, a cup of borax and a cup of white vinegar along with your regular laundry detergent to the wash cycle set on Hot. Rinse, then rinse again. If this doesn't remove all traces of stain and odor, nothing will.

Glycerin soap

To remove a stain from clothing, dampen it with water, rub well with glycerin soap (like Neutrogena), and rinse. You can see the stain disappear in seconds; rarely do you need to repeat the procedure. This really works on most types of stubborn stains.

Cold water wash

Baby shampoo is an excellent substitute for more expensive Woolite for washing delicate hand washables.

Delay dryer repairs

Use the low heat setting on your clothes dryer. The element lasts longer and your clothes will dry in about the same amount of time.

Vintage fabrics

To one gallon of water add 1/4 cup borax and 1/4 cup liquid chlorine bleach. Allow stained vintage linens to soak a few minutes. Rinse and allow to dry.

Great smelling laundry

Although laundry does its job of cleaning your clothes and making them look great, the smell of your clothes may dissatisfy you. Try adding a few drops of herbal shampoo to the wash cycle of your laundry to make your clothes smell delightful.

Distress jeans

Are your new jeans too stiff and look too new? Put them in the dryer along with several sheets of coarse sandpaper. Allow to tumble for a while. No heat necessary. This will soften and distress your new jeans all at the same time.

White deodorant marks

Hit those pesky deodorant marks with a clean cloth soaked in rubbing alcohol. Dries nearly instantly and you're ready to go.

Summer drying

During the hot summer months, to save on utilities—and to take advantage of the higher inside temperatures—hang freshly washed clothes on hangers spread out on the shower curtain rod. When your clothes are dry they are ready to be hung in the closet.

Money and Finance

Money and Finance

Price matching

Carry store ads with you when you shop, even if you don't plan on visiting that particular store. If a store will honor a competitor's price you have proof of the lower price right with you.

Fund your 401(k)

If you haven't maxed out your 401(k) then you can save money by doing the following: Increase your W-4 dependents and increase your 401(k) contribution. Go to the IRS website at *www.irs.gov* and use the IRS Withholding Calculator to figure your Federal income tax withholding so your employer can withhold the correct amount from your pay. Because your tax situation may change, you may want to refigure your withholding each year. This way you will immediately be saving the money you used to loan to the government interest-free!

Budget with scrip

If your kids' school sells scrip for fundraising, use it as a tool to stay on budget. At the beginning of each month, purchase scrip for the grocery stores, gas stations, department stores and fast food places you frequent according to your budget. When the scrip is gone, you know you're done spending in that category until next month. You won't overspend and your school will benefit, too.

Save on electricity

If you end up turning on all the lights in the house at night just so people won't trip in the dark, buy a couple of low wattage night-lights and plug them in everywhere. They will give you enough light to find your way and they don't use much electricity.

Bouncing checks

If you are a regular check bouncer, here's a way to kick the habit: On the day before you get paid, write out what bills that you need to pay, underestimating the amount you expect to receive on your paycheck (never overestimate). On payday, go to the post office or a convenience market and buy a money order for each bill that you plan to pay. Write the company name on the money order right away. This gives you no other choice but to pay the bill. It is guaranteed money so the order won't bounce, and it keeps you from spending it because it is too much hassle to get your money back. The small fee that you pay for the money orders is no comparison to the fees you will avoid for bouncing a check.

Keep receipts

Keep your receipts for all your major purchases in a place where you can easily find them—stapled to the inside back cover of the item's user manual. You can staple the warranty there, too. If you ever need to repair or return an item, you don't have to search for the receipts.

Info on the 'net

The website *www.bankrate.com* has great information about money management, including a section where you can look up CD, money market, and bank rates by state. Internet banks are also included in the state list if they have a high return rate. The site helps you understand investment lingo and make educated choices, too.

Paralegal help

If you are going through a divorce, a paralegal company can save you from some of the high attorney fees. Many charge much lower rates than attorneys and help you settle without going to court.

Shopping timer

Is it hard for you to stick to a time limit when shopping? Buy a small oven timer and set it to the desired time you wish to spend shopping. Stick it in your pocket or purse, and when the time goes off, it's time to go home. You can also set an alarm on your cell phone or watch, too.

Personal overdraft protection

To put the brakes on overdrafts, get in the habit of entering your reoccurring expenses into your checkbook the month before they will occur. Then you won't forget to write them in your checkbook during the following month. You can find out the date the payment is taken out on the previous statement. Enter that date in your checkbook register.

Download your charges

If you have a bank credit card, you may be able to download your charges on a daily basis into your check register using a computer check register program in Quicken or Microsoft Money. When your charges start getting close to your budgeted amount, then you can quit using the card for that month. It's also a great safeguard against a stolen credit-card number.

Money and Finance

Traveler's checks

If you are a AAA member, you can get no-fee traveler's checks. Even if you are not traveling, you can carry these in your wallet instead of cash. Most local merchants accept them even if you only live a mile down the road. And they're still replaceable if lost or stolen.

Check medical bills

Don't assume that a medical provider has the right to recoup payment from you for all expenses that your insurance did not reimburse. Always call your insurance company to verify that you are responsible for a payment and not the provider.

Free textbooks

If you are appalled at the cost of textbooks, try your public library first. You can save hundreds by checking the online card catalog for the textbooks you need. You can usually keep renewing the books for the duration of the class—and never spend a dime.

Tax class

Check out the tax classes that are being offered by nationally-known financial companies. You can save a lot on taxes by learning how to prepare your own return. If you have to pay for the course, it is a complete write-off when you itemize your tax return.

Never hurts to ask

A simple call to the credit-card company asking for a better interest rate can save you hundreds of dollars a year. All it takes is a few minutes and a little nerve. Call the Customer Service number on the back of your card. If they say no, ask to speak to a supervisor. Still no? Try again in a month. When they do offer you a better rate, it won't reduce your debt but it will allow more of your monthly payment to pay down the principal. And that will help you breathe easier.

Financial education

The USAA Education Foundation provides consumer education to the general public on the subjects of finance, auto, family, home, lifestyle and insurance. You can find resources on everything from investing and eldercare to inventory worksheets, health, home business and college financing. The information is in printable format online, or you can request free booklets to be sent to you. Check out the site at *www.usaaedfoundation.org*.

Expiration date

If you have taken extreme measures to ensure that you won't use a credit card (freezing it in a block of ice or cutting it to smithereens), make sure you still keep a record of the card number and expiration date while you are paying it off. If you need to call the credit-card company for some reason, they will need both pieces of information before they can help you.

Save on car insurance

Some insurance companies charge an installment fee each time they send out a statement for a bill. If you send in your payment before they send out the payment statement, you will not be charged for it. Check with your insurance company to see if this is their policy. Every little bit helps.

Saving receipts

Beware of the thermal paper that many stores use to print their receipts. It only takes a couple of months before the ink begins to fade and disappear. Before long, there is no longer a sales transaction on the receipt. So copy your receipts for big ticket items on a copy machine using regular paper so you can be sure to always have a record of your transactions.

Utility savings

At least once a year call each of your utility companies and ask them if they have any energy efficiency programs. A lot of companies either have programs (or know of state-sponsored programs) that offer free or low-cost weatherization materials, energy audits, water conservation programs and discounts on items like fluorescent light bulbs or new HVAC equipment. Often, it's just a phone call away.

Track long distance

Write all long-distance calls on the calendar on the date they are placed. Then you can check your phone bill for errors and also see if you need to cut back on your long-distance calls. Help keep calls short by putting a kitchen timer by the phone—when it goes off, time's up.

Writing checks

When writing checks use a pen with colored ink like pink, green or purple. It is harder for a crook to find a pen that color if they want to change the information on a check. Write as far as possible to the left of all lines and make sure you use the complete line so no one can make changes. If you do have room on the right side put in x's or a line to fill the extra space.

Money and Finance

Fun fund

Start a "fun fund" with your family. Each week put your accumulated change in the jar and tell your kids that they can either buy a treat with the money or save the money for an upcoming vacation or trip. You will teach the kids about saving and making good choices at the same time.

Free enrichment classes

If you are a lifelong learner, you may not want to spend all of your money on another college degree, especially if you've already earned a degree in the past. Instead, contact your local continuing education schools and inquire if they have scholarship programs or discounts for distributing their brochures. They get free publicity and you get a cheaper class.

Tip for tips

When tracking expenditures don't forget to count tips for your server, hairdresser and other service people. If not, you may throw off your budget.

Dollar a purchase

If you don't like dealing with change jars, commit to paying yourself a dollar every time you make a purchase. Think of it as charging yourself a service fee for shopping. You'll think twice about unnecessary stops at the mall and end up saving a lot in the bargain.

Free banking

Are you fifty-five or older? Want free banking? Check with your bank or another bank and see if they offer free banking services for seniors.

Online payment

One way to pay your credit-card bills quickly is to pay online. Most credit-card companies encourage you to go to their website and pay your bill online for free. Banks offer online bill pay features, too. It will save you late fees as well as the cost of a stamp.

Tax deductibles

Whenever you write a check that you know will be deductible on your income tax, use a red pen in your check register. When it's time to record your deductions, all you have to do is look at the red entries.

Read your plan

Read your health insurance annual booklet to familiarize yourself with your coverage. Busy health professionals and insurance claim representatives make mistakes. Don't pay the doctor's bill until the insurance claim has been processed and you have double-checked the Explanation of Benefits. If you find a mistake you can always call and get it corrected.

Car insurance claims

Do some research before you meet with your insurance representative to discuss the value of a claim. You will know if your insurance is offering you a low amount and you will have the knowledge and confidence to ask for more.

IRA savings

If you can't make the maximum IRA contribution each year, at least put in something. Some mutual funds will let you open an IRA for smaller amounts and at lower rates. A low interest rate may be better than none, especially since your money will be able to grow tax free.

Savings trick

Sometimes it is hard to save when money can be transferred between accounts too easily. So in addition to your regular savings, get another savings account at a credit union with no local branches and that is a couple of hours' drive away. You can send a check each month to deposit money, and you won't be as tempted to withdraw if you have to drive several hours or pay a bank transfer fee to get some money.

Kid's budget

Help your kids understand the value of budgeting. Each month give them an allowance to be used for clothing, lunches, and other expenses you identify. Help them set up an envelope for each expense and let them know they won't receive a bail-out from you if they blow it all on some toy.

Giving

Think of your giving as a reoccurring expense. Grab envelopes from your church or favorite charities and write out your checks for giving along with your bills. It will be easier to remain disciplined in your giving.

Unadvertised sales

Some local stores have sales that are not advertised in the Sunday paper. Keep a price notebook for your favorite stores and scan the aisles so you don't miss a bargain.

Hide money

To save money, "hide" it in your checking account by rounding the check total up to the next dollar amount. You can even round your deposits down to the nearest ten dollar amount. After a few months, you will have saved a bit and you can transfer it to a place where it will earn more interest.

Easy bill pay

Bills tend to come regularly and are for predictable amounts. Work out the cost of all your regular bills and divide that amount by the number of weeks in each bill period (12 for quarterly bills, 52 for annual ones, etc.). Then simply set those amounts each week in envelopes marked for utilities, insurance, etc. Make deposits in your savings account periodically if the money starts to pile up. If you save a little each week, you'll have enough for the bills when they come.

Charge yourself interest

If you don't have enough money for a necessity (make sure it is a necessity) in your checking account, don't run to your credit cards. Instead, borrow from your savings account or emergency fund and charge yourself interest. You'll be paying yourself and growing your savings account instead of making the credit-card companies rich!

Saving for improvements

Do you have a home that you'd like to fix up? Consider renting it out. Even if you only rent out a portion of the place it will help. The rent paid will supplement your remodeling. You can also deduct a percentage of the cost of improvements and repairs on your taxes, as well as depreciate both the rental property and the items purchased for it. If the combination of mortgage interest, maintenance, repairs and depreciation is more than the rental income, you can also reduce the amount of taxes you owe. If you're renting to a roommate, then you can take half of all of those expenses as deductions. Even if you break even tax-wise, you just added thousands of dollars of equity to your home that someone else paid for.

Break a habit

If you want to give up the credit cards but keep charging things you think you "have to have now," take your Rapid Debt-Repayment Plan, shrink it on your computer, print it out, and wrap it around your credit cards. You'll be reminded of your commitment to pay down your debt every time you want to reach for the credit cards.

Track credit cards

If you end up going into shock every time your credit-card bill arrives, track your charges throughout the month using an extra checkbook register. Keep it with your wallet and enter the amount charged every time you use the card. When the bill comes in, you can verify all the charges. You also won't go over your spending limit.

Stop charging habits

The next time you are tempted to charge something you can't afford right now, think about the amount of interest you would pay on that item. You can even write your interest rate on a piece of paper and wrap it around the card. Hopefully that sobering reminder will keep you on track.

Change jar

Every day, empty the change from your purse or pockets into a change jar. Make a habit of paying for small purchases with currency so you will accumulate even more change. Count it once a month and either deposit it in your savings account or use it for small indulgences like coffee or a newspaper throughout the next month. Either way, you won't break your budget.

Check safety

The next time you order checks have only your first initial (rather than your first name) and last name printed on them. If someone takes your checkbook, they will not know if you sign your checks with just your initials or your first name, but your bank will know.

ATM use

Each time you use your ATM card, keep the receipt in your wallet. For each purchase you make with the money, write the amount on the back of the receipt. You will be able to track your spending.

Monthly spending meetings

Meet monthly with your spouse to discuss your monthly spending plan. Discuss the results of last month's spending plan, identify areas of overspending and revise a new spending plan. This will help you both to stay on the same page with your finances.

Organize receipts

Have a file for each credit card and bank account you have and file the receipts for every transaction. You will know right where to find the receipt if there is a discrepancy on your statement. At the end of the year, store the receipts in separate manila envelopes and start over.

Check printing software

Did you know some computer programs allow you to print your own checks? If you decide to invest in this program, print a sample check and take it to your bank for verification of the format. You will get great rates on printing supplies, especially if you buy in bulk. And you'll never have to worry about running out of checks.

Paying down debt

If you are paying off credit-card debt, divide the set amount you have chosen for that bill and pay twice each month. By splitting the payment into two installments you cut the interest accrued on the debt since it is compounded daily.

Medical deductions

When itemizing your taxes, make sure you include any medical deductions for which you might be eligible. Keep track of the bills you pay that are not covered by your insurance. Track your mileage for doctor's visits, pharmacy trips and the hospital. Even if you don't have any major illnesses in a year, you may still be able to take the deduction.

Coffee indulgences

If you love a cup of expensive coffee now and then, budget for it. Decide on an amount that you are willing to spend on coffee in a month and put that amount on a gift card for your favorite coffee shop. You will be sure never to go over your budget.

Life insurance

Many people are paying too much for universal life insurance. Call your company and ask for a policy illustration. Then call three to four independent agents, give them some basic health info, and get them to mail you their best policy illustration. Compare the illustrations, looking at coverage, monthly cost, and cash value accumulation over the years. This can save you tens of thousands of dollars.

Free checks

When you open up a new checking account, sign up for one that offers free checks with your account. The checks aren't as pretty as others, but they work the same and you save a lot on check-printing fees.

Banking fees

Avoid a monthly maintenance fee at some banks by having direct deposits and making other deposits by the ATM. Also, open a savings account to link it to your checking account to avoid high NSF fees. Find out if you can avoid the monthly maintenance on your savings account with a low minimum by making at least one deposit per month and no more than one withdrawal a month. Keep close track of your accounts by tracking every penny you spend.

Organizing cash

If you don't like using envelopes to organize your budgeted cash in various spending categories, use colored paper clips. Assign a color to each category, and you can see at a glance how much you have to spend. You can keep all your cash in your wallet, too.

Long distance

Cancel your long-distance calling plan and buy each family member a prepaid phone card. Everyone can monitor their own long distance calls, and you won't have to worry about high bills.

Have kids help with bills

Teach kids about finances by having them help you pay the monthly bills. You can make out the checks for each amount and your child can address the envelopes and put on the stamps.

Where the money goes

Here's an easy way to find out where all your money goes. On payday put your paycheck stub in an envelope that will fit easily in your purse or brief case because you'll want to keep this with you at all times. Put every receipt into the envelopes after each and every purchase. If a purchase does not warrant a receipt (an item from a vending machine for example), write it on the outside of the envelope. You should also write what the purchase was for so you have no trouble knowing where to find the receipt if you need to make a return. On your next payday you will be able to look at your envelope and know exactly where every penny went. Another idea: If you prefer to track your money online, take a look at Mvelopes, *www.mvelopes.com*, a home budgeting system that uses the concept of envelopes to track your spending.

Stop "preapproved" applications

Tired of getting those pre-approved credit-card applications in the mail? Credit-card companies look to major credit reporting agencies for information on your credit. To take your name off the list simply call: 1-888-567-8688 and follow the automated prompts (you will be required to give your social security number, but they have it already so don't worry). Check the website at *www.optoutprescreen.com* for more information.

Free credit report

Check your credit report from Equifax, Experian and TransUnion. Don't assume these reports contain the same information. They may not, so you need to check all three. Go to *www.annualcreditreport.com* where you can get a free report from each company once each year. Caution: All other offers for a "free" credit report have strings attached.

Spending record

Instead of using 3x5 cards to keep track of your daily spending, use a pocket-size calendar/daily planner. It is the type that has a dated, lined, weekly spread over two pages. It fits nicely in a purse or pocket. Now you have no excuse for not keeping track of your spending. Also, the information for an entire year is kept in one place so it is easy to compare spending from week to week.

TV-free

For the cost of basic cable you can rent 2-3 movies per week. You may find this preferable to television because you can more easily monitor what you watch and regulate the amount of time spent in front of the screen. Chances are pretty good you'll spend more time talking to your kids, more time with friends and more time reading the paper and listening to the radio. And as a bonus you won't get bombarded by so many commercials.

Non-spending record

Every time you consider spending money but then refrain from doing it, write it down on your non-spending record. Add it up at the end of the month and give yourself a pat on the back. Now write a check for that amount and stick it in your savings, your kids' college fund, or special account.

Coin wrappers

If you save your change, you may think you need to buy your own coin wrappers at the office supply store. Before you do that, ask your bank or credit union. Most will give you all the wrappers you need for no charge at all.

Insurance discounts

If you've quit smoking, drinking or lost a substantial amount of weight, call your life insurance company and ask about having your premiums lowered. Also call your auto insurance company. Some offer discounts for non-drinkers and non-smokers, so find out what you need to qualify.

Want or need?

Before making any purchase, stop long enough to ask yourself if you're buying to impress or out of genuine need. You just might find yourself making fewer purchases for the purpose of impressing others.

Win-Win!

Do yourself and your favorite store a big favor. If you notice products in torn or damaged packaging, check with the management. Often they will be happy to reduce the price to remove the product from their shelves. They benefit by being able to maintain tidy displays; you benefit from the lower price.

Invest in your debt

Stash rebates, refunds and coupon savings in a secret place. When you have accumulated a few bucks, send it to the credit card at the top of your list. You can send it any time and for any amount and the company must, by law, apply that to the amount you owe. Every penny counts in driving down debt!

Cheap college

Consider attending a community college to fulfill the general education requirements for a four-year degree. Tuition at many community colleges is about one-fourth the cost at a four-year college.

Save deposit receipts

Always save your deposit receipts until you've reconciled them against your bank statement. You never know when you'll need to prove you made that deposit. Computer glitches and human mistakes do happen.

Private accounts

When paying by check, do not put the complete credit-card account number in the memo area of the check. Instead, just put the last four digits. The credit-card company knows the rest of the number, and anyone who might be handling your check won't have access to it with only four of its digits.

Mortgage principal pre-pay

Your mortgage lender is not likely to allow you to pay half of your payment every two weeks—also known as a bi-weekly payment schedule—without forcing you to pay a hefty fee for that privilege. And you don't want to do that because you will be locked into a biweekly plan. Here's what you can do: Divide your monthly payment by 12. Now pay that amount (1/12 of one payment) as an additional payment amount each month as you pay your regular payment. By the end of a year you will have paid 13 monthly payments—with the 13th going in its entirety to pay down the principal.

Know your stuff

Empty the contents of your wallet onto a photocopy machine so that you can make a copy of each item. Now turn each card over and take another copy of the backsides. Put this photo record in a safe place. In the event your wallet is lost or stolen you will have all the information you need (account numbers, expiration dates, phone numbers and so on) to cancel accounts and report the problem. You won't wonder what was in your wallet because you will have a copy of each and every item.

Too late, too early

Most retail stores have an unpublished policy that allows customers to receive the sale price for an item either a day before or a day after the beginning and the end dates of an advertised sale. But you have to know to ask.

Check register tips

Standing in line at the grocery store is not the best time or place to balance your checkbook. And hurrying to the car while chanting the total of the check you just wrote (but did not record) is not the best way to stretch your brain power. Relieve a lot of frustration by switching to duplicate checks. You always have an exact copy of the checks you write, providing a good record in the event you need to track down an occasional bank error, too.

Money management

If you find it difficult to consistently give from your income, do this: Start with $1 a week and increase it by $1 each week until you reach your goal. By the way, giving ten percent of your net income is an excellent goal and an activity that really will change your life.

Accountability

Agree with your spouse to each keep a small notebook with you at all times. Record every penny that you spend, then once a week or monthly—whatever works best for you—exchange notebooks. You can both see where there is over-spending and you will both see things about your spending that you might not have realized. This accountability of your spending to one another will make both of you more aware of your own spending. This is not easy to start but it really works if you are committed to getting your spending under control.

Yearly credit checkup

Never pay anyone to "fix your credit." Each year as you review your credit report (it's free, see a tip about that in this section), make a note of each and every error on it. Following the instructions that come with the report, dispute every error. Then follow up to make sure the corrections are made. By law, the credit bureau must respond to your request and either remove the errors or have proof that the information is indeed correct.

Check your checkbook

Now and then review your checkbook register. Place an X next to expenditures that were necessary. Place a Y by those that you now see were a waste of money. This is a simple exercise that will cause you to make better spending decisions because you will begin to see things as X or Y before you make the purchase, instead of waiting to review what's already happened.

Free energy savings

Watch for programs offered by your local utility company or community to help homeowners reduce energy usage. Some offer energy audits that will help detect leaks from unsealed windows or doors that do not fit tightly. Other campaigns to help lower energy consumption include coming to your home to wrap uninsulated pipes or to replace bulbs with ones that are more energy efficient. You just have to call to find out what your utility company is offering.

Sell your second-hand items

You can sell your second-hand books, videotapes, music CDs, DVDs, even trading cards at *www.half.com.* Best of all, the purchaser pays for the postage. Just list the items you have to sell online and wait for a buyer to request your item.

Free directory assistance

In exchange for you listening to a short commercial while they look up the number you need, 1-800-FREE411 will give you completely free directory assistance for any number within the U.S. Program it into your speed dial so that when you dial 411 it connects you to 1-800-373-3411.

Tax-free shopping

If there is a Veteran's Affairs (VA) hospital and medical center close to where you live, check out its canteen. Veterans Canteen Service (VCS) offers a variety of goods and services including quality brands for sale to the public, usually at costs considerably lower than retail chains. And it's tax-free, too. There is no extra hassle in buying anything. Plus, it's a great source for patriotic shopping. You won't check off your entire shopping list there, but for the basics, Veteran's Canteen Service (VCS) is hard to beat; *www.vacanteen.va.gov* has more details.

Easier sales

Have you noticed that toys and kids' clothes are the first to go at garage sales? At your next sale, have a sign-up sheet where you encourage your customers to leave their names and numbers so you can give them a call when you clean out your kids' toy boxes and closets next season. Who knows? You might have enough customers to sell out without hosting another public sale.

Cheap cable

Many cable service providers have a service plan they don't advertise: basic service for around $11.95 per month. Check it out. You won't get 500 channels, but you might get a lot more than regular broadcast TV and for a lot less than you're paying now.

Shop insurance

The Internet website *www.insweb.com* walks you through a series of questions regarding auto insurance and then presents you with companies willing to provide online quotes immediately. Try it, then select the cheapest. But don't agree to purchase it. Instead call your current insurance provider and tell them what you've found and that you're thinking about making the switch. Then wait. It's nearly guaranteed that they'll match that quote, but chances are good they'll even go lower.

Raise your rate

This only works if you pay your credit-card bill in full every month during the grace period. If you carry a balance, don't do this until you are debt-free. Open a savings account that attaches to your checking account and pays a relatively high rate of interest (*www.ingdirect.com* and *www.hsbc.com* are good examples). Keep most of your money in the savings account, leaving only enough money in your checking account for your mortgage payment and utilities. Put all other purchases on your credit card. Then when you get the bill, transfer enough from your savings to your checking to cover that payment. If you are earning 5% or more on your savings account, this allows you to keep that money in the account a bit longer each month and that means you earn more interest. This method requires financial maturity because it takes a lot of discipline to charge only what you can easily repay with in that grace period.

Mock shopping

When you feel the need to shop, pick up your favorite mail order catalog and go through it page by page, writing up your order. "Buy" everything and anything that catches your eye. By the time you are finished and add up the damage, you will be out of the spending mood, totally exhausted and shocked at the money you almost spent. This works especially well around the Christmas holidays.

Bill paying

To keep from paying bills after the due date record the due date and the payment above the stamp area on the outside of the envelope right when you receive it. For bills you pay with coupon books, put those coupons into envelopes and rotate them to the next month as soon as they are paid. Your due date needs to be a few days earlier than the date on the bill to preclude any late payments.

Finances in living color

A set of colored pencils will help you see things more clearly. Each time you write a check to a creditor, use the second line in the checkbook register to record how much of that payment was for interest (in red), the amount that is actually reducing the principal and attacking your debt (in green), and the new balance (in blue). This way you can see your progress at a glance. Red is a visual reminder of why you want to get out of debt.

Cut electric bill by $30

Go through your home and replace all 100-watt light bulbs with 75-watt bulbs. This could easily save 300 watts a month—or around $30 a month on your electricity bill. You cannot tell the difference but by doing this your bill will be lower immediately.

College costs

Most colleges and universities offer as part of their benefits package for full time employees tuition remission—meaning, a free college education. It gets even better. Many offer free tuition or reduced tuition for your dependents' undergraduate education after three years of service, too. It's really worth investigating. This might be worth it to a parent seeking a job change to work at an institution of higher learning in anticipation of a child attending that school.

Control the gimmes

Pulling the plug on your TV so you can cancel the cable or satellite bill could save $32 or more each month. But you're likely to benefit in other ways as well. You'll stop wanting stuff you and your kids see in commercials. Reports from families who have given TV the old heave-ho are quite amazing in terms of improved family times and more productive lives.

Overnight shipping

Before you pay for costly overnight shipping, check the UPS ground delivery schedule. Often if you ship within your state or region, the normal delivery is the next day. It costs about 1/3 the price of overnight—usually under $5 for a 1-pound letter (assuming you use a UPS shipping site that doesn't charge add-on fees). And you get free tracking at *www.UPS.com.*

Spread the risk

Individually, you and your friends are quite poor as investors. But collectively, if each of you were to put up $20, it's possible you'd have enough to invest in the stock market. That improves the likelihood that you can make back your original investment, and then begin to reinvest your profits. And if things don't go as planned, none of you have taken on too big a risk as to be devastated financially.

Benefit for military

Members and veterans of the U.S. armed services may purchase automobile, life and disability insurance through USAA, a company that deals only with individuals who have a connection to the U.S. military. Suppose you were never in the service, but a parent was—that may qualify you to join. As an adult child of a member, you may be eligible, too. USAA rates and benefits are excellent. Find out if you qualify at *www.usaa.com* or 1-800-531-8111.

Complain here

If you have a complaint or inquiry about a national bank, credit-card company, or national mortgage company, and are not getting resolution, contact the Office of the Comptroller of the Currency (OCC) for help. You can write them at OCC Customer Assistance Group, 1301 McKinney Street, Suite 3450, Houston, TX 77010. Include your name and address as well as the bank's name and address.

You can fax your inquiry/complaint, 1-713-336-4301, or call 1-800-613-6743. If the bank's name contains the word "National" or the letters "NA" in the legal title, it is a national bank.

Trial run

Before plunging into a new car payment, try it on for size for a few months to see if it fits into your monthly finances, as you assume it will. Start making those exact payments to yourself. Set a due date and then never be late writing that big check and placing it into your savings account. After six months, if it's as comfortable as you thought it would be, perhaps you can afford a new car. At the worst, you'll have saved a tidy sum in the process. This is an excellent tactic for a teen who is dying to have a car because it lets all of you test those waters.

Extra paychecks

If you get paid every two weeks, or 26 times per year, build your spending plan around two paychecks per month. Then those two times during the year when you receive three paychecks in one month, use those extra checks to build your savings account. Provided you stick to your regular budget, those two checks will be like found money.

Cut ten years

If you make the equivalent of one extra house payment each year and you have a 30-year mortgage, you will actually have your house paid for in about twenty years. Make sure the extra money you pay over your normal payment is directed to the principal, not credited toward future interest payments. Write the additional amount in a separate check and add "Principal prepayment only" in the memo line on the check.

Teens and money

Can't decide on how much allowance to give your kids? Set the rate at their age plus one (just because) per week. Or month. This means a ten-year-old would receive $11. By the time your kids are teens, they'll have enough to learn to manage, but not so much they can do anything that will cause financial harm.

Pain-free savings

Every time you get a raise, increase your direct deposit to savings by the same amount. If your company doesn't have direct deposit write out a check for each pay period for the next 12 months now, then simply date and mail a check to savings each time you get paid. The trick is doing it immediately, as soon as you get a raise. And if you can make it automatic, it will become a useful habit. You won't miss money you don't see in the first place.

Rebate routine

When you apply for a rebate, make a note in your calendar on the date you mailed the paperwork and the date the rebate is due (usually it is 4 to 6 weeks after the company receives it). If by the farthest date the rebate has not arrived, contact the company. Curiously some rebates never seem to come back on their own. It takes several calls or stern "reminders" to get that thing moving and on its way back to the customer.

Giving, saving

Give your kids their allowance in small bills and/or coins. Now it is easy for them to see how to give and save from the total without having to get change. That is a good lesson as well because it's better to take care of these two important activities—giving and saving—before you are tempted to spend all you have.

Online banking

There is a fringe benefit to online bill paying. If you schedule a payment and it somehow gets to the merchant late due to a bank error, most banks will reimburse any late fees and make any corrections to your credit report if needed. If you are still paying your bills manually by writing out checks and mailing them, you do not have that kind of a back up—even if your payment arrives late through no fault of your own. Naturally there are couple of conditions. First you must schedule a set time before the payment is due (the bank will include this in the online agreement and generally display it on the payment screen as well) and you have to provide correct information for the payment to be processed. Conditions may vary from one bank to the next depending on how they process payments, so always be sure to read the online legal agreement carefully as well as any payment instructions the bank provides.

Stop the bouncing checks

Don't use your ATM or debit card to purchase gas unless you are very clear on the process. The company will put a hold on your bank account for considerably more than your gas purchase—at least $75. This can wreak havoc on your account if you are running short. Gas companies can't know how much you are going to spend when you swipe your debit card, so they have to assume it will be the maximum, or about $75. It can take hours or days for the hold to be cleared, during which time if you try to spend that money your account will bounce.

CO2 to cash

Do not purchase or drink any carbonated drinks for a month (no sodas!). Instead, every time you want to reach for a soda, drop a dollar in a jar. That's the minimum that you pay at the vending machine or fast food restaurant. You'll feel better, will likely lose weight, drink a lot more water, and have anywhere from $60 to $120 or more in your jar at month's end.

Restaurant receipt

Snap a picture of your restaurant receipt together with your signature and the amount of tip you authorized using your camera phone. Now you will have proof if the charge goes through with an altered tip and total—something that's been reported to happen and without the customer ever knowing. Your photo gives you indisputable proof of what you really wrote in case someone gets sneaky.

Fundraisers

Many schools have fundraisers where kids go door-to-door. Ask the kids if they know how much the school receives per item and if you can make a donation to the school, via check, for that amount. For example if the fundraising item is gift wrap and the school gets $5 per order, write the student a check for $5 made payable directly to the school (not the fundraising company). You've made a donation to help the cause but you won't have to deal with fundraising stuff you don't really need or want.

Call before you go

When unsure about whether or not a business will perform a service (repairs, etc.), call and speak to someone first. Ask them specifically whether they can help you and what they figure will be the estimated cost. Get their name, too.

Unconditional return policies

Many retailers (especially mail order) will accept returns unconditionally with no time limit. So if you have clothes hanging in your closet that still have the tags, try to return them.

Easy save

To start saving money for the future, pay yourself the same day you pay your bills. Decide what you're worth and write yourself a check before you start paying the bills.

Money and Finance

Extra savings

At the end of each pay period, transfer the money left in your checking account into your savings. This way it gets saved and not absorbed. Sure, you'll feel broke but maybe that's a good thing. When you're broke you are not as tempted to spend as you might when you have what feels like extra money sitting there.

Read your meter

Call your utility companies and tell them you want to read your own meter. They will give you cards to record the information and you have to turn it in at a certain time of every month. They don't like allowing you to do this, but you may discover, curiously, that your bills are a lot cheaper when you read your own meters.

Off-peak credit

Check with your electricity provider to see if you qualify for lower rates if you choose to run your appliances during "off-peak" hours. If so, rethink when you wash clothes and run your dishwasher. Simply changing your routine slightly could net tremendous savings in reduced bills.

Credit for kids at college

If your kids live away from home for college—either with or without a car—report this to your automobile insurance provider. If you live in a large city and your child goes to a college in a smaller city, your insurance premium will drop to reflect this change.

Virtual campus tours

The cost of college begins long before your student even fills out an application. Sometimes the best school for your teen is not local, and when air travel is required for that first campus visit, costs can exceed $900 per city for just one parent and child. While nothing beats being there, perhaps the second best way to get a feel for a campus is to watch a videotape of someone else's visit. Collegiate Choice Walking Tours Videos are simple, straight recordings averaging one hour per college of everything a family would have seen and heard had they visited the campus that day. These are produced by guidance counselors. Go to *www.collegiatchoice.com.* The cost is $15 per campus— less than the cost of a textbook. This is a most helpful tool to winnow down the list of colleges on which to spend scarce travel dollars and personal days off from work and school.

Buy direct

Many companies offer you the opportunity to own their stock by buying it directly rather than through a commissioned brokerage. There is a transaction fee, but it is small. The initial investment requirement is typically $250 - $500 and you buy stock shares according to the amount you invest. Companies with direct investment opportunities are Wal-Mart, Home Depot, and Tandy—to name a few. Learn more about Direct Reinvestment Deposit (DRIPs) at *www.dripcentral.com.*

Fringe benefits

Check with your insurance company to see what kind of benefits they offer members. Geico has a privileges program that offers cheap movie tickets, discounts on hotels, online stores, and so on.

Stand-by power

Unplug the television, electrical heater, computers—any appliance that has a green light indicating it has an "instant on" feature. These devices pull electrical current even while idle, and that can add up on your electricity bill. They're costing you money even when you are not using them.

Loans to friends

If you are compelled to lend money to a friend or relative, do yourself a favor and lend only the amount you can afford to give that person as a gift. Of course you should expect repayment. And if that happens consider yourself fortunate to have received a bonus. You have to assume you will never see a dime, because that's more likely to be the outcome.

Learn from the pros

If you want outstanding, free advice on frugal living, talk to people who lived through the Depression era. They can teach you more than you could learn in a thousand classrooms. Most are at the age where they are flattered that a younger person wants to learn from them. So do yourself a favor and make a friend of an older person who can tell you the stories of financial survival.

Cash envelopes

You don't have to use credit cards to be an overspender. You can do that with a debit card. Here's a way to make sure you do not overspend: Withdraw cash from your account. Get a stack of envelopes and label each one according to the categories of your daily spending. For example, make envelopes for groceries, gasoline, entertainment and gifts. Divide the cash between the envelopes in the amounts you determine. As you spend, put the receipts into the corresponding envelope. When an envelope has no more cash, you're done spending. Such a simple visual reminder will quickly solve problems with overspending.

Home office

If you work from home while living in a one-bedroom apartment, convert the bedroom to an office and live in the living/dining area as if you had a studio apartment. Move your bed and all your personal items into the studio area. Check with your tax consultant to be sure your business qualifies for the deduction. One of the real benefits of this approach for the self-employed (besides saving money) is that you can literally "close the door" on your work when you need a breather, like on the weekends.

ORGANIZATION AND STORAGE

Organization and Storage

Record scan

Scan all of your important documents, then burn them to a CD or copy to a flash drive that you keep in a fire- and heat-proof safe.

Small containers

Save your empty prescription bottles to hold loose birthday candles, screws, washers, nails and other small items that get lost in the typical junk drawer. They're just the right size to hold small amounts of clutter.

Easy donation

Keep a couple of grocery bags or cardboard boxes in an out-of-the-way spot to hold old clothes, blankets, books or other items you run across that you no longer need or want. When the containers are full, call a local charity for pickup or wait for one to notify you of a regular pickup in your neighborhood. No more running around frantically the night before a pickup scrounging for things to give away. Once the items are gone, start a new box.

Organized craft supplies

Use an over-the-door hanging shoe bag to help organize craft supplies. Pockets are perfectly suited to hold paintbrushes, glue, markers and pens, fabric paints, scissors and so on. This saves valuable storage space for other things, and you can find your supplies at a glance.

Small storage

A plastic tackle box with trays and movable dividers is a great organizational tool for small craft items like beads, jewelry findings, buttons, needles and pins.

Moving boxes

When it's time to move, ask a local grocery store or supermarket to save their liquor boxes for you. The boxes have dividers that are great for packing glasses, vases, knick-knacks and other fragile items. You can place your breakables in the individual compartments with little or no wrapping material required.

Untangled necklaces

Keep necklaces and bracelets from tangles by hanging them from clear push pins.

Moving box labels

When moving to another home,

assign each room a color at your new house. Get a package of multi-color paper at the office supply and create coordinating labels so the boxes get delivered to the correct room. Place a full-size, colored "label" on each door, to correspond with the labeled boxes being delivered. As long as your labels are a full-size sheet of paper in the color of the designated room, you won't have to write too many other instructions.

Preserving newspaper clips

To preserve newspaper clippings, dissolve a milk of magnesia tablet in a quart of club soda overnight. Pour into a glass pan large enough to accommodate the flattened clipping. Soak for an hour, remove and pat dry. Now the clipping will not turn yellow over time because you have neutralized the acid in the paper.

Freezer storage

Heavy duty freezer bags can be reused, but if you've written on them it can get confusing. Instead, write the contents and also instructions for heating on a separate piece of paper that you slip inside the bag. You can see through with no problem, and the bag stays blank for its future jobs.

Family IDs

Create a wallet-sized card for each family member to carry in his or her wallet that lists that person's name, date of birth and Social Security number. Include parent's phone numbers, the child's school phone number and an emergency contact like a grandparent or neighbor. Laminate the cards (packing tape does a great job) so it will hold up to all kinds of potential abuse.

Art supply storage

Keep the kids' art supplies in a neat caddy with a handle. It can hold a lot of treasures and is easy to take in the car, to grandma's house, or wherever their little creative minds happen to go.

Earring organization

A perfect solution for organizing jewelry—particularly earrings—use foam egg cartons. Remove the lid; and the base part will fit easily in even the shortest drawer.

Beyond the obvious

If you need buttons check out the really cheap clothes at garage sales that have great buttons. A quarter won't buy many buttons in a retail store, but that same quarter will net a full set at a garage sale. Need fabric for pillows? Sheets, shower curtains and prom dresses all offer really nice fabric. Just think of the possibilities. Also be sure to make a list at home of the things you need for a project or gift and take it with you every time you go to a garage sale. This will keep you focused and able to look for potential items. Piles of unorganized stuff at a sale can be so overwhelming that you'll set yourself up for a mental block without a clear idea of why you're there.

Organizing meds

Organizing medications can be difficult, especially if the person is blind or has other health problems. Pill organizers are inexpensive and the best solution. After taking the medication leave the top open for that day. This way anyone will know that medication has been taken.

Padded cases

Surprisingly some glasses cases fit a cell phone or digital camera better than they do spectacles. Even more amusing—some padded cases created for cell phones or digital cameras are much better suited for eyeglasses! Just another way to use "this" for "that."

Craft storage

If you're into scrapbooking, quilting or other crafts that require lots of small intricate pieces, consider the lowly pizza box for keeping projects neat and safe. Typically they are 12x12 and just the perfect size for all kinds of craft projects. Everything stays nice and flat. Ask to buy a few from your local pizza shop. You might find that there is no charge for regular customers.

Tarnish retardant

A surefire way to keep silver jewelry from tarnishing is to store it in a box or zip-type bag with an aspirin or a piece of white chalk. Either of these will absorb moisture and your jewelry will retain that just-polished look.

Gift cache

Designate an area in a closet, basement or garage where you can keep a box or bag for each person in the family. Throughout the year put gifts into the receptacles. When you need a birthday gift, or a get- well gift, you're sure to have something that the person will enjoy. And by Christmas you may have a lot of your shopping already done.

Lid corral

A dish drainer is the perfect solution for neatly storing the lids for pots and pans. Just stand them up and arrange according to size so the small ones are at the front. The drainer will slide easily into a lower cabinet and keep all those lids corralled in on place.

Moving material

Don't bother with all the bubble wrap, newspaper and other packing material as you prepare to move. It's costly, takes time to get and has to be disposed of at the other end. You already have all the packing material you'll ever need in t-shirts, sheets, tablecloths and towels. Use these items to pack dishes, knickknacks and other fragile items. Provided the dishes and items you packed were clean to begin with, you can just fold the towels and linens and put them away.

Shoe boxes

Shoe boxes makes great inexpensive storage units. They hold kids' treasures and all kinds of small items. They also provide great "under the bed" storage.

Dorm storage

A hanging shoe bag is a great place to store items such as hairbrushes, blow-dryers, deodorant, etc. This frees up a lot of room in a dorm room because it hangs on the back of the door.

Magazine remind

Ever tried to find that special recipe or article you read in a magazine and can't remember which book or magazine it was in? Keep a few blank address labels handy to fix this problem. Simply place the label on the outside or inside cover and note the page number of the article or recipe you liked. Or tape a piece of paper to the cover for your notes.

Towel storage

A wine rack makes a perfect towel storage unit for even the smallest bathroom. Roll the towels and wash cloths and stick them in the holes designed for bottles.

Home index

As you clean closets and drawers, use index cards to record what's in where. Boxes in the garage or basement? Make an index card for them too, listing the contents and exact location. Now file the cards in one central location and you'll never again waste time looking for stuff.

Get off mail lists

If you are tired of receiving junk mail, you can register online at the Direct Marketing Association Mail Preference Service. The address is *www.the-dma.org*. There is a $1 charge for this. You can either go to the website and enter your information or print out a form to mail to DMS.

Organization and Storage

Know the rules

Before you post signs for your garage sale, make sure you check your city's zoning laws. Getting a $50 fine for posting signs illegally will wipe out a lot of profit and do nothing for your attitude.

Christmas in July

Summer—when the days are long and weather is warm—is definitely the best time to organize the house and clean out the garage. While you're doing this, take stock of your holiday decorations. What works and what needs repair? Need to replace a few bulbs? Discard a string of lights? Make a list of what you have and what to look for and you'll be way ahead of the game come December.

A tip for movers

When you pack tiny collectibles, it is a good idea to wrap them in colored tissue rather than newspaper. This assures you that you won't think it is just paper and throw it out. That can be costly, and you wouldn't want to throw out any family heirlooms.

Two-day sale

Don't skip the second day of a 2-day garage sale. Many times by the second day the owner is ready to call a charity to pickup what is left, so whatever you want is free. Sometimes the "whatever" is an amazing deal.

Prep for "saling"

The night before you plan to go garage "saling" pull out all the ads and plot your route on a map. Now you'll maximize your time and be first in line at the sales you're most anxious to visit.

Perpetual gift calendar

Create a simple sheet of paper that shows you all of the gifts you need to purchase during the year. Now you can see at a glance what your monthly obligations will be for birthdays, anniversaries and so on. Get really organized and create a holiday list as well, then divide the number of names on it by 12 to see how many gifts you need to purchase each month. This will really help you spread things out over a wider period of time and will ease the financial crunch.

Storage containers

Glass spaghetti sauce jars make excellent storage containers both for the refrigerator and the pantry. You can see what you have at a glance.

Space bags

To make your own cheap version of a "space bag" take a garbage bag, put your items in the bag, stick the vacuum nozzle between the items and wrap the bag around the vacuum shaft. Push the button and watch it compress. Turn the vacuum off and quickly take it out, twist the bag and twist-tie it closed. Works great to compress items for storage.

Big jars

If you need containers for large quantities of pantry items like flour or pasta, go to your children's school. Ask the manager of the school cafeteria if they will save some of the containers they throw away for you. Schools, like restaurants, get supplies in wonderful plastic and glass jars and tubs. Most of the time they are simply thrown away.

Moving boxes

Looking for moving boxes but refuse to pay the price for new ones? Go to *www.boxquest.com*. This is a nationwide network of people buying and selling their used moving boxes. When you get yours treat them carefully so you can turn around and sell them to someone else.

Organized closet

Hang an over-the-door shoe bag in your coat or entry closet. Now you have the perfect place for mittens, gloves, scarves, hats and umbrellas—in the pockets. No more crawling around on the closet floor to find a missing glove.

Household manuals

Owners manuals for everything from kitchen appliances to electronics, carpet, roofing and paint can be a real pain if you do not handle them at the very moment you get something new. This is the right way: The moment you get a new owners manuals, start a new folder in your Household Manuals File. Place the manual inside along with the warranty and sales receipt. File it. Now you have all you need for filing a claim, ordering a part, proving ownership in the case of loss, or selling the item.

Storage pillows

Do you love lots of throw pillows but hate the high cost of pillow "inserts?" Skip the inserts and think of those pillows as storage units. Neatly fold your winter blankets and slip one inside each pillow. You can do the same with bulky sweaters provided you fold them carefully so all buttons and zippers are tucked inside the folds.

Ice cream buckets

Most ice cream shops will sell empty 5-gallon plastic ice cream tubs that have a nice sturdy lid for as little as $.50. They're fantastic for organizing kids' toys, rolled towels and bathroom supplies as well as organizing the garage.

Gift P.I.

Use your day planner as a gift recorder. Whenever you hear someone on your gift list mention something they might like, write it on a post-it note and put it on the December page. If a person's birthday is coming look there to see if you have any ideas. As you purchase things also post them in December along with what it cost and where you stored it.

Guest book

Put a guest book in a conspicuous place in your home so you will remember to ask everyone who visits to sign it. You'll have a nice record of visits, but you'll have more than that. You'll have addresses and phone numbers, and nice comments. People who sign in the future can see who's come before.

Your trash, their treasure

Go to *www.freecycle.org* and join the Freecycle chapter near you. Freecycle is a non-profit Internet network that allows people to give and receive free stuff that others don't want, but stuff that still has a useful life. What a great way to declutter your home by giving away things to others that you do not need. You will see everything from lawn mowers and cars, kids' toys, clothing, baby items, small appliances, furniture, kitchen cabinets, carpet and computers—you name it and it's likely been available at one time or another at Freecycle.

RV needs

Keep a notepad handy in your motor home or camper. Now when you're off in some remote campsite and you realize you've run low on some item or supply, jot it down. Also make a note of repairs or maintenance items that need your attention. Once back in civilization you can quickly take care of your RV needs so your next trip will be even more relaxed. If that's even possible.

What you own

To keep track of what you own, make a video while walking through your home, narrating the description of everything you see—or you can write it down in list form, giving as many details as possible. Store your record in a safe place away from your home. It may seem tedious, but it is absolutely vital. If you should ever lose your house to a fire or flood it will be easier to be compensated for your belongings. Check your coverage amounts, and ask for replacement value on your policy.

Shoe boxes

When you purchase a new pair of shoes don't throw the box out. Instead snap a photo of the shoes and tape it to the outside of the box. This prevents shuffling through every box of shoes you have to find the right ones. Stack them neatly on the shelf, and avoid the shoe racks that take up so much space.

Bed linen kits

Store a sheet set—flat, fitted, pillowcases and a blanket—neatly folded together inside a pillow sham. It looks just like a pillow but serves a second purpose if you are short on storage space.

Big and bright

Don't bother putting your address on your Yard Sale signs. No one going 35 mph can read that. All you need is great big bright signs that say Huge Yard Sale Next Right or Big Yard Sale, Follow Arrows. That is the key to a successful yard sale.

Marker life

To extend the life of a marker and to keep the writing tip from drying out, store it upside down. The ink is always on top.

Storage boxes

Rather than writing a list of the items in your storage boxes, attach a photo or picture that is representative. For example if you have stuff for Easter, tape an Easter card to that box. No question about what's inside. Ditto for Christmas. You don't even have to take a picture of the exact contents. Clipping pictures from magazines and catalogs will do the trick quite nicely, too.

Accordian file

Get an expandable file folder to organize your shopping. Write the names of the stores where you shop on the tabs. Now place that store's current sales circular in its slot. Save the front section for rebate offers. Now when you go to the store, take your file with you. You will have all you need to qualify for price matching, to look up any rebate details you've forgotten, and so on. And since you have a slot for coupons and one for rain checks, you will have everything you need to be a savvy shopper.

Film developing

When you finish a roll of film from an event like a graduation or christening, write the event or person's name and how many sets of prints you want right on the film canister or cartridge itself. Then, no matter when you get around to taking the film in to be developed, you'll know exactly what's on the roll.

Unique labeling

Affix one of your regular return address labels to the film developing envelope. It's different so it stands out when you pick up your photos and you or an employee has to rifle through so many envelopes that all look alike.

Bags are best

When you have a garage sale it's not unusual for toys and parts to get scattered, lost or misplaced. To remedy this, put small toys and smaller like objects in zip-type sandwich bags. Group similar objects together such as cars, beauty items and so on and then label with the contents and price. Also, fill bags with miscellaneous things and sell them for a flat price like $.50 or $1. You'll be surprised how well they will sell because they are neat and tidy and represent a real bargain.

Save the memories

Whenever you mail undeveloped film or pictures, be sure to attach return labels to everything—the canister that holds the film, and the film roll itself; and on the back of each photo, if sending finished pictures. Do this for anything else you mail like shirts, cell phones, books and gifts. Every year the U.S. Postal Service has to destroy rolls of films, tons of photographs and other items because they've become separated from their envelopes as a result of the imperfect flow of mail. However, before doing that they do make every attempt to return the items to their rightful owners.

Compressed memories

Kids love to bring home the artistic creations they made in school and typically they're quite large. Instead of putting that into your album or scrapbook—after it has had its time on the refrigerator—take a picture of your little artist holding the masterpiece. This way you have captured the moment and the creation. You can fit lots of photos on one page of an album and it's fun to look at it and reminisce over and again.

Fireproof and waterproof

Only those who have suffered the heartbreak of a leak in a waterbed under which one's fireproof document safe was stored knows that fireproof does not mean waterproof. Here's the way to alleviate this unfortunate truth: Place all important papers into heavy-duty zip-type bags to increase the chances of your documents surviving the elements.

Gardening gear

When you're done in the garden shake your gloves out, brush off the dirt, and put them in a large plastic zip-type bag. You'll be able to store them in your garage or shed, safe from unwanted tenants who might like to live inside of them—like spiders.

Grab and go

Keep tote bags in your coat closet—one for each organization to which you belong—with all the necessary paraphernalia for the next meeting. If you're rushed when it's time to leave for the meeting, all you have to do is grab the right bag and go.

Electrical cord trick

If you have one of those 50-100 foot electrical cords that always seem to get tangled up, try a new way to secure it. Make a loop and pull the cord through it long enough for another loop, then pull the cord through that loop—similar to a crochet chain. When you need to use the cord it will unravel quickly without tangles.

EZ makeup storage

Plastic silverware trays make great organizers for bathroom drawers, which tend to be narrow. Makeup, cotton balls, cotton swabs and other supplies fit neatly in the compartments.

Gift record

To keep track of gift giving, use a spiral notebook—with one page for each month and holiday. Write in your recipients' names and descriptions of the gifts. Start over each year with fresh sheets. Now you have a concise record so you can look back to see what you've given in past as well as what you have purchased for future gifts.

Important info

Print out the exact information that a 911 operator would need to reach your house: the exact address, phone number, contact information for friends and family, and the numbers and names of repair people you often need to reach. Make copies for the refrigerator (you never know when you'll need help and the only person standing at your phone is a friend or relative who doesn't know your exact address or other important information), the glove box in each car and your wallet.

Garage sale re-fresh

After the first hour of a garage sale, your tables might be depleted of things. Refresh the display with things from the back of the garage sale so that it does not look like you've run out of inventory.

Artwork overflow

Do you wonder what to do with all of those precious pieces of artwork that your children bring home each week from school? Cut these images down and use them in scrapbooking. Just a snip of a face or other item is all that's needed to add unique character and charm to a scrapbook page.

Seasonal storage

When switching your wardrobe from winter to summer and vice versa—try rolling your clothes. Roll your shirts, sweaters, pants and skirts around empty paper towel rolls. This eliminates wrinkles. Rolled clothes do not take up much room. Store them in trunks, boxes or plastic bins.

Bring in the crowds

Post your big, bright garage sale sign a day or two ahead of time to create a buzz. Provided your community allows postings ahead of time, this will really help to draw the crowds. On the day of the sale add a couple of brightly colored balloons to each sign for added attraction.

Garage sale secrets

If you're planning a garage sale, get organized! First, buy inexpensive, clear plastic storage bags. In them place your pillowcases, sheets, tablecloths, throw pillows, or anything that would get dirty or separated with handling. Place them in laundry baskets so they are easy to go through. Instead of stickers that fall off, make tags by cutting index cards into small squares, hole punching and tying them on with dental floss. These are easy to work with and cheap because you probably already have some. Also, to create your own jewelry cards: cut index cards in half, place two small holes in the card and put earrings, pins, etc. on separate card.s Hand the shoppers an empty grocery bag when they arrive for shopping ease.

Tackle jewelry tangles

A plastic tackle box with shelves that pop out when the lid is opened makes a perfect jewelry box. Everything has a place and if you are careful to return each item to its place, nothing will get separated, mismatched or tangled.

Shoe space

Need space for shoes in your closet? Mount hanging shoe bags to the wall behind your clothes. You'll triple the space for shoes without taking up any additional closet space. And they're hidden from sight once the clothes are drawn across the rod. Cuts down on complaints from others who might not understand your need for so many shoes!

Flag store

Roll your special occasions flags around the pole, then slip into an empty cardboard tube from a roll of gift wrap. Label the name of the flag on the roll itself with a marking pen, e.g. U.S. Flag, Valentine, Birthday, Football, Halloween or Christmas.

Frozen safe

Keep your important documents like birth certificates, marriage license, insurance policies, and so on in heavy-duty freezer zip-type bags. Make sure they are zipped completely, then affix with tape to the back or side wall of the freezer. In case of a fire the inside of freezer will not likely burn and thieves would not be drawn to peruse the inside wall of your freezer. Now you don't have to buy a fireproof safe.

Plastic comforter bags

Use the large plastic zippered bags that sheets, comforters and blankets come in to store your out-of-season clothes, clothes that are designated for your next garage sale and hand-me-down clothes you are saving for a child who will soon be that size. The bags are sturdy and just the right size.

Film canisters

Empty film canisters are great storage devices. They can hold nails, safety pins and paper clips. Keep coins in one for all the times you need change. They keep earrings safe for travel and hold just the right amount of aspirin and vitamins, too. When you need more than the film you use—or you don't even buy film anymore because you have a digital camera—you can get all you need at any film developing counter where empty canisters are simply tossed into the trash.

Organization and Storage

Kid toy covers

Recycle your old shower curtain to cover bikes, backyard toys, the sandbox and so on in anticipation of inclement weather. Bungee cords or twine slip through the holes along the top side for ease in tying down the curtain so it won't blow off.

Shopping list

Keep a list of the items you need or want. But don't be so quick to rush to a store to purchase them. Instead keep this list in hand as you visit garage sales. You will stay focused, you'll save time because you won't have to look through everything they have and you won't be so prone to purchase impulsively. You'll be surprised what you might find if you simply ask the seller if they have any of the items on your list.

Hidden files

If you need a lamp table and filing space, too, get a 2-drawer metal filing cabinet. Cover with a floor-length round tablecloth and a decorative small square cloth. Add a lamp, and use as a bedside table or a reading table by your favorite chair. No one will ever guess that under your pretty cloth is a two-drawer filing cabinet.

Socks organizer

Use a shoebox in your dresser drawers to keep socks or hose separate from other clothes in that drawer.

Paint bottle organizer

An empty baby wipes container works perfectly to hold bottles of acrylic paint, plus it helps to contain any leaks or spills. You can get quite a few bottles in a box, too.

Storing craft beads

Clean contact lens cases are great for storing tiny craft beads like those used in cross-stitch projects. The screw-on lids help prevent lost or spilled beads.

Washcloth cubbies

An old wooden soda pop crate attached to the bathroom wall makes a handy storage unit for 24 rolled-up washcloths. Works great and looks even better.

Bathroom calendar

The bathroom is a great place to display your calendar that features appointments and a record of everything from when you bought that mascara to what you wore last week.

Item locator

Take a picture of every item that goes into each of your kitchen cabinets. Print out in "thumbnail" view, placing all the pictures of the items that go into one cabinet on one page. Tape these handy reference guides to the inside of the cabinet or drawer. Not only is this a quick reference for where things should be put away, it's also a reminder of what's stored in the back of low cabinets.

School calendar

Take your kids' school calendar and reduce it to pocket-size on a photocopy machine. Now you have a handy reference of all school functions right in your pocket or purse.

Garage clutter

Here's a solution for all those half-full bags of fertilizer, potting soil, kitty litter and pet food that can make a garage a real mess: frosting buckets with lids. At most bakeries they're free for the asking. Thoroughly cleaned, they make excellent containers for all kinds of garage items that need to be stored and kept dry.

Clothes storage

During the summer months keep your winter sweaters and coats packed away in your luggage. Tuck a dryer sheet or two between the items to keep them fresh. Moths will not be able to get into the suitcases, and you'll have additional closet space. When it's time to unpack, repack all your summer things and make the switch.

Multiply, don't divide

If you have a single wedding album or other collection of photos that more than one child would love to inherit, don't worry. Simply make as many color photocopies (even if the photos are black and white) as you need. Then recreate that album in multiples. Color photocopies are so good you will have a difficult time deciphering the copies from the original.

Family history in stone

As you visit the grave sites of your ancestors, snap a photo of the headstones. Once you have a complete collection you will have your family's history right there in a photo album. Have your journaling include the specific location and directions together with memories you have of those who have passed on.

PETS

Pets

Ear Infections

If your dog or cat is prone to ear infections, flush the ear canal once or twice a week with a mixture of equal parts of white vinegar, water and rubbing alcohol. This is great for animals that swim or get bathed often.

Cleaner filters

When feeding your fish unplug the filter during feeding time for about 15 minutes. The filter won't pull the food into it keeping it clean much longer.

Pet meds

Need an alternative to paying top dollar for heartworm medication? Check *www.omahavaccine.com*, which might have their price even cheaper than at *www.petmed.com*.

Pooper scooper

Don't toss out the cardboard French fry container next time you eat fast food. Instead flatten it and save it for your next dog walk. When Fido leaves his mark, pull it out, pop it open and scoop up the mess. Transfer to the plastic bag you also carry with you, and drop the whole thing into the nearest trash can.

Cheap flea prevention

Many dog owners have great success ridding their animals of fleas by using Lever 2000 deodorant soap instead of pet shampoo for routine bathing. Check with your veterinarian to make sure this is appropriate for your pet.

Pass the salt

You can rid your pet of fleas, but they may still be living in your home's carpet. There are lots of expensive methods for alleviating this problem, but none as cheap as table salt. Sprinkle it on all carpeted areas including the stairs and leave it on overnight. Vacuum well the following morning and repeat the process every day for a week. This is most effective provided you are vacuuming up every bit of salt.

Toy ropes

Instead of paying upwards of $15 at a pet store for a toy rope for your dog, go to a home improvement center or hardware store, and buy a length of rope for about $2 and tie a knot in each end. Your dog won't know the difference but you will.

Off the furniture!

A great way to keep dogs and especially cats off of upholstered furniture is to put sturdy double-stick tape on the areas you want to prevent the animal from scratching or sitting. This will not hurt the animal or the furniture in any way. It is inexpensive and very effective. In time you will train them what areas of your home to avoid and then you can remove the tape.

Out of the plants!

To keep cats from digging in your houseplants, cover the surface of the plant's soil with decorative pebbles or small stones.

Big dog beds

Pick up a comforter (not down or feathers) from a thrift shop or yard sale to use as a bed for your larger dog. Cut the comforter in half and bind the raw edges with a piece of fabric. Fold each in half or thirds and you have very nice dog beds that are washable and will dry quickly—all for just a few dollars.

Pet hair in washer

After laundering pet bedding, you may discover a lot of pet hair remaining in the bottom of the washer. It's not easy to wipe out, so do this: Allow the machine to dry out, then use your vacuum hose to remove all of it easily and quickly.

Cheap natural litter

If you prefer natural and healthy Feline Pine (pine pellets) to clay cat litter because it is natural and odor free, you may have also discovered that it is quite expensive—about $.50 per pound. You can save a bundle by purchasing woodstove pellets which are virtually the same thing, but much cheaper—about $.10 per pound during the winter months at home improvement centers and stores that sell wood stoves.

Pet poop pickup

Save the plastic bags from your newspaper—they're the perfect size and weight to carry on a dog walk. Simply stick your hand in the bag, pick up the refuse, turn the back inside out, knot it and dispose.

Dog bed

Instead of throwing away old pillows and pillowcases, use them for beds for your pets. They're already broken in and washable. Using household items for your pets gives items a second life before they hit the landfill.

Pets

De-skunking recipe

Here's a recipe from a pharmacist for how to de-skunk a dog. Mix well 1 pint hydrogen peroxide, 1 cup baking soda and 2 teaspoons liquid dish soap. Rub this into the dog's coat with no water. Leave on for 10 minutes, and then rinse thoroughly. The skunk odor will vanish.

Litter box liners

To save money and make litter box cleanup much easier, pull a kitchen-sized plastic bag over your cat's litter box to act as a box liner. Now fill it with scoopable or "clumping" litter and scoop as normal. When it's time to change the litter, you just need to turn the bag inside out, knot and toss. Your litter pan is still clean. This is much cheaper than buying litter box liners and works even better.

Dog treats

If you look on the ingredients list of dog treats specially formulated as rewards for obedience, you will see they are made of 100% beef liver. Why pay a premium when you can purchase liver from the meat counter and cook it up yourself? Cut it into small pieces and store in the refrigerator. Your dog will go nuts for these homemade treats. Beef liver is quite cheap, so you can plan on saving a bundle.

Shred donations

If you produce a lot of paper shredding as a result of protecting your privacy, don't throw it out. Donate it to your local animal shelter where they can use it for lining cages. Of course you should call ahead to find the best time to make a delivery.

Tuna liquid

When opening a can of tuna, drain it over your cat's food. It's a huge treat and quite healthy as well.

Hold the onions

If you choose to make your own pet food never use onions. Onions are toxic for many animals.

Pet odors away

Is there any odor worse than cat urine? Yikes. Many commmercial products from a pet supply store work for a while but do not produce a permanent solution because the pet it attracted back to that same spot. AtmosKlear Odor Eliminator, is the most permanent solution because it is not an air freshener, and truly eliminates the odors so your pet can't find the same spot again. Find it at *www.atmosklear.com.*

Dog treats

Forget those expensive dog treats! Fill a small plastic container with dry dog food and give your dog a bite-size portion for a snack or reward. It's better for your dog's health and a great way to give pets on a restricted diet a treat, too.

Miss Behavior

To keep your cat from jumping on the kitchen counter or other forbidden places, purchase a small spray bottle and fill with water. When your cat misbehaves, give her a few sprays. She will immediately stop. This discipline is completely harmless but most effective.

Cheaper inoculations!

Vets charge a lot to administer puppy shots and annual boosters. Most reliable pet stores and grooming shops sell puppy shots that owners can administer. It is easy and cheap, too. Shots from vets can range from $25-$45 each. The same shots from the same companies purchased from groom shops or pet stores can be less than $10 dollars each. It is legal in most states to administer inoculations to your pet. Check it out.

Cat shampoo

Word has it from a professional animal groomer that the best shampoo on the market—especially for long-hair cats and dogs with greasy coats—is not shampoo at all, but a product called "Goop," which is a hand-washing preparation found in auto departments. Follow with blue Dawn dishwashing liquid and then a white vinegar rinse—1 cup white vinegar to 1 gallon water. Check this out with your veterinarian.

Cool water

During hot summer days fill your dogs' water bowls with ice cubes. They'll have nice cool water throughout the day.

Smelly dog

If your dog comes in from the rain or snow smelling like a wet dog, here's a quick remedy. After wiping your dog off take a used dryer sheet and gently wipe over his fur. After a few rubs, he will smell dryer fresh.

Less is more

Feeding your pet premium pet food may appear to be very expensive. But look at the recommended daily feeding chart. You will see that the recommended amount per day is 30% less than recommended amounts for regular food. Less food means a healthier animal, fewer vet visits, a shinier coat and less skin problems.

And there's less waste in the yard for owners to contend with.

Snuggly fresh

If you hate the way your dog smells even after his bath, rinse him with just a little liquid fabric softener in the rinse water and he will smell great for days. His coat will also be softer than ever. No more smelly pets.

Pet hair off furniture

A simple and inexpensive way to remove pet hair from your furniture is to take a damp sponge or old washcloth and rub it over the surface. The cat hair (or dog hair) will ball up and is easy to collect with the rag.

Poor horse owners

You can save a great deal of money by using a self-care stable instead of a full-care facility. You not only get to know your horse better (horses respond better under saddle for people they know and love well), but the exercise you get from mucking your horse's stall is terrific. If your riding instructor is also a reputable horse trainer and your baby needs work, ask her if she can alternate between the two of you—a lesson for you one week, a lesson strictly for the horse the next.

Horse rinse

Add a cup of white vinegar to the rinse bucket when grooming your horse. It makes her coat gleam and helps to remove manure stains, especially on the white areas.

Shiny horses

Instead of purchasing expensive coat conditioners and sprays for your horses, here's a simple trick: Use a dryer sheet and rub this over a freshly-bathed horse. Keeps the dirt from sticking and is not harmful to the coat or skin. This will also add an excellent shine.

Liquid meds

Ask your vet to give you a small plastic syringe-type liquid medicine dispenser in case kitty or pup needs a dose of medicine. This device squirts the meds right into the mouth. It is much easier to measure and administer the dose.

Cheap pet bedding

A small bag of pine shavings to be used as bedding for small pets cost about $6 for two pounds. If you really want to save a ton of money go to the local feed store and buy a bag of compressed horse bedding. It is the same pine shavings, in a bag that weighs about 40 pounds, contains about 40 pounds and enough to cover the floor of a 10x10 horse stall about three inches deep. That ought to be enough to last your little fur baby forever. And the price? About $4.

Repairs and Maintenance

Repairs and Maintenance

Wallpaper repair

When old dark colored wallpaper has separated at the seams and the wall color can be seen underneath, fix it this way: Make a small amount of eggshell finish latex paint in the same color as the background color of the wallpaper. Take a 1-inch brush and a damp cloth. Paint the seam 1/2 way down and then wipe seam with damp cloth. Finish the lower half then wipe off. You'll have a new looking wallpaper job. Do not do this if the seam has already lifted. Do not paint more than half the seam at a time. If the paint dries on the wallpaper it will be difficult to remove.

Product warranty

Take advantage of a manufacturer's warranty program, even if you believe the warranty period may have expired. If the item is truly defective you may still be able to have it replaced or at least repaired.

Nail hole filler

If you need to fill some nail holes but don't have wall patch material on hand, mix cornstarch with water until you have a smooth paste. This will be a good option for filling small holes because it dries hard and can be sanded.

Vertical blinds

Don't throw away your old, faded vertical blinds until you have first considered refurbishing them. Even if they are cloth covered, you may be able to paint them to match the room décor. Test one slat with a roller and flat latex paint. Hang to dry. You may be surprised to see just how great it looks, especially when you consider what you won't have to spend to replace them.

Easily fix cabinets

If your kitchen cabinet doors stubbornly refuse to stay closed, here's a quick fix that should get you through the interim time until they can be replaced: Velcro. No kidding. You can buy this at a hardware or fabric store. You can get it with self-stick adhesive or you may wish to attach with small brads or heavy-duty staples. Whichever way you choose, you can be sure that those doors will stay closed.

Hardwood floor

A cheaper alternative to traditional hardwood flooring is 8x4 foot sheets of hardwood plywood. Once installed and finished you will not believe just how beautiful your hardwood floor is. And at one-fourth the price of engineered hardwood flooring or even laminate—you'll love it even more.

Fix a torn shower curtain

If you have family members who don't know their own strength when opening and closing a shower curtain, here's an easy way to fix a curtain that is torn away from the hooks: Use clear packaging tape to cover the hole, punch a new hole, replace the shower ring and it's good as new. Double the tape and your repair will last twice as long.

Look like new

Just because you paint all the walls a new shade doesn't necessarily mean you'll have to also switch out all the electrical outlets and light switches, too. Even if they're the wrong color—almond and you need them to be white—try this: Remove all the outlet and switchplate covers. Make a template that fits perfectly around the receptacles so you can spray them with white (or your choice) epoxy paint (must be epoxy). If you prepare the template well, you'll be amazed at the result.

Satellite dish care

Extend the life of your new satellite dish and coax cables by buying lifetime guarantee GE silicone clear caulk. Wearing a latex glove, squeeze some clear silicone on every coax connection and on the coax connector itself. Cover the whole connection with silicone. This will ensure a watertight connection and prevent corrosion, which will inevitably happen to unprotected cables. You can also cover every bolt, screw and nut used to mount the dish. If you ever need to take it apart it is a simple matter to peel off the silicone to disconnect the cables.

Appliance repair

Websites like *www.sears.com* and *www.repairclinic.com* have a wonderful feature. Simply type in the model number of your appliance, and you can see a breakdown illustration of the appliance to help you locate any replacement parts you need. Both websites will help you find the model number if you're having trouble.

Bunny ears

If you live in or near a major city, consider getting rid of satellite or cable TV in favor of an amplified set of rabbit ears for your TV. For about $20 you'll be able to get up to 14 channels. Total cost for the rabbit ears from Radio Shack: $25 or less, which is about $275 less than the cost of satellite for one year.

Bath mat renew

Don't throw out bathroom rugs that have lost their rubber backing due to multiple launderings. Slip a piece of rubber shelf liner under the mat. That will keep it from slipping and extend its useful life.

Paint the Formica

If you can't replace the Formica counters that you think are out of date, consider painting them. There are several methods you can use, so check with a good paint store. Products such as Kilz for the base and then Stone Creations by Rust-Oleum for the new color are good optoins. Stone Creations has an interesting texture that will update your look for a very reasonable cost.

Shoe polish for scratches

Use brown shoe polish for covering scratches on wood cabinets, shelves, furniture, trim or anything wood. It blends in well even if it is a darker shade. Apply and wipe off with a dry rag.

Glue in a tight spot

If you need to repair or reinforce a piece of furniture that seems to be falling apart but can't get the glue to run into the seam, try this: Get a drinking straw, pour some glue into the tip while you pinch it closed two or three inches down (to keep it from running down the other end). Now pinch the top of the straw completely, and insert the now-flat tip into the area to be glued. Once you have it far down in the crevice, begin to squeeze the glue, forcing it into the seam. You can now press the parts tightly together.

"Frosted" glass

Here's an inexpensive way to cover a window, but still allow for diffused light. Measure and cut waxed paper to fit the window and affix with double stick tape on the inside. The paper is translucent enough to allow light to come through and thin enough that you will still be able to open the window, regardless of the configuration. It's a temporary measure but one that you might find lasts for a long time. For sure the price is right.

Paint brush anti-clean

When painting you can avoid cleaning your brushes if you still have more painting to do the next day.

Wrap them securely in a plastic bag, sealing the plastic around the handle of the brush. Now pop them into the freezer. In the morning they'll be ready to use. You can do the same thing with paint rollers. Just make sure the bags are sealed well.

Fix drafty windows

For less than $10 pick up an indoor window insulation kit from the home improvement center. It's a clear vinyl sheet that attaches to the inside of your window with double-sided tape. Once you put it up, you shrink it taut with a hair dryer. For best results, put it up when the area you are taping it to is warm. It gets rid of the drafts. It is available at home centers and hardware stores.

Wallpaper cutting board

Use your sewing cutting board and rotary cutter for cutting wallpaper. With the grid lines you can cut perfectly straight edges with few problems at all.

Jewelry maintenance

To prevent the loss of your treasured diamond or other gemstones you should have them checked every three to six months by a jeweler. The settings wear down over time and the stones can come loose and fall out. Most jewelers will check and clean the ring at no charge. A minor repair to the setting is much cheaper than replacing a diamond.

New walls

If your walls are uneven, fraught with cracks or other problems—and you don't mind a stucco-like texture, get a bucket of all-purpose joint compound. Apply it directly to the walls with a trowel or wide putty knife—no prep required. It will look like stucco and you can experiment with the type of texture you want, all the way from quite smooth to stippled or even swirls. The compound is relatively cheap. You'll need to apply a base coat before the final paint.

Marine paint

Use "marine" paint for the window trim in bathrooms. It is formulated for damp areas and will hold up very well. It's also great for patio furniture and other outdoor applications. It is a bit more expensive, but a real bargain when you consider you won't have to repaint as often because it is so durable.

Cell phone rescue

So you dropped your cell phone in the pool [puddle, tub, sink]. Before you trash it try this: Turn it off if you can. Open it up and and dry it off as well as you can. Place it in the refrigerator. Leave it at least 12 hours (24 would be better). It seems as though the humidity control in the refrigerator dries it out better than placing it near hot air.

Wood cabinet finish

Cabinets or furniture (stained, not painted) can be made to look like new. If the finish is dull or has water spots, make a paste of salt and vegetable oil. Rub it into the area—-or on the entire surface—-and let sit for a few minutes. Wipe off with a towel. Chances are your cabinets will look brand new with no evidence of any water looked brand new with no evidence of any water stains.

Nail hole fill

White toothpaste—any brand as long as it's all white—-makes a dandy filler for small nail holes. It dries as hard as concrete, can be sanded and accepts paint readily.

Down the drain

Have you ever dropped an earring or a ring down the drain? Instead of calling a plumber, which can be very costly, get out your wet/dry vacuum and put it over the drain opening. Chances are excellent that whatever you dropped will be sucked into the vacuum for easy retrieval.

Fix-it notes

The best time to see all the little imperfections in your house is when you're cleaning—cracks, loose grout, chipped paint, loose molding, etc. Making "mental" notes doesn't usually work. So keep a pocket notebook with your supplies and make a list. Now you know exactly what needs to be done.

Free paint

Most counties have Hazardous Household Material programs and collection sites where residents can drop off items that should not end up in landfills. They get all types of paint, ranging from latex, oil-based, primer, interior, exterior and stain. Sometimes the paint dropped off at the site is brand-new—never even been opened. Some sites have a policy that allows anyone to take what he or she can use, provided they sign a waiver stating that they will use it appropriately.

Hardened paintbrushes

Wait, don't toss that old hardened paintbrush in the trash. You might be able to restore it to the softness of its youth. Heat white vinegar in the microwave and then submerge brush in the vinegar all the way up and over the top of the bristles. Allow it to sit there until the vinegar cools. Wash the paintbrush in soap and warm water, working out the dried paint. There. Should be almost as good as new.

Special Occasions and Holidays

Special Occasions and Holidays

Cool decorations

Keep your eyes open as you shop in stores like Target and Kmart—any store that has in-store decorations. Those decorations all land in the trash once the holiday campaign is over. So if you see something that would be perfect for a kid's-themed party or a school function, talk to the manager. Ask if they might save some of the pieces for you.

Wedding photos

Instead of hiring a wedding photographer (which can cost many thousands of dollars), supply disposable cameras for your guests to take candid shots. In addition ask guests with their own cameras to send you copies. Any good editing software will allow you to crop and manipulate digital photos for a keepsake album. Chances are great that you will have the best photos ever because they will be unique—not so posed and staged.

Free wedding favors

There are lots of great ideas for how to make sure each wedding guest leaves with a small gift from the bride and groom, but none quite as unique as this: Buy miniature flower pots from the craft store for less than $.50 each. Paint them to match your theme colors. Plant an apple seed in each tiny pot so it has sprouted by your wedding day. You might want to write, "Grow Old Along With Me …" on the pots as a special memory of your day. Who wouldn't love to bring home a tiny apple tree?

Kid's Christmas gifts

If it's time to put the brakes on runaway Christmas expectations, here's an idea: Make a rule that each child can expect three gifts, in keeping with the three gifts the Wisemen brought to the Christ Child. Now everyone knows what to expect and the kids know they'll need to reduce their gift lists accordingly. Don't feel guilty about not giving them an abundance of things. Grandparents and others will still be giving to them.

Simply divine

Go to the thrift store and buy a fancy evening gown. Cut off the bodice, tuck the cut ends into the skirt and secure by sewing or with a hot glue gun. Place skirt over your tree stand before putting up the tree and presto! You've got a gorgeous designer tree skirt for a few dollars. Of course if you can find a gown in Christmas colors, all the more festive. If you're lucky you might even have a white crinoline peeking out from underneath. This is nothing, if not unique.

Stuff a piñata

Instead of paying major bucks to stuff a Birthday piñata with individually-wrapped candy, go to yard sales several weeks ahead of time and purchase a large quantity of small toy cars, etc. You can usually get entire boxes of them for about five dollars or less. At home wash toys in a bucket of water with a little bleach and choose the best ones. Use these to stuff the piñatas instead of all or part of the candy. The kids love it and the parents will thank you, too.

Frosting palette

When you are frosting all of those Christmas sugar cookies, use a muffin tin to hold the different colors of royal icing. All the colors will be close at hand, and easily covered and saved if you get interrupted.

Wedding gift

Try this inexpensive wedding gift. Make up a gift basket based around a favorite recipe. Put the recipe in the basket with all non-perishable items and tie a bow on it or decorate it in your own unique way.

Sensible bridal gown

If you shop around a bit you can find a previously worn (for what, five or six hours, tops?) wedding dress that looks perfect—like it has never been worn before. A good seamstress is able to alter the dress—even take it down by two sizes until it fits you well. You'll have a fabulous gown and money to spend elsewhere.

Not just at Christmas

A favorite tradition in many areas is for friends and neighbors to exchange Christmas cookies and candies. If that is not possible for you, don't be afraid to change up that tradition in this way: Wait until January or February when life is less hectic, and make cookies for your friends to enjoy along with a "Thanks for being our neighbor" or "Happy Valentine's" greeting. By that time, the excess treats of Christmas are just a memory and a sweet surprise is welcome during what some people consider the dreary winter months. Everyone's a winner.

Fun foods!

It doesn't have to cost a lot of money to make holidays like Valentine's Day, St. Patrick's Day or Good Report Card Day, a little festive. Making food fun using a little food coloring and cookie cutters goes a long way to making the day memorable. For St. Patrick's Day, make green French toast cut into shamrocks and served with green "slime" syrup and green milk. Shamrock-shaped sandwiches, fresh veggies with green dip, and cookies can be a fun lunch. For Valentine's Day, heart-shaped meatloaf, heart-shaped pizza and red syrup for breakfast will send the message. Ranch salad dressing turns a very pretty shade of pink and green for Easter. Be creative, use what you have and you can make it a fun day for everyone.

Wedding replies

Send postcards for wedding replies instead of a reply card that requires a separate envelope. You'll save on stamps, printing and paper.

Prom attire

Prom wear gets cleared out at bargain prices but not until after the spring formal season is over. And that's exactly when you should be buying next year's prom dresses. You'll have to anticipate growth perhaps by buying up a size. But you'll save so much on the dress. Even if you need to have it altered, you'll still be way ahead.

Off the wall invitations

Wallpaper sample books are readily available from home improvement stores and other specialty home decorating shops. Get your name on the list to have a book or two when the new ones come out. They're typically free for the asking and have all the promise of wonderful craft projects. Because the sample sheets are quite large you can make envelopes, notebook covers—even unique and elegant shower invitations.

Gift exchange

If your gift exchanges have become burdensome, think about scaling back a bit this year without eliminating any of the fun and anticipation. Instead of exchanging gifts, exchange ornaments. Who doesn't love Christmas tree ornaments? With an ornament exchange there are no master lists to keep track of, no busted budgets and everyone gets a yearly keepsake.

Christmas lights

An easy way to store Christmas lights is to wind them around a cardboard tube from gift wrap or paper towels. This keeps the lights from tangling and compacts them for easy storage.

Memories

For each holiday you celebrate with your family members, get a nice, large size tablecloth. Purchase a permanent marker. Place the day and year on the tablecloth and invite each person to write or draw something they want to remember on that day. As the tablecloth gets filled, start a new one. These bring back great memories and they are great heirlooms to pass on to the kids. When you use the tablecloth reflect on your many blessings!

Fabric "jars"

Jar gifts are really popular, but those jars can be heavy for mailing. Here's another idea: Use leftover fabric to sew up a little sack. Then place your soup or cookie ingredients inside a zip-type bag and then into your fabric sack. Tie with snippets of ribbon, tiny rope, or raffia. Punch a hole in the card that contains the recipe and directions for the contents and thread the ribbon through.

Grab Bag exchange

Every adult brings three gifts costing $1 to $3 each. The men put their gifts into one big box; the ladies' gifts in another. As turns come up adults reach in and without looking grab three items. It's cheap, fun and at times funny, too. It's amazing just how clever people can be with their gift giving. Kids get to advance to the Grab Bag exchange once they turn 13.

Low-cost celebration

Need a low-cost way to celebrate a special couple's anniversary? Create a scavenger hunt. Divide into two teams and race to see which team can finish first. Items listed should be reflective of the couple's marriage. And don't forget an anniversary card that must be signed by 20 strangers. Of course you will think of your own ways to make a unique celebration even more enjoyable. This could be expanded and tweaked to cover almost any special occasion.

Shower idea

Ask each shower guest to write her full name and address on an envelope supplied by the host. Use these to draw door prizes. Gather the envelopes and give them to the guest of honor to assist with mailing her thank-you notes.

Birthday cake kit

Just because you are not geographically close doesn't mean you can't bake a cake for someone special. Here's the plan: Bake a cake in the size and shape you like. Allow to cool then wrap well in plastic wrap. Get a box and pack the cake, a can of icing, paper plates, a plastic knife, decorating tubes, candles, sprinkles, napkins and forks. Your surprised recipient will have the time of his or her life—no matter the age or gender—assembling, decorating and serving his or her very special birthday cake.

Keepsake ornaments

Can't bear to part with your babies' pacifiers, bottles, booties and other keepsakes? Turn them into Christmas tree ornaments. Getting out precious items every year makes Christmas an even sweeter celebration.

Christmas family book

If you have a large extended family and need a good gift for each family, try this: Several months ahead of time send out a questionnaire to each person inquiring about their favorite and least favorite color, movie, music and so on. Also ask what their greatest blessing of the year was, their favorite family traditions and activites. Get creative to stimulate thoughtful and hilarious responses. When you get back all of these questionnaires, make copies, embellish and then bind one set for each family within your large extended group.

Wedding dress tip

Brides don't have to wear bridal gowns. They can be just as beautiful in a bridesmaid's dress ordered in white or ivory. You will be able to expand your choices of style and design. And here's the bonus: Bridesmaid's dresses are only a fraction of the cost of the typical bridal gown.

eBay for brides

Here's a little-known fact: Many discontinued bridal gowns are sold on eBay for as little as $50. Provided you are sure of your measurements or have a good alterations person available, you can get a fabulous designer gown for next to nothing.

Bridal accessories

You can get all your wedding accessories at wholesale prices online—jewelry sets, bracelets, headpieces, gloves, and so many other things you won't believe it. There is usually a minimum order, but you won't have trouble meeting that once you find it's a one-stop shop for many things on your list.

Wedding flowers

To save money on flowers for your wedding, find out who will be using the same church or reception site later or earlier in the day. Suggest that you share the flowers and split the cost.

Change of wedding protocol

If you long to have a reception no one will forget and in which everyone can be involved, look no farther: In lieu of gifts, ask your guests to bring a fabulous potluck dish for the reception. And in lieu of cards, ask that each participant bring the recipe—printed out and signed by the cook. You have to admit, it sounds like a delicious detour off the beaten path of wedding traditions.

Cost of weddings

Worried about the cost of your kid's wedding? Worry no more. Figure out what you are willing to spend, then write the check to your daughter (or son). Make sure they know this is the budget; there will be no more. And what they don't spend is theirs to keep for the honeymoon or whatever they decide. You're going to be amazed how quickly a bride-to-be is able to learn the fine art of frugality.

Don't forget the kids

If you know there will be children at the wedding, plan ahead. Create a craft table for them with lots of things they can do to keep busy and fairly quiet.

Co-ed baby shower

Here's an idea: A Dipe and Wipe Party. Guests bring gifts of diapers and or baby wipes. It's easy and always greatly appreciated—and a reasonable solution for the latest craze in couples' baby showers. Most stores will allow the parents to exchange diapers for a larger size if they turn out to get enough diapers to last until their baby is potty trained.

Head start on Christmas

To make Christmas less hectic, make cookie dough throughout the month of November and drop onto cookie sheets as if to bake. But instead of baking, freeze. Store the frozen cookies in dated and labeled freezer bags. Take a day in December to bake all the cookies without the mess or annoyance of running out of ingredients. Your cookies will taste fresh since they were just-baked.

Special Occasions and Holidays

Ditch one envelope

Save on wedding invitations by eliminating the double envelope. No one except your very proper aunt will mind, and she is going to find a problem no matter what you do.

Christmas tip

When you buy a Christmas gift early in the year, you might forget about it unless you take a few minutes to store it with your holiday decorations.

For another time

On the days following Halloween, Easter and Valentine's Day gather together all the candy that has not been consumed and earmark it for future movie nights or other special occasions. The non-chocolate candy will keep for over six months. And the chocolate? You can probably think of something to do with it.

Birthday tablecloths

For a child's birthday, instead of buying a themed tablecloth, cover your table with butcher paper or unprinted newsprint. Scatter crayons, markers and stickers on the table as the children arrive, and they can decorate the table. Alternatively, you can decorate the centerpiece yourself, and draw "placemats" for the kids to color. At the party's end, either throw it away, or cut in pieces so each guest can take home their own piece of the party.

Christmas photos

Find a vintage photograph of parents or grandparents when they were young. Make color photocopies and use them to decorate your tree. Be sure to have the camera ready when the subjects of those photos see it for the first time. There are some memories that money just can't buy.

Wedding flowers

Save a ton on wedding flowers by renting silk flowers. Many major retail stores and craft stores rent bouquets and some even provide delivery.

Generous kids

Teach your kids the joy of giving by requiring that they go through their toys, animals, games, books and so on and pare down. Identify and then clean up the things they have decided to give to others. Help them decide on a donation site—perhaps a local shelter or mission project.

The sweetest idea

Shortly after Halloween many stores have candy on sale for up to 90% off. This is a great time to stock up on candy for holiday Gingerbread Houses, school parties, birthday piñatas and other events you know are on the calendar. Lollipops and hard candies can be crushed to make stained glass sugar cookies, and chocolate candies can have their useful lives extended in the freezer.

Treasure hunt

Turn Christmas Day into a treasure hunt for your kids. Write out clues and riddles, hints and suggestions to help them find their gifts. Make it really hard by hiding the biggest and best at the grandparent's house. Now Christmas will last longer and not become a frenzied blur.

Get real

Keep a trash can nearby as you unpack your holiday decorations. Give yourself strict instructions that if you don't love it, if it doesn't make you smile or it's hopelessly tangled in knots—it's history. Out it goes.

Family Christmas Club

Find a large container such as a large coffee can with a lid. Glue the lid in place and then decorate in a festive way, cutting a slit on the top. Keep the Club Can in a safe place known to everyone in the family. Each pay period contribute a set amount. Additional contributions can be made at anytime during the year and in any amount. On Thanksgiving Day, open the Club Can, count the bounty and make plans for how you will spend your cash so that you really do have a debt-free holiday.

Santa bulbs

When you have a light bulb that blows, don't toss it out. Paint it white, turn it upside down and paint a face near the base. Paint the base to look like a cap, add a fabric scarf and you have a snowman to hang on your Christmas tree. You can also paint Santas or holiday colors with glitter finishes. And the candle shaped bulbs make great Santas.

Wedding day survival kit

Create a wedding day survival kit for the bride-to-be. Include items in a special gift bag or basket that she might need the day of the wedding as she is getting ready, such as a can of Static Guard (or a dryer sheet), a travel-size sewing kit, a large pack of safety pins, bobby pins, breath mints, a small box of tissues and a disposable camera.

Count down to Christmas

Change your child's top bookshelf to twenty-four Christmas-themed books. It's a good idea to make sure each book can be read in one night. Write a number (1-24) on red and green construction paper and place one on the spine of each book. Be sure the last book is *Twas the Night before Christmas*. Each night read the designated story. This is a fun and inexpensive way for the family to count down to Christmas. And if you don't have 24 books, you can find these very cheaply at used bookstores. Or start this tradition next year, and ask relatives to give the kids Christmas books this year.

Lights out

Take pity on your electricity bill that gets a serious jolt from all of your Christmas lights. Add an automatic timer to your holiday display. A reliable schedule to consider is lights on at 6:00 pm and off at 11:00 pm.

Debt no more

After each credit card you pay off, cut it into a star, bell or some type of Christmas shape. Punch a hole through the top, add a ribbon and put it away with your Christmas ornaments. At the end of the year, take out these credit-card ornaments, put them on your tree, and let them be a reminder of the great job you did paying them off. Let it also be a reminder not to get into credit-card debt next Christmas.

12 days tradition

Before the start of the Christmas holidays secretly select a family with children that you will make the recipient of your annual Twelve Days of Christmas tradition. Next, figure out what you want to do for each day such as: Day 1: A poinsettia with pretty red leaves. Day 2: Two quarts of eggnog. You get the idea. Carry this out as a secret and try really hard not to get caught delivering the different days' goodies. Deliver to school, work, home, church—anywhere you can. The last day go to the family's house with Day 12's bounty. If you can, sing your own version of the "Twelve Days of Christmas," using your gifts in the lyrics. It's great fun and suspense for the family giving as well as the one receiving.

Vintage formals

All of those prom, bridesmaid's and party formals hanging out in the back of your closet need to come out into the light of day. Be brave. Cut them up and make new party dresses for your little girls. Or let the kids play dress-up in them. Another idea: Use the beautiful fabrics to make throw pillows or other decorator items for your home. It's a pretty good bet that you'll never wear them again, so you might as well get some use out of them.

Reception sites

These days a wedding reception can be ridiculously expensive. But there are some options that come in on the lower end of the scale: Private clubs, Women's clubs, hunt clubs and college campuses are more likely to be within your budget.

Just for kids

Here's a fun idea for making treats to take to a school or other group party. Save the cardboard from toilet paper rolls and cut colored tissue paper into rectangles. Roll the tube in the tissue paper, use curling ribbon to tie one end and fill the open end with candy and tiny treasures like erasers, plastic jewelry and balls. Tie the other end with curling ribbon and you have adorable presents for kids' holiday parties.

Decorating with leaves

Every year when the leaves begin turning gather the most colorful. Press them between the pages of heavy books for two days so they are dry and flat. Glue stems to ribbon and make garlands and a table runner. You can leave your decorations up for two months. There. You've decorated for both Halloween and Thanksgiving for free.

Melted wax cake?

To protect the frosting on your birthday cakes from being coated in wax use miniature marshmallows for candle holders. If you have larger candles use the large marshmallows.

Floral arrangements

You do not need to buy flowers from expensive florists to have beautiful arrangements. Sam's Club and Costco sell beautiful bouquets for cheap. When put in a vase they make a beautiful display on the altar for a wedding or on the tables at the reception.

Wedding savings

Professionals who provide wedding services often charge outrageous sums because of their names, not necessarily for their exceptional expertise. To save money on food and pictures, find a culinary arts school and ask the instructor to recommend a student or students who may have had some experience in catering. They will often take the job for a little above cost just to get the referral. Inquire at a photography school or college photography department, too.

Christmas cookie swap

Get your friends together and plan a Cookie Swap. Here's how it works: Set a date and a time for the event. In anticipation each participant bakes one dozen cookies for each participant, including herself. Include a copy of the cookie recipe with each dozen cookies, which are packaged separately. For example, if there are six participants, each one bakes six dozen cookies from a favorite recipe, and makes six copies of that recipe. On the day of the cookie swap, cookies and recipe cards are swapped with each participant. Each participant ends up with six different kinds of cookies (1 dozen of each variety) and six different recipes. This is a nice way to have a variety of cookies for the holidays without all of the expense and hassle of baking so many varieties.

Fab fireplace

If you love having a fireplace but hate the mess of ashes, logs and soot—do this: Clean out your fireplace and remove the grate. Arrange candles of all sizes right where you would normally place the logs. Before you light the candles, open the damper because this is going to give off more heat than you might think. Light the candles and enjoy the beautiful warmth and cozy display of a well-controlled fire.

Jack-o-lantern smarts

If you're tired of burning your hands trying to light jack-o-lantern candles or right fallen flashlights, try cutting the bottom out of the pumpkin instead of the top. You can carve out a level place in the cut-out for the candle. Light it and simply place the cleaned and carved pumpkin over the top.

Photo tin

A metal cookie tin makes a great container for photographs—particularly those that are holiday-related. Just bring them out year after year. No one seems to tire of enjoying the memories.

Family photo

If you love to send family pictures with your Christmas cards—but hate the high reprint charges, try this: Take a fresh roll of film and shoot off 24 or 36 pictures of the same pose. Most kids can manage to stay still for the few minutes this takes. Have the roll developed with double prints so you get 48 or 72 pictures for a lot less than reprinting one favorite shot. Now everyone gets a slightly different take on your photo session. The pictures are more candid than staged, and that's what makes them so great.

Holiday tradition

Once Christmas is over why not plan for next year and add a new tradition? Throughout the year look for ornaments that have a significant meaning for the recipient. On Thanksgiving use them as place cards, indicating each person's place at the table. If you have small children they will have a wonderful collection for their first Christmas tree as an adult. It's a fun way of recalling memories of one's childhood.

Saving on Christmas

If your mall has a big holiday kick-off when they offer 20% off on mall gift certificates or something similar, take them up on it! Buy $100 gift certificates for $80 with your Christmas cash. It's going to stretch a lot farther. Now shop as you normally would, but pay with the gift certificates you have just purchased. There will probably be a limit of say $200 in gift certificates per person, so plan ahead. Take a spouse or friend with you to buy additional gift certificates for you.

Wedding on a budget

Huge wedding, no debt. The groom bought a suit instead of renting a tux. The bride bought her dress in the formal section of a department store. She approached a florist in her neighborhood and said she had only a limited amount to spend and no more. She had a formal bouquet and also one to toss. Her sister's was identical, but with different ribbon. Having one attendant each was a real saver, financially and emotionally. The florist made eight simple boutonnières and corsages for ushers, parents, siblings and grandparents. The church was so beautiful it needed no decoration. Their reception centerpieces were small terracotta pots with ribbons and votives inside. It was gorgeous. The couple had a formal wedding for 300 guests with dinner, live music, and open bar for less than $8,000—in Chicago.

Sweet costume

Use a brown trash bag, some poster board and felt-tip markers or paints to make a great costume for a small child. Cut head and arm holes in the bag, and decorate with the M&M logo cut out of the poster board. For added color, cut out circles and color with paint or markers to resemble candies; attach to the front and back of the bag. This costume works very well in cold weather, since it can be worn over warm clothing. You may want to add a bright colored hat and gloves to match.

Travel and Entertainment

Travel and Entertainment

Friendship potluck

Get a group of friends or relatives and pick a day or week of the month when everyone's cupboards are pretty lean. Get everyone to bring an item that they have to share and have dinner together. Saves money on going out with friends, and you can have some fun with some of the surprises on the menu.

Fly like royalty

If you are on your honeymoon and traveling by air, be sure and let the gate agent know. Be sincere, polite and friendly when asking for the upgrade. You just might get it. In addition, ask for the gate agent's name so you can write the airlines about his/her professionalism. These types of letters go into a personnel file and are used to justify promotions.

Traveling meals

Traveling with kids can get expensive if you don't bring your own food. Since kids like the same things for breakfast no matter where they are, buy large boxes of cereal. Store the cereal in zip-type bags when traveling and bring along plastic spoons, bowls and napkins. Just stop by the store and pickup some milk before you stop to eat. Add fresh fruit from home and you've got a great breakfast. For lunches, pack cheese, crackers and fruit. Add fresh veggies and dip and you've got a rolling feast that's a great alternative to plain sandwiches.

Buddy packing

Packing can be tricky, especially when trying to figure out how to allow for any traveling mishaps. Always pack one change of clothing in another family member's luggage. This way, if the airlines lose your luggage, you will still have fresh clothing until your luggage is found.

No more lost luggage

Put a note inside each piece of luggage that lists your name, cell phone number and/or email address. That way you can be found, and your luggage returned without giving out your home address or other personal information.

Family vacation

Plan a stay-at-home vacation this year. Visit all the tourist attractions in your own city. Do something different every day. Stay up late, sleep in late. Unplug the phone. Eat out, cook in. Just change it up in every way and you'll have a vacation you'll always remember.

Camping timesaver

Before you cook over an open flame rub a coating of liquid dish soap all over the outside of your pans. The soot from the flames will stick to the layer of soap and will rinse right off when you wash the pan. This prevents your pans from getting blackened by the camp fire.

Ice for travel

Rather than making a stop at the grocery store to buy bags of ice for your cooler, several days before you start your vacation or day trip fill empty two-liter soda pop bottles with water, place in the freezer and make your own ice "blocks." Not only does it save time and money, these large containers of solid ice last two or three times longer than cubes and the melted water is contained so the items in the cooler don't get flooded.

Extra room on the plane

When booking a flight that has three seats together, ask for the aisle and window seats if there are just two of you traveling together. Other passengers are usually reluctant to take a middle seat. When no one sits there just flip up the arms and you will have lots of extra room. In the event that someone does take it, you can offer to switch one of the seats so you can sit together.

Cheap entertainment

Before you take off on a road trip stop at the library and check out books on tape. If you have kids, get lots of stories that will interest them along with music, too. Even if there's a rental charge of a buck or two, that's a lot cheaper than renting from the video store or buying them outright.

Cheap case

Need luggage for a kid who's traveling? Check the thrift store. You'll find a big selection and you won't have to be concerned about it getting beat up on the trip because it's already been there, done that.

Adhesive tape play

Got little ones on a long plane trip? Take a roll of adhesive tape. They have so much fun playing with it, and it keeps them occupied for what seems like hours.

Condo rental

If you have kids you will find that renting a condo or apartment is better than staying in a hotel room. It's not so confining, there are more things for kids to do and you'll be able to eat a few meals in. Check online for house or condo rentals in your destination of choice. You may be pleasantly surprised to see the cost is not only competitive—it could be a lot less.

Priceline for hotels

Using *www.priceline.com* for hotel accommodations is not that tricky. You just determine what grade of hotel you want (they use the star rating system) and the specific area and then place your bid for the per-night charge. Remember that the price you name, if accepted, will not include tax, which can be significant, especially in large cities like New York or Chicago.

Bring proof

If a city offers free or discounted services to its residents and you live outside the city limits you may be able to qualify for certain services or amenities if you can prove that you pay taxes or any utilities to the city. Show pay stubs or documentation.

Packing for a trip

Make a list of all the things you need to pack in your suitcase. Now throw the list in your suitcase, too. It will be a handy check on the other end when you pack to come home. You don't waste a lot of time wondering what you forgot to pack.

Cheap sleeps

If you are over 50, consider joining the Evergreen Club (*www.evergreenclub.com*). You stay in other members' homes for just $25 per night. The hospitality network includes nearly 2,000 Bed and Breakfast home stays in North America, so almost anywhere you want to explore, you'll be welcome at an Evergreen Club home. You'll find an amazing organization of wonderful folks all across the country who not only love to be guests, but hosts, too.

Cheaper movie night

Instead of paying for movie rentals, record all the television shows that you don't watch during the week, and watch them on your weekend family "movie" night.

Luggage I.D.

Mark your luggage in some unique way so it will be clear it's yours when it comes down the luggage belt at the airport.

Kid travel

About 30 days before traveling with small children, take some of their favorite small toys and wrap them in colorful gift wrap. Place them in a bag all their own. In the bag, also add crayons, coloring books, plain index cards and "garage sale stickers" (round colorful stickers). Now you're all ready for a fun-filled road trip with kids on board.

Join a ski club

If the high cost of skiing is enough to give you a heart attack, consider joining a local ski club. Most cities have at least one ski club, and many are family oriented. Even if you don't ski often, it's worthwhile to pay the modest membership fee because ski clubs are eligible for significant group discounts on lift tickets, hotel rooms and equipment rentals.

Contact number

Make sure the airline has a contact number for you, not the travel agent who might have made your reservations. With no contact information they cannot reach you with a schedule change or cancellation until you get to the airport.

Travel kit

Keep a travel kit in the car that contains gallon-size zip-type bags, paper napkins, straws and antibacterial soap. It's amazing how many times you will need to use your kit, especially if you have kids.

Traveling seniors

Be sure to check if the airline has a senior rate. Most do and not only will you get a lower fare, the restrictions will not be so limiting. For example, one airline doesn't require an advance purchase and will leave your return date open.

Free tickets to the fair

If you have a hobby or craft that you enjoy doing, enter one of your finished products in your local county fair. As an exhibitor you will be given free tickets to the fair. If you've been to a fair lately you know just how expensive it can be to take a family. Call your county office to find out how to get a fair handbook for your area. The handbook cites all the rules you must follow to enter an exhibit.

Rental car insurance

Before buying that additional insurance offered by rental car companies, check with your own car insurance company and find out if you have coverage for rental cars. Chances are you do, so you can say "No thanks" to the salesperson who tries to scare you into purchasing additional insurance. Remember: The commission is significant on insurance add-ons. So expect some amount of pressure.

Family food

When traveling as a family, choose a lodging that has a refrigerator in the room. Buy cereal and milk, sandwich fixings and juice boxes. Freeze the juice boxes. Next morning have breakfast in the room. Pack a simple lunch that will stay cool, thanks to the frozen juice boxes. Then, enjoy your dinner at an interesting restaurant.

Bubble envelopes

Take along a large, self-addressed and stamped padded envelope with you to the airport. If security decides to take something away like sewing scissors, or who knows what else, they will mail the item(s) to your home if you have this envelope ready for them.

European car rental

Compare car rental rates months before your European holiday. Three sources to compare are car rental brokers with U.S. offices such as Kemwell; the airline's fly-drive packages; and world-wide car rental companies like Hertz. Also compare the rates between different European gateway cities you could fly into. Rental rates for cars and vans may vary widely between locations and companies, but it's not that difficult to figure out. Just start planning early.

Picture perfect

If you like to take photographs on vacation of historical sites and landmarks, buy a bulk pack of postcards instead. Usually you can buy these from street vendors at tourist spots. You can get several postcards for one or two dollars. This has many benefits. You never have to worry about lighting or lenses. You don't have to wait for the crowd of people to move who are blocking your shot. You don't have to wait until you get home and develop your pictures to realize you left the lens cover on or that your thumb was in the way. They are already perfectly sized and centered for photo albums and scrapbooks. But most of all, you save on the cost of film and developing.

Travel prep

It's always good to keep a small travel kit in your car even if you have no plans for an overnight stay. Get travel sizes of toiletries and a spare change of clothes. You just never know when you will be called upon for an overnight emergency and it's sure nice to know you have your stuff with you.

Entertainment book

Entertainment books are filled with great coupons and discounts for everything from entrance fees to food and gasoline. Go to *www.entertainment.com* where you can buy a book for the cities you will be visiting at a greatly-discounted rate, because you'll be there for only a short time.

Date night

Getting a night out with your spouse is sometimes hard to arrange, and expensive if you happen to need a babysitter. So create a Date Night at home. After the kids have gone to bed break out the candles and special dinner. So what if it's really late? That was never a problem back before you had kids.

Instant picnic kit

Get a big basket and load it up with canned meats, crackers, bottled water, juice boxes, paper supplies, Frisbee and a tablecloth—all non perishables. Now all you need to add is a a sunny day with two or three hours to spare. You've got a picnic all ready to go.

Jumbo bags

Use the large zip-type bags when you pack the family for a trip. Pack one complete days' outfit for each person in a bag and zip it up. Everything is clean, neat and separate from the other things in the suitcase. Squeeze the air out by rolling the bag up before zipping closed. It's so much easier to pack your suitcases when everything is neatly organized into big plastic bags.

Roll your own

When packing your suitcase, roll your clothes instead of laying them folded flat. They will be less wrinkled and you'll maximize your space.

Free theater

Local community and broadway theaters always need good-sized audiences during previews when critics and reviewers will be attending. To that end, theaters often do what's called "papering the house," which means that they'll give out free tickets. You can either call the theater box office and see if they're offering complimentary tickets or if you're anywhere near a university or school with a drama department, check out the bulletin boards, which usually list the dates and shows when theaters are doing this.

Minimize jet lag

During the week before traveling outside of your time zone, go to sleep later than normal when traveling east. When traveling west go to sleep earlier than normal. During that week, gradually increase these bedtime changes until you are experiencing the exact destination times. While en route on the aircraft, change your watch time to the destination time and start living in that time zone.

Strategic travel

When you travel you need to compare airfares for alternative airports. For example, when traveling to New York City, you may discover it's a lot cheaper to fly into Philadelphia, rent a car and drive the two hours to the city. Even with the cost of the car, the difference in airfare could save you a lot of money. Check all kinds of options and you'll see how this can work out for you.

Vacation memories

When you travel take a little time to mail postcards back home—to yourself. Describe where you've been and what you've been doing—in detail. By mailing the postcards, the date gets stamped on them. Now you have the perfect record of your trip complete with dates, pictures and specific details that might otherwise slip your mind once you arrive back home. Just pop your postcards into a photo album and your vacation scrapbook is complete.

Cheaper and better

When you travel, try out a studio hotel. The kitchenette allows you to prepare meals, there's a laundry room, and many times it's cheaper than regular hotels. If there is not a studio hotel where you need to stay, ask about a room with a kitchenette at a chain hotel. You pay much less because you receive only one maid visit per week, and they know that those who want this type of room are usually not the type who damage rooms.

Avoid traffic

If you are in a real time crunch getting to the airport, use the Arrivals instead of Departures to reach your terminal. This saves a lot of time though you may have to take your luggage up the elevator. Again, this is not the proper way to enter the airport but certainly a viable option if your other choice is to miss your flight.

Free to win

If your area has a radio station that offers phone-in contests, get involved. If you are persistent in time you're bound to win something like movie passes, lunches, games, CDs, trips, vehicles and merchandise. It only takes being the right number caller to win. These little extras can put a lot of fun into a frugal household.

Cheap dates

Many cities have bookstores or malls that feature free music "in house" by live bands on the weekends. The mall may even send you a copy of their booking schedule. At that price (free), you can take the whole family.

Loose change, family fun

Set up a central change collection receptacle with the rule that everyone in the family empties their pockets in the Family Vacation Jug. Once everyone is on board you'll be amazed how quickly it adds up. When you're ready to get away from it all, the kids get to count the money to see how far the family can go.

Saving money feels good

Before you book your next vacation call your local public television station and find out when they are having their next pledge drive. There is almost always a travel package to bid on. For example, an all-inclusive Alaskan cruise for four valued at $3,100 can go for as low as $1,000. Weekends at bed-and-breakfasts, family dude ranch vacations, ski packages, Caribbean travel, and much more—all are typical travel auction items during public television pledge drives. You will also be supporting your local public television station and the programs they offer to you and your family, so you can feel good about yourself and get a vacation out of it to boot.

After midnight

Buy the cheapest airfares after midnight. Most airlines only hold reservations until midnight in the time zone where the airline is headquartered. For example American Airlines is based in Dallas, so that would be midnight Central Time. Call the airlines' reservation numbers after midnight (once those seats reserved for the day have been released again) or go online to the airline's website to have the best selection of cheap fares.

Camping trick

When heading out for a camping trip, fill a couple of your pump-style hand soap containers with shampoo the and hand soap.

Travel and Entertainment

Affordable vacations

Gather the family and plan a vacation twelve months out that everyone can start working to contribute to. Even the little ones can do something. Pick a place within 200 miles. Calculate gasoline for the trip, approximate price for the hotel, food, entrance fees and so on. Write it all down, add it up and divide it by twelve to get the amount you need to save each month. Show it to the family and say that this is the goal for a debt-free vacation. Adjust the plans accordingly. Everyone contributes with babysitting money, yard work money and garage sale proceeds. You can make up the difference and everybody can watch the dream grow. When someone whines about never getting to go anywhere, reiterate the vacation goal. It will make the vacation more anticipated and you won't hear too many complaints about being bored when vacation day arrives.

Free passes

The library is an excellent resource for free passes to local museums, science centers, and aquariums. If you have a library card in an area where these wonderful attractions are located, generally they have free day passes. Call your local library and check out what they have.

Family outings

Purchase memberships to the museums and zoos in your area. The cost is reasonable, and well worth it if you have a large family. Full admission for the entire family is included in your membership and could extend to other interesting venues as well. In New York City one membership will get you into the Museum of Natural History, the Bronx Zoo and the Hall of Science. And you can go as many times as you want.

Free concerts

Many theaters and concert halls have a need for volunteers and will often repay them with free tickets to events. Volunteer opportunities can range from stuffing envelopes to ushering at events—sometimes ushers even get paid. Call your local theater to find out if they need any help. All it will cost you is a little time.

Free movie rentals

Find out if your video rental store advertises that new releases are guaranteed—meaning that if they run out, you get a rain check to rent the movie for free when it is available. Be sure you visit the store the first weekend a movie comes out and when the store is out (which is almost always) you get your rain check.

Hotel incentives

Even if you think you might never stay at a hotel chain again, sign up for their club so you get points for staying. You might discover the hotel is part of a larger network and who knows, you just might be back. Those points can add up to a free night or two in not much time at all.

Vacation long distance

Always take a prepaid long-distance calling card with you so you never have to make a call from the hotel room. Charges of $30 for a 10-minute phone call are not unusual. Of course you can call the toll-free number from your room so you can use your prepaid card. Or if you don't have a card, walk down to the lobby and use a public telephone. At least you'll pay the going rate— not some inflated rate with all kinds of add-ons and mystery fees.

Flight cancelled? Try this

For whatever reason, airlines are always canceling or rescheduling flights. The airline announces the change and most passengers rush to get in line at the counter to rebook. If this happens to you, get on your phone or go to the nearest telephone and call the airline's toll free customer service number, usually found in your reservation packet. These service agents know of cancellations and can get you immediate access to available seats on other flights.

Restaurant tab

Ordering drinks in a restaurant— even lemonade or soda— can boost the tab by about $3 a person when you consider tax and tip. For a family of four, you've just spent $12 before you even look at the menu. Agree to order water. In fact, pay the kids a buck each when they do. You'll all be way ahead and the kids will think they've just discovered a gold mine.

Free firewood

When camping, don't plan to buy firewood once you reach your camping destination. It will cost you a fortune for just a small amount of wood. Instead, plan ahead. Go to a local lumber yard or home improvement center that offers "free wood" i.e. the ends of 2x4s, broken pallets and other scrap lumber. Make up your own bundles of firewood, being careful to not include any treated wood.

Travel and Entertainment

Packing for the road

Rather than packing a suitcase for each person in the family when taking a car trip, use small laundry baskets. They hold a lot, they are easy to stack, and it's easy to take items out en route. It's also easy to consolidate into one basket when stopping overnight rather than lugging one suitcase per person to the room. Sadly, this method does not work for plane travel.

Yard and Garden

Yard and Garden

Stubborn lawn mower

After sitting unused for a few months it is difficult to start some lawn mower engines. One trick to get a stubborn gasoline engine running is to remove the spark plug, dribble a few drops of gasoline into the spark plug hole, replace the plug and then try starting the engine. Often, this will get things running, and save time and a trip to a repairman.

Bye-bye aphids

Plant 4 or 5 peeled cloves of garlic near the base of your rose bushes and in a couple of days all the aphids will have vanished. This non-toxic treatment is completely natural and remains effective for a long time.

Hose bin

Instead of purchasing a garden hose hanger for the garage make your own by recycling a large plastic bucket. Nail the bucket to the wall with the open side facing outward. Wind your hose around the bucket and place sprinklers inside of the bucket. Nice and tidy.

Container gardening

Pots for container gardens are usually deeper than necessary. Filling the entire pot wastes soil and makes the pot heavy. Save the plastic packs that the annuals come in and turn them upside down in the bottom of the pots to take up room. Fill the pot with soil and plant your flowers.

Hummingbirds, no bees

If you apply Vaseline to the feeding spouts of your hummingbird feeder, the bees will not bother it. The Vaseline makes the bees get stuck, which they don't like, but the hummingbirds are unharmed by this sticky situation.

Marking territories

Place cut oranges or lemons in the areas around your home where you would just as soon the neighborhood cats not "mark" as their territory. Apparently they are not interested in a lovely citrusy scent and it repels them. It really works well.

Sharing yard tools

It's unlikely that any one family will use all of their yard and garden tools all the time. That's why it makes sense to share the cost and then share the item. Of course you'll need to decide who services the shared lawn mower or stores the rakes and leaf blower. But if you are flexible, it's a great way to reduce the cost of homeownership without sacrificing the price of ownership.

Birdseed holder

An empty 2-liter soda bottle is perfect for storing bird seed. It stores easier, pours easier and doesn't attract mice.

Perfect hose filter

Position a piece of nylon hosiery or a knee high over the end of a garden hose, tying it securely. While filling your swimming pool this will act as a fine filter to catch all of the sediment from the pipes that you do not want clogging up your pool filter.

Free mulch

Tree trimming services will often need a place to dump their wood chips. See if they will let you pickup a truckload of wood chips or even dump a load at your driveway. Use it as mulch in your gardens to save on watering costs because mulch slows down the evaporation process, leaving the soil moist and plants alive. It's much less expensive than paying three dollars a bag for store-bought mulch to cover your plants. And fresh wood chips look great and will fragrance your yard, too.

Cheap compost

Here's the way to make an inexpensive compost bin. Buy a 32-gallon plastic trash can. Drill holes in it around sides and the bottom because compost must be able to "breathe." Add your grass clippings and pine needles; kitchen refuse like melon rinds, carrot peelings, tea bags, apple cores, banana peels—almost anything that is not protein or high in fat; wood ashes, garden clippings; and other compost material. Put the lid on and let it do its thing. About once a week, give it a good roll around to stir things up. When it's ready, work it into your garden. See *www.compostguide.com* for more information and details.

Dirt cheap!

Next time you are at the home improvement center or garden store, ask them about their "ripped bags" containing dirt, mulch and 3-in-1. Typically, when the bags become torn, contents are re-bagged and sold for half price.

Sheer coverage

Stop buying flimsy, expensive row covers to protect garden veggies from hail, cabbage butterflies, leaf miners and other airborne menaces. Instead, purchase old nylon sheer curtains at garage sales and thrift stores. These are usually cheap (or even free from family and friends, if they know you'll take them off their hands) and will last for many years. Sheers repel hail and hot sun, yet let in plenty of light, air and rain. After harvest, simply shake out the dirt, launder in hot water and store for next season. Sure beats throwing away tattered commercial covers every year and, best of all, bug—free harvests encourage families to eat homegrown organic produce.

Sprouting driveway

If your driveway or patio seems to sprout weeds through the slimmest of cracks, here's a very cheap way to alleviate the problem: Pour boiling water on the cracks. Kills 'em dead.

Houseplant miracle juice

Ever wonder how some people make those houseplants shoot up like bottle rockets? Well wonder no more because you can be one of those people. Just add one tablespoon of apple cider vinegar to one gallon in your watering can when watering all flowers and foliage. Don't overdo. Just measure carefully and your plants will respond.

Fencing for the frugal

Need a new fence but can't see your way clear to pay $25 per fence panel (the going rate in most areas)? Stop into a home improvement store and ask the manager if they ever discount their fence panels. You may learn that if one or more slats is broken, they price it for clearance. Bingo! That's what you're looking for. If you can get the panels for half price, it's quite simple to replace a broken slat. If you're patient, you should be able to pay as you go for all the fencing you require.

Broccoli care

To protect the broccoli in your garden from cabbage worms, place one leg you've cut from an old pair of pantyhose over the forming head and secure with a rubber band. This is a cheap substitute for "floating row covers" and provides a way to recycle ruined pantyhose.

Cheap scarecrow

Take those CDs you get in the mail or attached to magazines and loop a string through the center. Hang from a flexible pole or a clothesline stretched across your garden. The sun flashing on the shiny CDs annoys the birds.

Ashes for fertilizer

Take the ashes from your fireplace or fire pit and spread underneath your evergreens, bushes, pines and roses. A thin spread over all of your biannual flowers also makes a big difference the next spring. Greener, fuller foliage and beautiful flowers.

Almost never water again

To avoid watering except in very dry times, mulch. Here's the routine: Plant your vegetable seedlings. Surround them with four layers of newspaper. Pile grass clippings up to 8 inches deep on top of the newspaper. The grass will supply nitrogen, smother weeds and hold in the dew and rainwater. Your seedlings will have no trouble growing through all that mulch and will offer you a bountiful harvest.

Lawn mushrooms

If you want to get rid of mushrooms permanently sprinkle a small amount of powdered laundry detergent on them. They should be gone in a week or so.

Compost boost

Coffee grounds are like candy for a compost heap, and that's great for coffee drinkers. If you aren't one, but want great compost, ask if you can provide containers to a local café or coffee shop. Most will be more than happy to dump grounds into your containers. Just make sure you retrieve them daily.

Perk up with castor oil

Instead of buying expensive fertilizer for plants, mix 1 tablespoon castor oil (from the drug store) with four cups water. Use this to water the plants once a month for lush, green foliage.

Friendship landscaping

New home in a new community? Instead of purchasing flowers and bulbs for your landscaping, place an ad in the local community newspaper. Let readers know that you've just moved in and would love to have the unneeded plants and bulbs removed from their gardens when thinning and dividing. Not only can you end up with a yard full of beautiful plants and flowers, but you will meet many new friends. Both the landscaping and the friends should last for many years.

Almost free landscaping

You can get shrubs and other plants for your yard and garden for free (or just the cost of transporting and transplanting) if you know where to look. Many nurseries have "boneyards" where they toss plants they deem unworthy of sale. Neighbors and strangers alike will often give you cuttings, seeds or divisions of plants you admire. And if you know anyone who is part of the grounds crew of a large college or university, ask him or her to pass along any goodies they remove at work.

Cheap weed killer

Weed killer can cost a bundle. Guess what works and costs less than $.50? Plain old table salt! Generously sprinkle on the weeds and then water. Beware, however that salt will permanently sterilize soil, so you don't want to do this where you want anything to grow in the future.

For the birds

If you have a porch railing where birds love to congregate and make a mess, try this: Stretch a length of fishing line tightly from post to post about 1/2 to 1 inch above the railing. The fishing line is too thin for the birds to grip so they'll find a new haunt. This technique works well for any place that birds love to sit. Even on roofs.

Bargains in gardening

In September, October, and November, nurseries and garden centers typically reduce prices by 50% or more. They need to make room for Halloween pumpkins and Christmas trees.

No cost fertilizer

Once a week water your houseplants using a milk jug that has not yet been rinsed. The little bit of milk left in the container gives the plants a shot of nitrogen and makes them grow better than ever. Save money on fertilizer and don't waste the water that would normally go down the drain while rinsing out the jug for recycling. Your plants will look great.

Weed control

Combine 7 parts rubbing alcohol and 3 parts white vinegar in a spray bottle to kill unsightly weeds. Be careful to avoid spraying plants you want to keep. This combination is not toxic and safe around pets.

Cheap ant killer

About 1/2 teaspoon of borax dissolved in 16 ounces of hot water and 2 teaspoons of sugar will stop ants dead in their tracks. Use it in a spray bottle and spray as you would a pesticide wherever you see ants.

Snow shoveling

Before you start to shovel snow, spray your shovel with cooking spray, and it will help keep snow from sticking to your shovel and ice building up on it. Reapply as needed.

Saving water

Place a new inexpensive sponge in the bottom of a container or garden pot before filling with dirt and adding the plant material. You won't have to water as often!

Starter bed

Plastic deli/bakery containers that have the lid attached make perfect starter kits for growing vegetables from seed. Add potting soil and seeds and—Presto! Instant mini greenhouse.

Tomatoes go bananas

Throw your banana peels on your tomato plants and see greener plants. Bananas add potassium that tomatoes need.

Cleaning pruning shears

Spray your pruning shears with nonstick cooking spray before using them, and the sticky stuff that accumulates from pruning will clean up easily.

Tool maintenance

Find a cheap galvanized bucket in the garage. Fill it 3/4 full with play sand. Add enough motor oil to see a change in color but still keep it mostly sandy. When you are finished with your hand tools for the day just put them in the bucket. They will be clean, oiled and ready to go for your next gardening adventure.

Propagating roses

In the fall, cut off a rose bloom with a stem that has a "Y" shape. Place it in rich soil and compost. Place a quart jar over the rose, giving the jar a twist to press it into the earth for stability. In the spring, after the last frost, uncover and leave your new rosebush in place for one to two years before moving.

Free flower seeds

Each year when your flowers dry up and die save the seeds found just below the bloom. Remove them with your fingers and make sure they are dry. Place seeds in a plastic bag and keep them in the freezer until you are ready to plant them next spring. Try this method with cosmos, zinnias, marigolds and bachelor buttons. You really get a lot more seeds than the amount you get out of those small store-bought seed packets.

Seedlings

The proprietor of the produce stand in your community may be an excellent resource for vegetable seedlings. It can't hurt to ask. Best of all you'll be able to mix and match without having to buy a whole flat of any one kind.

Yard and Garden

Yard lights

Ask any food business that uses bulk food for a few of their 3- to 5-gallon white buckets. Cut a small hole in the lid and run an electrical cord through the hole with a standard bulb socket attached on one end. You can set these out on the ground or hang them from things. The amount of very white light you get from even a 40-watt bulb is astounding.

Want trees?

Before you run out and spend a lot of money on saplings for your yard, call your city's public works department to inquire about its landscape programs. Some cities will plant trees wherever they can find homeowners who want them. You might even be given the choice of several different types of trees.

Slow melt

To save your potted plants when you're gone for a day or two, put ice cubes on top of the soil of your plants. With the ice slowly melting your plants will stay moist until you return.

Winter blooms

Geraniums will bloom on your kitchen windowsill while snow is still covering the ground. All you have to do is bring in the plants before they get killed by the first frost of the season. Geraniums are particularly hearty and don't mind coming in from the cold.

Beautiful free flowers

Nurseries and stores that carry bedding plants are happy to get rid of the pots of blooming bulbs they haven't sold once the blooms have begun to wilt. Offer to take them off their hands and you will probably have a deal. Now you'll have bulbs galore—and that means free flowers in the spring.

Plant tonic

To one gallon of water add 1 teaspoon baking powder, 1 teaspoon Epsom salts and 1/2 teaspoon ammonia. Use this for your once-a-week watering of all your plants.

Flat-out full

Look carefully when selecting a flat of plants to place in your garden. Many flats that look full can be missing plants and it's difficult to see if the others are in full bloom. Without careful inspection expect to miss 3 to 4 plants. It is worth the effort to check. Buyers beware.

A Final Word

There's a good reason why this book is not titled *The Complete Tiptionary.* That's because as far as I'm concerned, Tiptionary will never be complete.

As long as people like you discover new ways to do things cheaper, better and faster there will always be another great tip right around the corner. And as long as I live and breathe, I'll be out there searching for tips.

I'm concerned that as you dined on this *Tiptionary 2* smorgasbord, dozens of tips came to mind. Would you share them with me? I'd love to hear from you. I'll tell you how to contact me in a minute.

But first, and in the spirit of Tiptionary—quick and easy, grab-and-go information—there are three things you need to do before our time together comes to a close:

1. Read *Debt-Proof Living.* Yes, this is a book—my book—that you need sitting right next to your *Tiptionary* collection. You will want to refer to it often. In it I tell you how to get out of debt, how to stay out and how to manage your money well. It is the complete guide to living financially free.

2. Join *DebtProofLiving.com.* You need to make this website your new home in cyberspace. You can always stop by as a visitor, but why? At Debt-Proof Living Online, membership has its privileges. You need to become a subscriber. And to thank you for buying *Tiptionary 2*, I have a gift for you. Keep reading.

3. Get *Everyday Cheapskate Daily Email.* Love tips and daily inspiration to help you manage your resources? Then you want to wake up to *Everyday Cheapskate* in your email inbox, Monday through Friday. Sign-up information follows. And don't forget, it's FREE!

And so my frugal friends, our time together has come to an end. Or maybe not. Every time you pick up this book to learn, laugh and enjoy, I'll be right here handing you yet one more way to use a dryer sheet. Or Dawn dishwashing liquid (*has* to be blue), or vinegar, baking soda, plastic bags ....

Debt-free wishes,
Mary

P.S. Look for my contact information at *DebtProofLiving.com*, keeping in mind that I can't promise a personal response.

New Revised Edition

DEBT-PROOF LIVING

The Complete Guide to Living Financially Free

MARY HUNT

Getting out of debt takes courage, commitment and a simple plan that works.

Staying debt-free is remarkable and what debt-proof living is all about. Thousands of people have done just that following the plan outlined simply and logically in *Debt-Proof Living.*

In *Debt-Proof Living,* originally published in 1999 and revised and updated in 2005, Mary Hunt tells her story of how she got into terrible financial trouble but managed to work her way out of more than $100,000 of consumer debt—and lived to write about it. With warmth and humor she convinces her readers it is possible to live a rich fulfilling life without consumer debt and she shows them exactly how to do it.

By applying her simple principles and specific methods readers learn what they never learned growing up—how to manage their household income effectively and how to create a simple get-out-of-debt plan using her trademarked Rapid Debt-Repayment Plan. But getting out of debt is only part of "The Plan." Readers learn how to give, save and build wealth using the Contingency Fund and Freedom Account along with her sound and proven principles.

Millions of readers agree ...

Debt-proof living is like giving yourself a raise!

DPL Press, Inc. (2005) ISBN 978-0-9760791-1-8

Available **NOW!** at *DebtProofLiving.com* Bookstore

Also Available from Best-Selling Author

MARY HUNT

Debt-Proof Your Marriage
08007-5850-1

In Stores NOW!
$12.99

Debt-Proof Your KIDS
978-09760791-4-9

In Stores NOW!
$14.99

Everyday Cheapskate's Greatest Tips
978-0-7624233-5-4

In Stores NOW!
$12.95

Tiptionary 1

Re-Release Coming Soon!

The Financially Confident Woman

Re-Release Coming Soon!

Debt-Proof The Holidays!
978-0-9760791-8-7

In Stores August 2007!

Available wherever fine books are sold or call 1-800 550-3502

Live Your Life For Half The Price

Award-Winning, Best-Selling Author

Mary Hunt

Now that you have the basics of debt-proof living under your belt, Mary wants to help you take it to the next level. It's time to learn all her secrets for how to live your best life on 80 percent of your income!

DPL PRESS

ISBN 0-9760791-0-0

INDEX

Index

12-Day Tradition 321
401(k), funding yours 255

A

AAA member benefits 6
accident info 8
accordian file 288
acne 177
address book 148
address box 197
address labels 200
advent calendar 154
aftershave stretcher 181
air conditioning 9, 212
air freshener 50, 214
  white vinegar/water 50
air freshener, all natural 199, 202
airport arrive and depart 335
ammonia, as oven cleaner 51
Angel Food Ministries 157
anniversary scavenger hunt 316
ant killer, cheap 347
ant repellent 195, 202, 206, 208, 211, 214, 215, 217
antibacterial kitchen spray 45
antiperspirant solution 181
antique furniture polish 56
aphids 343
apple handles 127
apples with lemon juice 120
applesauce
  for recipes 101
  oil substitute 90
appliance
  colors 233
  safety 23
  repair 306
appreciation gift 141, 143
artwork
  calendar 20
  children's 17
  garage 16
  on loan 218
ashes for fertilizer 345
astringent 176
auto
  buying 6
  car shades 6
  floor mat cleaning 247
  heat control 10
  mystery leak 11
  notebook 5
  scent, fresh 7
  tire traction 194
  trash bag 11
auto insurance 11
  rental car 332
auto parts, where to buy 6

B

baby
  bath tub 18
  bib 28
  bottle, cleaning 15, 48
  bottle, storage 29
  dressing 29
  food 15, 17
  formula 24
  formula samples 18
  kit 150
  rash 186
  toy 29
  wipes 23, 28
baby shower
  co-ed 318
  dipe and wipe 318

Index

backseat cover 9
bacon prep 107
bacon, baked 104
bacon, by George Foreman 108
bag organizer 238
bakery goods 161
baking soda
  cheaper price 212
  non-abrasive cleanser 59
  tar remover 8
banana
  for shoe polish 103
  freezing 126
  ice cream 103
  sandwich 89
  stash 117
  storage 84, 127
  store 103
bananas on tomatoes 348
bang trim 168, 169
banking
  free 259
  fun fund 259
barrette grippers 169
barstool covers 21
baseball cap cleaning 248
bath for dry skin 175
bath gel 174
bath mat, renew 307
bath oil 172
bathroom
  bucket 200
  candles 197
  decorating 211
bathtub
  back rest 174
  kneeling pad 26
  paint 25
  seat 26
  toys 26
batteries, watch 190
battery life 198
beads, craft storage 293
beauty college savings 169
bed linen kits 288
bedsheet centering 204
bee sting relief 187
beef
  beef broth extender 124
  day-old 96
  degreaser 96
  ground beef alternative 125
  ground meat stretcher 117
  purchase at university 95
  side of 83
  steak substitute 96
  tenderizer 97
bees, hummingbirds 343
beet tricks 95
bell peppers, freeze 105
belt ends 73
belt, men's designer 76
bench seating 217
beverages, quick cooling 120
big jars 286
bill pay, easy 261
bill paying 270
bills, kids help with 264
bin for garden hose 343
bingo, grocery 163
birdfeeder 27, 142
birds, keep off rail 347
birdseed container 344
birthday
  cards 146
  club 151
  gifts in bulk 142
  party 19

Index

cake kit 317
tablecloths 319
blazer, proper hanging 76
bleeding of minor cuts 186
blemishes 176, 177
blinds cleaner 53
blinds, vertical 305
blow-dryer cleaning 170
body powder 173
boil food together 116
book website 34
bookends 196
bookmark momentos 213
bookmarks 37
books
for sale 35
on tape 22
online 33
books for teachers 149
booster seat 21
boot stuffers 73
bottle labeling 55
bouncing checks 273
bowl caps 238
bowl covers 89
box and bag storage 234
brass, cleaning 224
bread
breadcrumbs 127
freezing buns 114
fresh 87
frozen 87
heel uses 87
prep for freezing 111
pudding 87
soften in oven 133
stale for melba toast 88
breading 113
bride's tool kit 139
bridal accessories 317
bridal, gown sensible 314
broken glass pickup 62
brown sugar
DIY 117
softening 85
brownies, cutting 129
bubbles
bath 22
party 17
to go 17
buckets, ice cream 287
buddy packing 329
buffet space 205
building supplies 208
bulk food packaging 91
bulk wrapping paper 152
bumper stickers 6
bunion treatment 187
burned pot cleaner 61
burned-on spot 57
burner covers 206
burnt-on 239
butter mixture 117
butter wrappers 121
buttermilk, freeze 107
button
holder 69
repair 69, 70
surprise 69

C

cabinets, easy fix 305
cable, cheap 269
cake
carrot 98
cutter 128
decorating 126

Index

- frosting-free 86
- ingredient substitutes 112
- pan, greasing 85, 133
- tester 124
- transport 133
- wax candle drips 127
- weepy icing 83

cake tester 232
calendars
- art 204
- recycle 16
- in bathroom 293
- lasting 222

calling, long-distance 264
camping food 113
camping timesaver 330
campus bargains 5
campus tour, virtual 275
can opening 85
cancelled flight 338
candles
- decorating 214
- lighting 223
- long-lasting 201
- mess 43
- no-burn 223
- noodle 224
- removal 50, 62
- smoke remover 47
- stabilize 196, 213
- trimming 196
- unwanted 206
- votive jars 214

candy bouquet 154
cappuccino 125
caps, easy off 231
car seat cover 21
card organizer 146
card table repair 209
caretaker information 188
carnival fun 15
carpet
- candle wax 46
- cheap 204
- cleaning 49, 50, 54
- fleas, in carpet 47
- indentations 201
- nail polish 47
- remove odor from wet 50
- spot remover recipe 55
- stains 60
- static 215

carrot cake 98
carrot pancakes 113
cart shopping 163
cases, padded 283
cash
- envelopes 276
- register for kids 25
- organizing 264

cast iron cookware 229
castor oil, fertilizer 346
cat shampoo 300
cats, make them scram 343
cats, misbehaving 300
caulk cleaner 53
CD cookbook 141
CD repair 45
ceiling cleaning 45, 61
ceiling fan paint 196
celery storage 83
cell phone rescue 308
cereal
- savings 92
- storage 128

cushions, chair 225
champagne flute 42
chandelier, cleaning 63

Index

change jar 262
changing table 27
chapped lips 185
charcoal recycling 89
charging habits 262
charitable gift log 155
check register tips 267
check safety 262
checkbook 268
checking accounts 28
checks
  bouncing 255
  free 263
  writing 258
cheese
  chill first 128
  flavoring 119
  grater 128
  grating 84, 101
  mold prevention 120, 125
  slicing 113
  storage 116
cherry pitter 102
cherry substitute 128
chicken
  deli deals 119
  de-skinning 84
  frozen singles 89
  meals 100
chicken stock 129
children's books 35
chilled drinks 120
china finds 211
chocolate
  baking squares 97
  for grating 101
  syrup 118
chore cards 19
Christmas
  card photo album 154
  family book 317
  gift, 3-Gift Rule 313
  gifts 152
  in July 285
  lights 316
cinnamon rolls, use floss 110
clams, easy-open 96
cleaning
  bucket 51
  clothes 216
  photos 41
  solution 42, 57, 58, 61
  timer 57
cleanser
  granite countertop 46
  scrubbing bubbles 43
  soft scrub 44
  stovetop 45
cleanup, easy 232
closet curtain 205
closet, organized 286
cloth napkins 221
clothes
  donate 77
  dye 248
  for kids 72
  mens for women 78
  plan for a month 80
  relocate "temporarily" 78
  wrinkled 77
clothes hamper fragrance 247
clothespins 201
clothing
  buy from dry cleaner 74
  little girls 75
  mens shirt, recycle 75
  one more use 69
  shopping with tape measure 74

Index

club soda 41
clutter, garage 294
coasters 139, 224
coating mix recipe 113
coffee
  cappuccino 125
  carafe cleaning 47
  creamer 84, 116
  flavored 120
  flavors 128
  gourmet 86
  gourmet instant 86
  iced 88, 130
  storage 97
  vanilla 96
coffee filter substitute 98
coffee grinder,
  clean 63
  free 105
coffee stain magic 65
coin collection 141
coin wrappers 265
cold pack 186
cold sore remedy 184, 187
college costs 270
college, cheap 266
college, credit for kids 275
color pallette 72
comforter bags 292
compact powder sponge 179
complain about credit cards 271
compost, cheap 344
computer
  books 34
  screen cleaner 33
  software 34, 36
  software exchange 37
concerts, free 338
conditioner, shave with 180
congratulatory certificate 153
contact reuse case 183
container refill 94
cookie dough
  chill 132
  gifts 138
cookie swap 323
cookies
  for newlyweds 148
  no chips 115
  softening 119
  swap 125
  sandwich in a flash 107
cooking in bulk 83
cooking oil 89
cooking oil brush 95
cooking spray bottle 123
cooking spray zone 122
cookware cleaner 44, 48, 53
copper pans 230
cord organization 36
corn husks 90
corn, frozen on cob 105
cornbread, baking alternative 111
cosmetic storage 179
costume box 22
cottage cheese, storage 124
couch cushions 206
count down for Christmas 321
coupon 159, 163
Coupon Mom 162
coupons
  album 161
  clippers 159
  online 158
  organizer 162
  reminder 159
  where to find 160
  with list 163

Index

crafts
- beads, storage 293
- projects 207
- storage 283
- supplies, organize 281

crayons
- cleanup 24
- long lasting 27
- marks 50

cream cheese flavoring 85
cream of tartar 46
credit cards, tracking 261
credit checkup, yearly 268
credit report, free 265
credit, off peak 275
crevice cleaner 62
cross-stitch cleaning 49
crowds for garage sale 291
cruise control 9
cucumber
- storage 96
- tricks 129

curtain rod 196, 197, 206, 219
curtains 210
curtains, hanging 222
cuticle cream 179
cuticles 189
cutting board 235
cutting board, disposable 239

D

dandruff 171
date night 334
Dawn dishwashing liquid
- miraculous bathroom cleaner 55
- spot remover 251

dealer's invoice 6
debt
- invest in yours 266
- paying down 263

decorating
- bedroom 219
- dresser 219

decoupage plate 137
deductions, medical 263
denim
- patches 29
- softening recipe 80

deodorant soap 181
deodorant solution 181
deposit receipts 266
designer clothes for kids 22
designer deals online 72
diaper pin cushion 17
diaper rash cream 18
dinner 217
dinner plate size 111
dipe and wipe baby shower 318
director's chair gift 152
directory assistance, free 268
dirt cheap 344
disaster bag 210
dish cleaner 53
dishwasher
- as heater 207
- flatware 236
- Kool-Aid clean 49
- repair 235
- rinse aid 51
- soap bubbles 59
- soap savings 54

dishwashing liquid 200, 230, 233
dishwashing trick 234, 237
dog bed, big dogs 298
dog, smelly 300
dollar bill roll 149
donation as gift 145

Index

door squeaks 198
double coupons 158
drain cleaner 45, 237
drapes 223
drawer organizers 22
drawer storage 234
dress-up 27
drink blender 236
drinking glass 207
driveway sealing 205
driving routes 10
dry feet soother 175
dry hand soother 175
dry skin 174
  solution for 172
  bath for 174
dryer maintenance 252
dryer sheet 7, 214
dryer sheet rationing 251
dry-erase boards 42
drying flowers 201
dump 212
Dust Buster filters 53
dust cloth 61, 62
dust mittens 55
dusting brush 59
dusting sheet 65
dustpan, made from foil 63
duvet cover 218
dye 219

E

ear infections, pets 297
earring
  fix 189
  organize 282
  storage 167, 168
  for sore ears 168
egg carton recycling 94
eggnog freezing 85, 117
eggs
  chopping 112
  cleanup 49
  deviled 103
  food coloring 93
  freezing 84
  freshness 83
  hard boiled 94
  non substitute 109
  peeling 83
  prevent cracking 237
  substitute 95
electric bill, cut it 270
electricity, save on 255
energy
  conservation 197
  freezer 97
energy savings 226, 268
Entertainment Book 334
envelopes 151
envelopes, cash 276
eraser cleaner 62
exercise and get paid 183
exercise balls 183
exfoliant 177
exfoliator 176
expired coupons 160
eye makeup 178
eyebrow and ear numbing 179
eyebrow brush 178
eyeglass
  cleaner 61
  frames 182
  repair 182
eyelash curler 178
eyeliner sharpening 177
eyeliner trick 177

Index

eyeshadow blush 178

F

fabric 201, 219
fabric jars 316
fabric paint 76
fabric softener 244
  sponges 247
  substitute 245
fabric storage 221
face mask 173
facial 173, 176
facial powder 178
facial scrub 176
fair, free tickets 332
Family Christmas Club 320
family
  conversations 26
  greeting card 145
  history, headstones 294
  outings 337
fan blade 41
fashion show 17
fees 263
fencing, for frugal 345
fertilizer, free 347
fiberglass
  cleaner 49
  cleaning 46
fireproof 290
files, hidden under tablecloth 293
film
  I.D. 204
  in the refrigerator 194
film developing 289
filter, aquarium 297
financial education 257
fingernail
  file 180
  repair 189
  stains 180
fire starter
  half a log 212
  lint 215
  magazine 194
  pinecone 199
fire station birthday party 19
firewood cover 200
fitness videos 35
fix-it book 221
flag cleaning 247
flags, store 292
flatware help 220
flavored oils 88
flavorings, by mail order 114
flawed packaging discounts 158
flea prevention, cheap 297
flea repellent 216
fleece blanket 151
flies and garbage cans 195
floating row covers 345
floor cleaner 44
floor mats 9
floor, hardwood 305
flour pest control 125
flower
  cutting 199, 216
  drying 214
  food 196
  ordering 138, 151
flowers, cut 221
flowers, free 349
foaming soap refill 20
foil liner 230
food
  chart on refrigerator 104
  coffee filters 109

co-ops 162
dates 132
donate 106
packaging 25
saver 108
food storage 87
area 83
freezer 91
chips, snacks 87
foot
soak 174
wrap 173
fork beater scraper 230
Formica, paint it! 307
foundation color 177
free fertilizer 347
free firewood 338
free flower seeds 348
free flowers 349
free landscaping (almost!) 346
free movie rental 337
free mulch 344
free passes 337
free trees (maybe) 349
freezer
bags 114
containers 126
defrosting 229
labels 84
freezer storage 282
French manicure 180
French toast 112
French toast sticks 106
friendship landscaping 346
friendship potluck 329
fringe benefits 276
Frisbee bowling 26
frosting palette 314
frosting saver 129
frozen cookie dough 123
frozen dinners, homemade 107
frozen doors 7
frozen beef in slow cooker 98
frozen water bottles 237
frozen yogurt 91
fruit fly catcher 213
fruit, to freeze 121
fruit-pops 121
fudgesicles 102
full flats 349
funnel 8
furnace checkup 200
furniture
ads 216
new from old 209
polish 56
furniture, pets off 298
furniture, rented for sale 196
fuse box 194
futon pad 207
fuzzball remover 73

G

garage rental 10
garage sale
prep 285
re-fresh 291
secrets 291
garbage disposal 236
garden hose storage 343
gardening bargains 347
gardening, no spill 220
garlic
chopping 130
no stick 127
slicer 231
garment tags, relocation 246

Index

gas cap 7
gelatin to-go 90
George Foreman grill cleaner 47
gift
 bags, cheap 141
 basket 146
 basket wrap 153
 baskets 142
 box 138, 140
 budget 148
 cache 283
 calendar, perpetual 285
 card shopping 139, 140
 cards on eBay 148
 creative 154
 certificates 141
 exchange 145, 150, 315
 in a jar 138
 notebook 148
 labor of 150
 P.I. 287
 packaging 152
 planner 146
 questionnaire 147
 record 290
 reminder 145
 savings account 138
 stash 153
 tag 155
 wrap 151
gift wrap storage 140, 142, 143, 147, 150
gift,
ginger storage 119, 130
glass, "frosted" 307
glue gun cleanup 52
glue in tight spot 307
glycerin soap 252
grab and go 290
grab bag exchange 316
graduation photo frame 150
grandparent's gift 147
grape storage 100
grapefruit slush 84
gray hair touch-up 171
green onions, grow your own 105
greeting cards 152
 display 140
 recycled 155
 website 35
grinding teeth, stop 182
groceries, carry load 163
grocery
 bags 236
 delivery 158
 gift card 157
 gift certificate 161
 list 159
 savings stash 158
grocery bingo 163
Grocery Game 162
grocery hauler 163
grocery shopping
 coupons for kids 18
 donations 160
 floor plan 162
 list 160
 with family 162
grocery store, small markets 158
guacamole 86
guest book 287
guestroom goodies 209
gum in the refrigerator 100
gym membership 183
gym shower 183

Index

H

habit, how to break 261
hair
  conditioner 170
  conditioner pump 170
  detangler 172
  dye 169, 171
  highlights 169
  product build-up 167, 169
  rollers 170, 172
  static 170, 171
  towel 170
  treatment 170
hairbrush 170
haircut 169
haircut kit 168
hairspray 171, 172
  remove overspray buildup 63
Halloween candy 320
ham for less 84
ham glaze 92
hand
  cleaner 56
  de-greaser 44
  sanitizer 50, 65
  scrub 173
  soap 173
hand wash prep 239
handmade gifts 140
handprint tiles 149
hanger marks 71
hanger organizing 71
hangers, free 76
hardwood floor 305
headband holder 172
headband slipping 170
headboard 197
headliner 7
heat, extra from dryer 194
heating bills 194
heating pad 185
herb
  savings 102
  storage 88, 124, 127
history scrapbook 151
holiday
  decorations 138
  memories 149, 152
  mugs 145
home index 284
home office 277
home party gifts 143
homemade play dough 22
homemade weights 183
homework box 27
honey, no waste 104
horse owners, poor 301
horse, rinse 301
horse, shiny coat 301
hose, toughen for run resist 75
hose filter 344
hospital
  gifts 137, 146
  stays 188
  visits 187
hostess gift 150
hot chocolate gift 146
hot water heater, timer 226
household manuals 286
houseplants 202, 211, 213, 217, 219
houseplant watering 226
Hula-Hoop fitness 183
humidifier 193, 218
hummingbirds, no bees 343
hydrogen peroxide 63, 64, 65, 183, 195, 245

Index

I

ice chest snacks 234
ice cream
- banana 103
- cone storage 95
- dripless cones 89
- freezer burn 93
- shakes 133
- storage 131
- toppings 88, 230

ice cream cone cupcakes 102
ice cubes 231
- freeze in egg carton 103

ice for travel 330
ice pack 186, 190
ice tea flavors 85
ice tea jars 144
icing 83
illness prevention 186
important info for emergencies 290
ink
- remove from hands 63
- with hand sanitizer 65

inoculations, for pets cheaper 300
insect repellent 185, 195
insect sting relief 185
inspirational calendar 148
insulated food bags 95
insulation 203
insurance
- auto, save on 260
- disccounts 265
- life 263
- shop around 269

interest, charge yourself 261
internet
- provider 33
- shopping 35

inventory list 208
IRA savings 260
iron cleaner 53
ironing board cover 252
ironing, seasonal clothes 249
itchy skin relief 187

J

jack-o-lantern 323
janitorial supply store 60
jar, to open 240
jeans
- distress 252
- how to dye 77
- repair 69

jet lag 335
jewelry
- care 168
- cleaner 42
- jewelry 167

jewelry maintenance 308
juice 'soda pop' 111
juice cocktail 115
jumpy computer mouse 36

K

kerosene heaters 204
kids
- art 18
- artwork scrapbook 29
- artwork storage 29
- clothing sizes 20
- consignment 23
- travel 332

kitchen
- floor 233
- timer, for chores 25
- towels 235

kitty litter, cheap 298
knife caddy 229
knife safety 240
Kool-Aid dye 69

L

label removal 222
labeling, unique through P.O. 289
ladder 199
laminate countertops 49
lampshade
  clean with roller 64
  cleaning 52, 60
  scrapbook 144
landscaping, friendship 346
laptop computer 35
latte 122
laundry
  baby shampoo for delicates 252
  baseball cap 248
  basket on wheels 249
  bleach 247
  carrier 251
  chewing gum remover 250
  cold water 247
  color-fast treatment 249
  delicates, machine wash 248
  deodorant marks 253
  detergent measuring cups 251
  extra spin to dry 250
  hang to dry 253
  inside out clothes 247
  odors 252
  piggy bank 246
  reminder 198
  scheduling 246
  sock bags 248
  sorting clothes 251
  stroller 249
  wash rayon 250
  wool sweater wash 250
laundry soap (liquid) 244
laundry soap (powdered) 245
lawn mower, starting stubborn 343
leather, renew 75
leftovers
  coffee 115
  containers 90
  dips 131
  directory 104
  labeling 130
  no more 117
  party 116
  turkey 118
  wine 230
leg cramps 187
lemon
  cleaner 51
  freeze 94
  harvest 121
  juice 101, 131
  juice substitute 126
  zest 126
letters for baby 24
lettuce, don't chop 110
lettuce storage 86
lettuce wrap-up 86
library
  for new books 36
  information 33
  summer fun 37
  website 33
lid corral 283
light bulb 219
light bulb adapter 203
light bulb, efficiency 222
light timers 198

Index

lights, Christmas 316
line-drying 249, 250
linens, organize 223
linens, storage 212
lint remover 74
lip gloss 178
lip wrinkle cream 178
lipstick colors 178
lipstick stretcher 178
liquid hand soap 45
liquid pet meds 301
loans to friends 276
locator, items picture list 294
long distance 258
loofah sponge 60
loss leader tracker 161
lotion stretch 174
lotion warmer 22
luggage ID 331
luggage, lost 329
luminaria 196
lunch 21
  once-a-month 110
  pack for all 21, 30
Lysol, cleaning tires 8

M

macaroni and cheese 127
marinade, recipe 108
magazines
  deals 36
  recycle 34
  remind 284
  shared subscription 33
magnet recycling 209
mail lists 284
mail, fragrant 222
makeup application 177
makeup companies 179
marinade 120, 131
marine paint 308
marker life 288
marshmallows, non-sticky 121
massages 175
matching game 30
mattress shopping 202, 205, 213
meal kit stretcher 114
meal planning 92
measuring cups 234
meat sandwich filling 84
meat wrappers 86
meatloaf
  for meatballs 122
  in a bag 85
  muffins 103
  on the barbecue 111
medical deductions 263
medical supplies 188
medication
  accuracy 186
  information 188
  organizing 283
  pet liquid 301
  reminder 187
  samples 187
melon picking 96
memories, compressed 289
memory mug 149
menu planning 158, 159
meter, read your own 275
mice repellent 195
microwave cleaner 59
military, benefit for 271
milk
  mixing 99
  mixture 116
  scalding 238

Index

mini brownies 91
miracle juice, houseplants 345
mirror messages 21, 207
mitten extenders 76
mock shopping 270
moisturizers 176
money management 267
money, hide 260
money, where does it go? 264
monthly shopping 159
mortgage principal pre-pay 266
mosquito bite relief 188
mosquito repellent 185
moth ball odor 64
moth-proofing 71
moths, pantry repellent 122
mouse pads 35
mouse stopper 210
movers 285
moving box labels 281
moving boxes 281, 286
mud pie kit 150
muesli, designer 106
muffins
  liners 114
  low-fat 118
mulch, free 344
mushrooms in lawn 346
mylar balloon wrapping 142

N

nachos 131
nail hole filler 305
nail polish
  drying 180
  removal 179
  storage 180
nail, removal 223
necklace storage 168
necklaces, tangled 281
necklaces, untangle 189
neighbor gifts 142
newspaper clips, preserving 282
newspaper subscription 37
newspaper wrapping paper 147
newsprint for windows 57
night-light bulbs 199
noodle pancakes 124
noodles, pot of 224
no-stick krispie treats 125
notepads, cheap 221
nuts, chopping 129

O

oatmeal 130
  extender 119
  tricks 115
  to-go 128
odor control 60
odors, pet 299
off-peak credit 275
oil carafe 99
oil spill 10
oil temperature 95
oily hair refresher 171
oily skin blotters 173
omelets, big 92
onion flavor 94
onions
  chopping 86, 100, 105
  odors 123
  storage 238
onions, pets 299
online banking 273
online coupons 158
online groceries 158, 162

Index

online payment 259
opt-out credit card junk 264
orange pith 126
orthotics, squeaky 79
oven cleaning 51, 59
overdraft protector 256
overnight shipping 271
owner manuals 286

P

pacifier habit 28
packing for kids 19
packing material 198, 200, 202, 284
paint 5, 214
- can lid 224
- cleanup 224
- container 203
- storage 220
- striped walls 217

paint bottles, organize 293
paintbrush
- anti-clean 307
- clean-up 42
- hardened 309

paint color swatch 195
paint goofs 195
paint thinner, recycle 64
paint tray liner 195
paint, free 309
paint, marine 308
painting 225
painting drop cloths 208
pajama substitute 24
pancake batter measuring cup 102
pancakes, really fun! 130
pantyhose 69, 71, 73
paper dolls 16
paper towels 216
papermaking 30
paralegal 256
parking meter 10
party decorations, free 313
password storage 33
pasta 132
pasta, cooking 99
pastry, make ahead 98
pattern weights 73
paychecks, extra two 272
peas 15
perfume applicator 181
permanent marker 42
peroxide spray bottle 184
pest control 208
pet bedding, cheap 301
pet hair on furniture 301
pet hair, in washer 298
pet odors 299
pet toy 297
pets, out of the plants 298
phone book saver 10
photo
- art 212
- delivery 153
- gifts 146
- holder 179
- pillows 154
- swatch 213
- tin 323

photos, occupy baby 19
photos, wedding 313
piano storage 201
picnic kit, instant 334
picture frame 138, 149
picture, digital 224
pie
- cleanup 94
- crust 118, 237, 238

Index

mat 240
protectors 121
vent 238
pillow
cloth napkin 206
covers 196
re-fills 204
storage 286
pillowcase wrapping 144
pin holder 69
piñata 314
pizza
buy leftovers 97
cutter 22
deals 99
disks 101
kits 93
pizza cutter (for everything) 238
placemats 214
plane, extra room 330
plant exchange 212
plant tonic 349
plants, protecting from pets 224
plastic bags, storage 24
plastic mattress covers 25
plastic storage containers 232
plastic wrap 100, 125, 231
play dough 22
plush toys 26
pocket calendar 141
poison ivy relief 185
ponytail holders 77
ponytail rubber bands 18
pool chemicals 207
poop, pet in French fry box 297
poop, pet pickup 298
popcorn
bag 93
freezing 115
leftover 90
packaging 143
popsicle dripping 90
popsicles, homemade 98
porcelain sink cleaner 48
porcelain sink, clean 46
pork patties 89
portrait package 23
postage stamp borders 225
postcard 143
postcard-a-month 147
potato chips, casserole topping 101
potato chips, freezer 94
potato salad 101
potato storage 115
potatoes, pressure cooked 101
potluck, friendship 329
potpourri 143, 197, 202, 204, 218
poultry seasoning 88
powdered milk 88
powder-puff 174
preapproved applications 264
prescription co-pays 188
pretzels in cookies 132
price comparison 161
price matching 255
principal prepay, mortgage 266
printer cartridge 34, 36, 37
printer cartridge refills 33
printer paper 34
prize box 16
produce bags 239
product praise 160
product warranty 305
prom attire 315
promotional codes 33
pruning shears, cleaning 348
puffy eyes 184
purse 78

Index

renew 78
saver 70
security 160
pushpin hanger 189
pushpins from earrings 221
puzzle storage 29

R

rabbit ears, TV 306
raffia ribbons 153
rain checks 162
rainy day sandbox 25
rake toys 22
razor saver 180
razor storage 180
rebate gifts 145
rebate routine 273
recalls 5
receipt, restaurant 274
receipts 256
check printing software 262
organize 262
saving 258
reception sites 322
recipe
cards 140
ingredients 100
hang 239
laminate 240
organizer 107
recipe 100
storage 132
website 110, 112, 161
record scan 281
recycle envelopes 24
redhair conditioner 171
refrigerator
photos 144
beauty storage 176
care 203
light 28
mold 235
odor 233
shelf paper 54
re-heat rolls 237
remnant shopping 70
remodeling 210
remote control on treadmill 201
rename foods 99
repair appliances yourself 306
repair manual 8
replacement tires 7
repo sales 6
restaurant supply houses 159
restaurant tab 338
return policies 274
reusable grocery bags 161
reusable worksheets 20
reversible wrapping paper 147
ribbon from florist 138
rice
DIY recipe 102
microwave 98
rice cooker cleanup 132
ring remover 168
roasting bag alternative 120
rolling pin 233
roses, propagating 348
row covers, floating 345
rubber band 207
rubbing alcohol remove hairspray 54
rug liners 197
rugs 220
rust rings 48
rust stains 60
RV needs 287

S

salad dressing 124, 133
salad leftovers 93
sales ads 157
sales, unadvertised 260
salt
scrub 175
shaker 96
whipping cream 120
salt, for fleas 297
salt, rid fleas 47
sandbox 214
satellite dish 306
sauce
freezing 91
pasta 108
healthier 109
savings, extra 275
savings, pain-free 272
scarecrow, cheap 345
scarf hanger 72, 73
school assistance programs 15
school calendar 294
school supplies 20
schoolbook exchange 35
scissor sharpening 236
scrapbook 216
scrapbooking 201
scraper cover 113
scrip, use for budgeting 255
seam ripper 77
second-hand items 268
secret code 140
security system 225
seedlings 348
senior gifts 144, 152
senior pictures 25
septic tank 235
septic tank activator 46
sewing cleanup 197
shampoo
cleaner 43
pump 27
switch 171
warning 171
for cat 300
shaver saver 180
shaving legs 181
shaving with conditioner 180
sheer curtains, garden 344
sheet set kit 288
sheet, sleeping 225
sheets 209
sheets for decorating 15
shelf displays 160
shelf liner 217, 218, 232
shelf-paper removal 232
sherbet 91
shipping books 34
shipping costs 72, 211
shoe
boxes 284, 288
cleaner 74
odor eater 70
polish 72
protection 70
re-soled 74
scuff cover 79
scuff marks 47, 75
sizes for kids 23
space 292
stretch for too tight 78
waterproof 70
shoes for less 70
shoes, dress 75
save wear and tear 75
white, 78
shoes, white 78

Index

shopping list 293
shopping organization 159
shortening mess 90
shorts from pants 71
show shoveling 347
shower cap covers 89
shower cleaner 52
shower curtain
  fabric 218
  fix torn 306
  rod 215
shower door 41, 56, 57
shower floor cleaner 52
shower gel 177
shower invitations 315
shower soap dispensers 175
shower timer 212
shower, bride or mom 316
shreds, donate them 299
silk flowers 41
silver cleaner 43, 56
sink cleaner 52
sink liner 231
sink waxing 51
sippy cup cleaner 43
ski club 332
skunk, de-skunk recipe 299
sliding door tracks 62
slip shortener 72
slipcovers 207
slow cooker turkey stuffing 92
smelly dog 300
smoothie 26, 133
smores frosting 112
snacks
  clips 124
  prep 83
  to-go 124
  workplace 99
snap tightener 73
soap, hand 50
soap dish scum 48
soap dispenser 236
soap stretcher 175
socks
  organizer 293
  spare pair 75
  uniform for whole family 79
soda 88, 129, 159
  fizz keeper 129
  fizz stopper 88
  savings 159
soda pop crate 293
soup
  flavor secret 94
  freezing 87, 121
  leftover recipe 122
  ready-to-serve 89
  salty fix-it 127
  tomato 98
  vegetable 133
sour cream
  imitation 88
  storage 124
spa treatment 172
space bags, make your own 286
spatter guards 240
spending meetings 262
spending record 265
spending record, non 265
spice
  buy 109
  container 93
  co-op 121
  grinder 93
  organizer 240
  savings 101
  storage 90

Index

splinter removal 184
sponge cleaner 48
sponge life 64
spray bottle 54
squeaks 214
stain pretreatment 245
stain remover 58, 252
  baby wipes 250
  Coca Cola 248
  Dawn dishwashing liquid 251
  hairspray 249
  hand sanitizer 251
  laundry detergent 246
  oven cleaner on coats 244
stainless steel sinks 230
stains
  berry 55
  blood 41, 246
  crayons 245
  ink 48
  lipstick 55, 60
  mildew 250, 251
  on vintage fabrics 252
  red clay 249
  rust 250
  wood pitch 246
  yellowing of vintage fabric 244
stand-by power 276
stars 21
static cling 79
static cling cure 74
steel wool scouring pad 44, 46, 58
stencil testing 198
sticker 58
sticker remover 65
stock certificates 139
stocking exchange 143
stocking stuffer 147
stockpiling 111, 202
stomach acid reflux 184
stomachache relief 184
storage
  boxes 288
  containers 285
  in dorm 284
  seasonal 291
  small 281
store stuff, freezer 292
stovetop splatters 234
strawberries
  how to hull 103
  slicing 109
straws 231
sports equipment 183
student sales 5
sty prevention 186
sunburn relief 184
sunglass clip 182
surface cleaner 46
sweetened condensed milk, recipe 110
Swiffer mop 57, 59
syrup, flavored 107

T

tablecloth 220
tablecloth wrapping 142
taco filling 87
taco mix 99
tailor 76
tape grabber 194
tarnish retardant 283
tax class 257
tax-free shopping 268
tea organizer 108

Index

tea, flavored 92, 99
teacher's umbrella 149
teachers, books for 149
teen, important lesson 79
teens and money 272
teeth
  brushing photos 24
  cleaning 182
  grinding 182
telephone, landline 34
  toys while on phone 16
tennis ball, clean vinyl floor 64
tennis shoe cleanup 21, 70, 71, 74
textbooks, free 257
thank-you notes 153
theater, free 334
themed wreaths 153
thermal carafes 122
thermos cleaner 62
thermos jug odors 101
thread pickup 213
tips 259
tire cleaner 7, 8, 9
tissue box 139
tissue paper wrinkles 153
toddler bib 154
toddler shoe 16
toilet bowl cleaner 43, 62
toilet paper conservation 216
toilet paper fragrance 54
toiletry donation 172
tomato freezing 112, 118
tomato paste, freezing 94
tomato sauce, baking soda 114
tomatoes, chopping 128
tool maintenance 348
toothache relief 182
toothbrush
  for free 182
  sanitizer 181
toothpaste 182
  baking soda 182
  clip 181
  saver 181
  toothpaste tube 182
tortilla chips, warm 'em 105
towel
  rationing 248
  rugs 220
  storage 284
towels, frayer 199
towels, homemade 222
toy age range 20
toy boxes 18
toy covers 293
toy library exchange 20
toys 21
  as ornaments 21
toys for grandparents 25
traffic, avoid at airport 335
trash 212
trash bag 232
trash can fragrance 234
travel 23
  kit 332
  meals 329
  packing 329
  with kids 19, 23
Traveler's checks 257
tree gift 152
tree sap remover 52
tree skirt, prom dress 313
trees, free 349
trophie recycling 30
t-shirt blanket 154
tube warmer 174
tuna liquid 299
Tupperware, cleaning 239

Index

TV rabbit ears 306
TV-free 265
Twelve Days of Christmas 321
two-day sale, garage 285

U

ultimate sales insert 163
under-eye bags 173
ungifting 144
uniforms for less 77
unplug cable lines 35
upholstery care 210
USAA Education Foundation 257
usable wrapping 147
used books 149
used car, buy from college student 5
used paperbacks 34
utility costs and kids 28

V

vacations, affordable 337
vacuum
  attachments 57
  bag fragrance 49
  care 65
  cleaner bag 45
  seal 233
vacuuming, easy 63
vase 209
vegetable
  garden 137
  juice 85
  stock 115, 123
veggie
  bags 122
  burgers 100
  cocktail 107
  pie 97
vertical blinds 305
vinegar, clean porcelain 46
vinyl floor 52
  scuffs 64
  ugly black marks 44
V-neck insert 71

W

wall borders 210
wall decorations 205
wall fix 225
wallpaper border 198
wallpaper repair 305
wallpaper, cutting 308
walls 43
  scuff marks 43
walls, clean with mop 63
walls, new 308
want or need? 266
warehouse club savings 160
warranty 8
warranty, product 305
washcloth storage 293
washing machine
  shut-off 202
  cleaner 59
  hose 200
  loading 244
  maintenance 248
  saver 245
washing soda 42
wasp spray 217
watch shopping 74
water 183
  cut usage
  flavored 106
  track drinking 183

Index

waterproofing shoes 70
wax treatment 175
waxpaper cleaner 56
wean to cup 27
website finder 36
wedding
  cost of 318
  dress 317
  favors 145
  flowers 318
  gift 139
  kids at 318
  on budget in Chicago 324
  photo 144
  photos 313
  survival kit 320
weed control 347
weed killer, cheap 347
welcome mat 141
whiteboard 19, 59
whiteboard cleaner 54
window
  cleaner 46, 56
  cleaning 61
  decal 7
  film 193
  screens 193
  snow cleaner 61
  toppers 211
  treatments 205
  drafty 308
windshield
  repair 5
  wiper 9
  wiper fluid 9
wine glass charms 217
wine pourer 126
winter blooms 349
wish list for kids 28
wood cabinet finish 309
wood scratches 43
wooden spoon 58
wool, unshrink 244
wrapping paper 147
wrapping paper envelopes 139
wrinkles, out of pans 78

Y

yard lights 349
yard tools, sharing 343
yeast dough, heating pad 125
yogurt drink 93
yogurt mix-in 102

Z

zippers, closed when washing 251

DPL
PRESS